David, I know
you'll enjoy this
book about the
Glory Days!
Love, Brenda
12-25-13

SEC
Football

75 Years of Pride
and Passion

SEC Football

75 Years of Pride and Passion

Richard Scott

Voyageur Press

Voyageur Press titles are also available at discounts in bulk quantity
for industrial or sales-promotional use. For details write to Special
Sales Manager at MBI Publishing Company, 400 First Avenue N,
Suite 300, Minneapolis, MN 55401 USA.

Library of Congress Cataloging-in-Publication Data

Scott, Richard, 1960-
  SEC football : 75 years of pride and passion / Richard Scott.
    p. cm.
  Includes index.
  ISBN 978-0-7603-3248-1 (hb w/ jkt)
  1. Southeastern Conference—History. 2. Football—Southern States.
I. Title.
  GV958.5.S59S43 2008
  796.332'630973—dc22

                              2008015166

On the front cover: (top row, left to right) Danny Wuerffel, *University of Florida Sports Information*; Louisiana State 2008 BCS champions, *AP Images/Nam Y. Huh*; Bo Jackson, 1985, *AP Images*; Coach Robert Neyland and the Tennessee Volunteers, *University of Tennessee*; (second row, left to right) South Carolina Gamecocks, *Southeastern Conference*; Rafael Little, 2007, *AP Images/Mark Humphrey*; Archie Manning, 1968, *AP Images*; Bear Bryant, *Paul W. Bryant Museum*; (bottom row, left to right) Uga VI, *Phillip Faulkner/UGA Sports Communications*; Dan McGugin and the Vanderbilt Commodores, *Vanderbilt University*; Arkansas Razorback mascot and crowd, *Southeastern Conference*; Jerious Norwood, *Mississippi State Media Relations*.

On the back cover: LSU players Demetrius Byrd (2), Carnell Stewart (71), and others hold the SEC Championship football trophy after beating Tennessee 21-14 at the Georgia Dome in Atlanta on December 1, 2007. *AP Images/Dave Martin*

On the title page: Alabama and Auburn square off at Jordan-Hare Stadium in Auburn, November 19, 2005. *Joe Murphy/WireImage/ Getty Images*

Editors: Josh Leventhal and Peter Bodensteiner
Photo Editor: Krystyna Borgen
Designer: Cindy Samargia Laun
Jacket Design: Brian Donahue

Printed in United States of America

CONTENTS

"*In the East, college football is a cultural exercise. In the West, it is a tourist attraction. In the Midwest, it is cannibalism. But in the South, it is religion. And Saturday is the Holy Day.*"

— Marino Casem, college football coach, 1963–1992

INTRODUCTION

It's an SEC Thing

The astute Marino Casem—who coached at Alabama State University, Alcorn State University, and Southern University during his thirty-year career—had it mostly right, with one addendum. He should have added the words, "particularly in the Southeastern Conference" when he mentioned the South. Nowhere is football a more vital part of the identity, culture, and economy than in the eight states where SEC football is played.

In the Southeastern Conference, football is more purpose than possibility, more commandment than suggestion. It's more than legendary coaches and players or monumental teams and games. It's every walk-on who ever showed up looking for a chance and worked tirelessly and unselfishly to help his team prepare for a big game.

SEC football is about more than season-ticket holders and all-night tailgating. It's about purchasing a recreational vehicle, driving it to the stadium days before the game, parking it on campus, and holding court until kickoff. It's 93,000 fans at Alabama's *spring* game.

It's not just the week of the big game or the morning after. It's signing day in February. It's the spring game in April. It's between pitches at a little league baseball game in May. It's between bites at a Fourth of July picnic. It's 365 days a year. (Don't believe it? Just eat Christmas dinner in a divided house and see what happens.) It's cradle to the grave.

It's been that way from the start, even before there *was* an SEC—back in 1881, when the *Knoxville Journal* reported, "The game of football is beginning to gain a foothold in Knoxville"; in 1899, when the Sewanee "Iron Men" defeated five teams in six days; in 1915, when Alabama All-American Bully Vandegraaff refused to leave a game against Tennessee, even if meant removing an appendage.

"His ear had a real nasty cut, and it was dangling from his head, bleeding badly," Tennessee lineman Bull Bayer recalled. "He grabbed his own ear and tried to yank it from his head. His teammates stopped him and the managers bandaged him. Man, that guy was a tough one."

Left: The Southeastern Conference is about historic rivalries—none is more passionate than Alabama vs. Auburn.

The SEC is about playing in front of packed houses of rabid fans—like Tennessee's Erik Ainge playing before more than 100,000 fans at Neyland Stadium.

People from outside the South don't understand. They can infiltrate the South with sociologists, anthropologists, and psychologists and expound on theories connecting the South's love of football with a supposed deep-seated regional inferiority complex stemming from its bloody loss to the oppressive invaders during the War of Northern Aggression.

Maybe so. But they would forget all about Gettysburg and Appomattox, Grant and Lee, when two SEC football teams draw battle lines in a sacred cathedral on an autumn Saturday.

"The folks up north and in other places around the country play college football, and they enjoy it," said Pat Dye, who played at Georgia, started his coaching career as an assistant at Alabama in 1965, and finished as Auburn's head coach from 1981 to 1992. "That's fine. But down here we don't play college football. We live it. And we live it every day."

That life manifests itself in a unique and profound dimension on game days when Ole Miss fans tailgate at the Grove on the campus of the University of Mississippi, or when the "Vol Navy" drifts down the Tennessee River to storm the beaches at Neyland Stadium.

It drifts on the winds through the parking lots of Tiger Stadium on the Louisiana State University campus as fans stir pots of gumbo, grill Cajun sausages, and growl as the opposing team faces off with Mike the Tiger.

It takes on mythical proportions at the foot of Bear Bryant's statue and in the handprints of Crimson Tide football captains at the Denny Chimes bell tower on the University of Alabama campus. It soars with the eagle circling the crowd at Auburn's Jordan-Hare Stadium.

It barks between the hedges at Georgia. It rings like a cowbell at Mississippi State. It craves Gator Bait at The Swamp in Gainesville. It calls the Hogs at Arkansas and crows like a fighting Gamecock at South Carolina. It clings to a healthy measure of hope and history at Kentucky and Vanderbilt.

The SEC is about fanfare and entertainment—here with musical accompaniment by the South Carolina marching band.

The SEC is about tradition and ceremony—such as Ole Miss fans cheering the Rebels as they walk from the Grove to Vaught-Hemingway Stadium on game day.

The SEC is about teamwork and game plans—which helped the Mississippi State Bulldogs pull out a victory in the 2007 Liberty Bowl.

It's barbecue, sweet tea, and fried peach pies. It's Bermuda grass and humidity so thick it can take your breath away.

It's little boys in plastic football helmets and jerseys, and little girls in cheerleader outfits, dreaming of a day when they will take the field in front of 90,000 screaming fans.

It's scheduling a wedding during an open weekend (or avoiding football season altogether) so people won't skip the ceremony to watch the big game—or perhaps worse, listen to it on the radio as the couple recites their vows.

Don't die late in the week, either, because no one is going to attend a funeral on Saturday. Save it for Monday.

SEC football is about generations coming together and passing down tradition from one to the next like a priceless family heirloom.

"Football's just always seemed to mean more here in the South," legendary Ole Miss quarterback Archie Manning says. Manning's been to every SEC stadium and has seen just about everything an SEC football fan can see. "The fans and their passions and allegiances to their schools; the administrators, especially the athletic directors who made sure there were great stadiums and money for great coaches; the players who've always played so hard and so well because they came from the South—all of that has contributed to what we have today."

Archie married the homecoming queen, and together he and Olivia gave the SEC three football players. Two followed in his footsteps to Ole Miss; one went to Tennessee.

"Olivia and I are obviously Ole Miss fans, and we were fans of Tennessee when Peyton played there, but we're really just fans of SEC football. There's just not a better way to spend a fall afternoon or night than at an SEC game."

The SEC is about reaching out and grasping for glory—which keeps hopes alive for teams struggling to beat the traditional powers.

The SEC is about coming together as one in pursuit of the ultimate goal.

The SEC is about putting rivalries aside for a common calling—as shown by these Arkansas and Auburn players kneeling together in a postgame prayer.

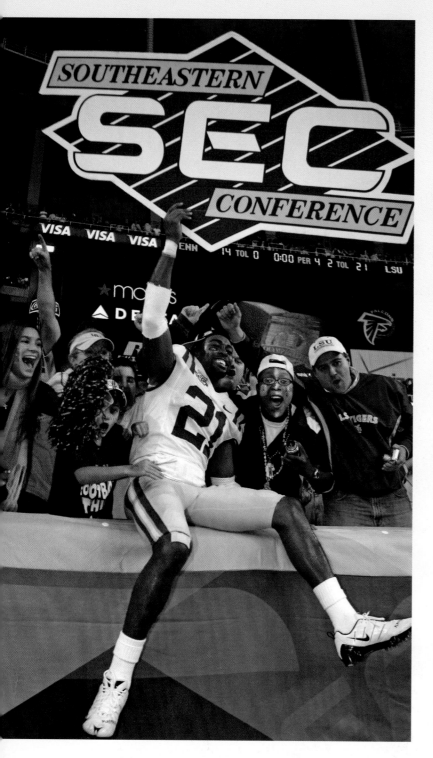

It's a connection with history, with tradition, with something that pro football can't touch. Long before there were Falcons, Saints, Buccaneers, Titans, Jaguars, Panthers, and Dolphins, we football fans in the South made sacred covenants with our schools and chose sides for life.

It's who we are. It's part of our identity. It's in our blood.

"More cars are sold on Monday after we win; more clothes are sold at department stores. There isn't any question that the psyche of the people is wrapped up in the football team," says Skip Bertman, who was born in Detroit and played baseball at the University of Miami, but who has come to understand SEC football from the inside as LSU's former baseball coach and current athletic director. "In Louisiana, we may be ranked forty-five to fifty in things that are good and in the top ten in things that are bad, but in athletics we rank very well."

It's an SEC thing. If you're not from here, you wouldn't understand.

Left: The SEC is about being the best in the conference—something the LSU Tigers have done three times since 2000.

Opposite: The SEC is about winning it all—and the conference has produced four champions since the inception of the BCS National Championship Game in 1998, including the 2006 Florida Gators.

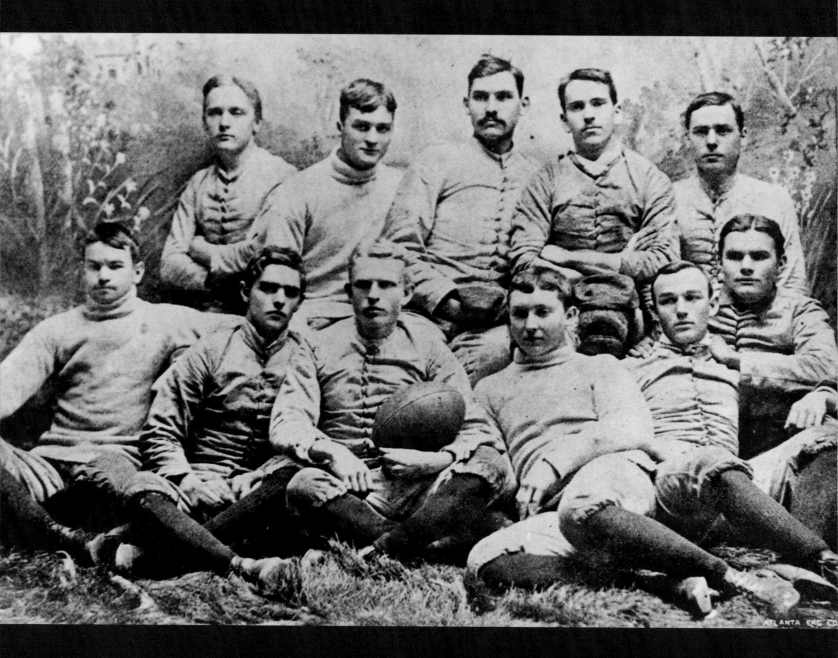

The Early Years

Southern Football Makes Its Mark

Within just a few years after the first college football game was played south of the Ohio River—a contest between Centre College and Kentucky (now Transylvania) University in April 1880—the sport was rivaling baseball as the sport of choice for Southern boys. The mutt of a game still resembled a mix of rugby and soccer, but by the time young men from the University of Georgia and the Agricultural and Mechanical College of Alabama at Auburn played before 2,000 fans at Atlanta's Piedmont Park on February 20, 1882, this business of football had become serious business indeed.

It didn't take long for administrators at universities in the South to understand the potential of college football in the region. At the suggestion of Vanderbilt chemistry professor Dr. William Dudley, faculty representatives from seven Southern colleges met on December 22, 1884, to discuss organizing a joint athletics association that would allow the member schools to establish some common ground.

Those faculty representatives from the University of Alabama, the Agricultural and Mechanical College of Alabama (now Auburn University), the University of Georgia, the Georgia School of Technology, the University of North Carolina, the University of the South (Sewanee), and Vanderbilt University formed the Southeastern Intercollegiate Athletic Association (SIAA).

In 1895, Auburn hired John Heisman as its football coach. He quickly set the bar for future Auburn coaches by beating Alabama 48-0. That same year, Glenn "Pop" Warner began his coaching career at Georgia. Soon, hiring a full-time football coach was a priority for every major institution with dreams of football excellence.

The University of Georgia football team, circa 1892, the year the Bulldogs and the Auburn Tigers first played in the Deep South's oldest football rivalry. The two coaches, Dr. George Petrie of Auburn and Dr. Charles Herty of Georgia, learned about football while in graduate school at Johns Hopkins. Before they brought football to Georgia and Auburn, football had not been played south of Raleigh, North Carolina.

The road to football glory wasn't paved with ease and simplicity. In 1896, the first attempts by Mississippi A&M (now Mississippi State University) to become a Southern football power were brought to a standstill by yellow fever and the Spanish-American War. The same war prevented the University of Tennessee from even fielding a team in 1898, and the death of a Georgia player in a game against Vanderbilt almost put an end to Georgia's football team.

Still, the group of schools that would become the Southeastern Conference survived, and ultimately thrived, during these formative years. Along the way, powerhouses such as the 1899 Sewanee team, the 1915 "point-a-minute" Vanderbilt team, and the 1917 Georgia Tech national championship team drove Southern collegiate football closer to national prominence.

By 1920, the SIAA included 30 schools. With so many varied interests among the institutions, representatives from 14 like-minded SIAA schools met in Gainesville, Florida, and established the Southern Conference. In addition to SIAA inaugural members Alabama, Auburn (then known as Alabama Polytechnic Institute), Georgia, Georgia Tech, and North Carolina, the original Southern Conference included Clemson University, the University of Kentucky, the University of Maryland, Mississippi State University, North Carolina State University, the University of Tennessee, the University of Virginia, Virginia Polytechnic Institute and State University (Virginia Tech), and Washington and Lee University. By 1922, they were joined by the University of Florida, Louisiana State University, the University of Mississippi, the University of South Carolina, Tulane University, Vanderbilt, and the Virginia Military Institute. Sewanee entered the picture a year later, followed by Duke University in 1928.

Southern football teams were making considerable progress with the forward pass and defensive strategy, while the fans attended games in increasing numbers. Newspapers began to devote more space to college football, even adding photos to illuminate their stories.

In 1924, Wallace Wade, Alabama's coach from 1923 to 1930, spoke to the *Birmingham News* about the state of football in the South and elsewhere.

Sectionalism in football is rapidly disappearing due to the interchange of coaching ideas. Coaching schools are being held and attended by coaches in all parts of the country. Coaches are coming into the South from other sections; also coaches are carefully studying the football books put out by the leading coaches of the West and the East.

More men are devoting their entire time the year round to the study of football. This and many other conditions are putting the standard of football of the South on a plane with that in other sections.

In spite of those conditions, Southern football continues to retain some distinctive characteristics. This fact must be recognized from the fact that few coaches who have come to Southern universities from the West or East have been successful until they have become familiar with conditions by a year or two of experience in this section.

There is more sentiment in Southern football; the coaches appeal to the affections of the players. There is less driving and more loyal conscientious effort. The Southern coach holds a higher position in the hearts of his players and of the entire student body than does the coach of the North. Instead of being called by the affectionate term of "Coach," as the Southern coach is, the Northern coach is often called by his first name and is too often treated with very little respect.

Yet, even with the success of Sewanee, Vanderbilt, and Georgia Tech against some of the nation's best teams, Southern football remained something of a regional and rural entity in the perception of the national media.

That changed in a dramatic way in 1926, when Alabama became the first Southern team to play in the Rose Bowl.

Opposite: Georgia hired Glenn Scobey "Pop" Warner as its new head football coach in 1895 at a salary of $34 per week. In their first two seasons in the Southern Intercollegiate Athletic Association, the Bulldogs won 7 of 11 games under Warner. Warner went on to win 319 games in 44 years as a head coach, but he is best known for founding a popular youth football organization.

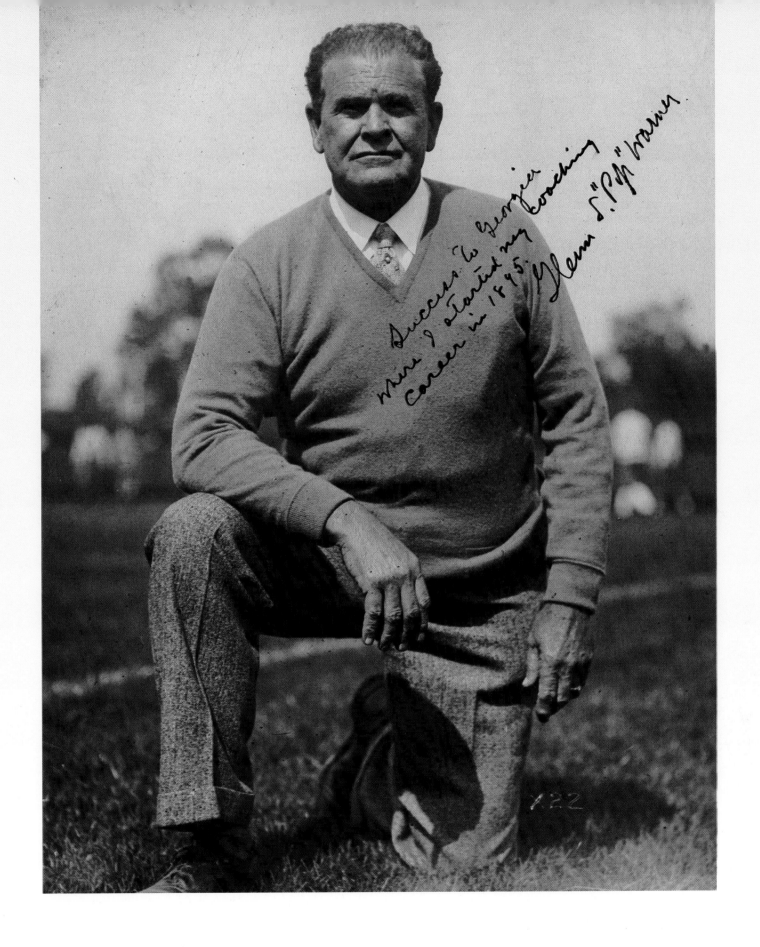

Success to Georgia
where I started my coaching
career in 1895.
Glenn "Pop" Warner

Above: This photo is believed to be the first Georgia-Auburn game, played at Piedmont Park in Atlanta on February 20, 1892. Only 3,000 people attended the game. Tickets were fifty cents for adults and a quarter for children. Auburn won 10-0. Since 1898, the Tigers and the Bulldogs have played every year except 1943, when Auburn didn't field a team due to World War II.

Left: At 6-foot-2 and 185 pounds, Tennessee's Nate Dougherty would not be a lineman in today's game. From 1906 to 1909, he was large enough to earn the nickname "Big'n." Dougherty was later instrumental in the rise of the Southern Conference and the Southeastern Conference. He is a member of the College Football Hall of Fame.

Robert "Bob" McWhorter played halfback for Georgia from 1910 to 1913. In his career, he scored 61 touchdowns, earned all–Southern Conference honors four times, and was an All-America selection in 1913. Later inducted into the College Football Hall of Fame, McWhorter chose law school and a career as a law professor over a career in sports. He also served as the mayor of Athens, Georgia, from 1940 to 1947.

Hall of Famer Vernon "Catfish" Smith played end for Georgia from 1929 to 1931 and earned All-America honors in 1931. His performance in a 15-0 upset of Yale in 1929 is legendary. Smith accounted for all the game's points by falling on a blocked punt in the end zone, kicking the extra point, catching a touchdown pass, and adding two more points on a safety.

Jimmy Hitchcock, a triple-threat halfback known as the "Phantom of Union Springs," became Auburn's first All-American in 1932. Alabama Coach Wallace Wade said of Hitchcock, "I have never seen a finer all-around back play against one of my teams."

W. T. "Bully" Vandegraaff (left) and his brother, Hargrove "Hog" Vandegraaff, were a formidable pair for the Alabama Crimson Tide in the 1910s. Bully was so tough that he reportedly once attempted to tear off his injured ear rather than come out of a game.

(Georgia Tech had been invited to participate in the Rose Bowl following a perfect 9-0 season in 1917, but the outbreak of World War I forced Heisman to turn down the offer.) The Crimson Tide caught the attention of the college football world on January 1, 1926, by defeating the heavily favored University of Washington 20-19 and winning a national championship.

Alabama offered further proof of its strength the next season by going 9-0-1 while allowing a total of 27 points throughout the course of the entire season. The Tide returned to the Rose Bowl for a second straight year and tied Stanford in the game to earn a share of another national championship. That same season, Georgia finished 9-1 and finished first in one national championship poll.

Georgia Tech brought further national acclaim to football in the Deep South when the Yellow Jackets went undefeated (10-0) in 1928 and then bested the University of California in the Rose Bowl on New Year's Day 1929 to claim the national championship. The game is perhaps best known for the blunder by Cal standout Roy Riegels, who in the game's second quarter picked up a fumble and ran toward his own goal line, only to be brought down by his teammates. Cal had to punt and Tech blocked it for a safety, which proved to be the difference in Tech's 8-7 victory.

As the quality of football improved, the cumbersome number of teams in the Southern Conference and constant disagreements over recruiting, academic scholarships, radio broadcasts, filming of games and practices, and scouting practices led to much divisiveness among the schools. In 1932, those problems culminated in a definitive split of the conference. During the annual Southern Conference meetings on December 8 and 9, the thirteen institutions in the western and southern segments of the region broke away to form the Southeastern Conference and elected Dr. Frank L. McVey of Kentucky as the first president. The ten schools east of the Appalachians retained the Southern Conference name.

By the time those thirteen institutions—Alabama, Auburn, Florida, Georgia, Georgia Tech, Kentucky, LSU, Ole Miss, Mississippi State, Sewanee, Tennessee, Tulane, and Vanderbilt—played their first season of football in the fall of 1933, the SEC was well on its way to becoming the nation's preeminent football conference. Tennessee had established itself as a national powerhouse, posting a record of 52-2-4 in its first six seasons (1926–1932) under Coach Robert Neyland. Alabama had added another national championship after finishing 10-0 in 1930 and beating Washington State 24-0 in the 1931 Rose Bowl.

With the formation of a conference featuring such a host of successful programs, the point had been made: Any team wanting to call itself a national power would have to prove itself the equal or better of the best the mighty SEC had to offer. It has been that way ever since.

The Sewanee Iron Men

"In six days, Sewanee beat Texas, Texas A&M, Tulane, LSU, and Ole Miss. On the seventh day, they rested."

In the history of a conference that has produced 23 official national championships and a multitude of unofficial titles, one of the most extraordinary teams might just be a team of giants from the smallest school among the SEC's original membership.

Thirty-four years before the SEC officially came into existence, and 41 years before the school dropped out of the conference, the University of the South—also known as Sewanee—outscored its opponents 322-10 on the way to a perfect 12-0 season in 1899. All 10 points that Sewanee gave up that season came during the Auburn game; the other 11 victories were shutouts.

That's impressive enough by any measure, but what really makes the season stand out in the annals of college football history is the way the Tigers won five road games in six days—an inconceivable feat in today's game. And the 1899 "Iron Men" of Sewanee did more than just win those games. They beat five of the South's best teams and shut them all out, defeating Texas by a score of 12-0, Texas A&M 10-0, Tulane 23-0, LSU 34-0, and Ole Miss 12-0.

As longtime Penn State coach Joe Paterno once said, "While there are some who would swear to the contrary, I did not see the 1899 Sewanee football team play in person. Winning five road games in six days, all by shutout scores, has to be one of the most staggering achievements in the history of the sport."

The 2,500-mile journey began on the Cumberland Plateau in Sewanee, Tennessee, at an institution founded by Episcopal bishops before the Civil War. Student-manager Luke Lea, who went on to become Tennessee's youngest U.S. senator at age 32 and also founded *The Tennessean* newspaper, put together a schedule that appeared to be more murderous than ambitious. In addition to the five-game road trip, he also added games against Georgia, Georgia Tech, Tennessee, Auburn, and North Carolina.

The travel party of 21 included future football Hall of Famer Henry "Diddy" Seibels and coach Billy Suter, who had just graduated from Princeton. Loaded with two barrels of local spring water for his players, the Tigers took the "mountain goat" train down to Cowan, Tennessee, on November 7, before boarding a Pullman car for Memphis and traveling to Austin, Texas. Along the way, Lea managed to leave the team's game shoes on a train platform, causing Lea to make a long-distance call that sent the shoes to Texas.

On November 9, Sewanee beat the previously unbeaten Texas 12-0 in front of 2,000 spectators. Less than 20 hours later, Sewanee beat Texas A&M with the help of a Texas native named Bartlet et Ultimus Sims and the intimidation of "Wild Bill" Claiborne, who made certain the Aggies saw his swollen, discolored eye and told them, "See this? I lost it yesterday in Austin. This afternoon I'm getting a new one!"

An overnight train brought the Tigers to New Orleans, where they spent the night. The team supposedly saw a play that night, but legend has it that some of the players actually attended a burlesque show.

Following a day of rest, Sewanee pummeled LSU before a crowd of 2,000. On the sixth and final day of the road trip, Sewanee defeated Ole Miss in Memphis. The next day, the Memphis *Commercial Appeal* reported, "The trip of the Sewanee eleven will probably remain unequaled for many generations."

More than a century later, it's safe to say the trip will never be equaled. After emerging as one of the South's early football powers and winning four SIAA championships from 1900 to 1910, Sewanee lost 42 consecutive conference games before withdrawing from the SEC in 1940, content to focus on academics without major athletics.

While Sewanee now plays Division III football and focuses more on Rhodes scholars than athletics, the "Iron Men" live on in legend and history.

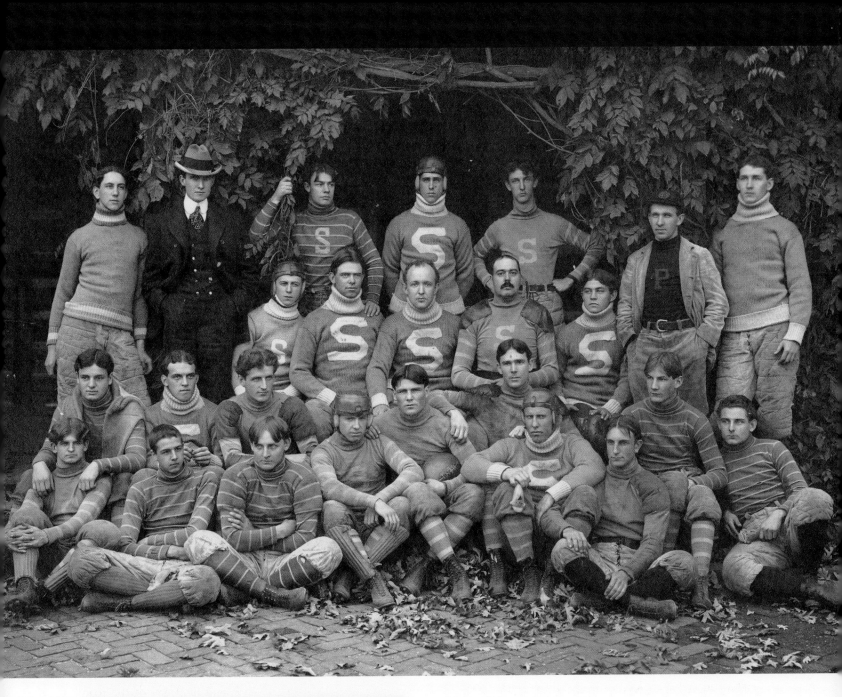

1899 Sewanee, 12-0		
October 21	Sewanee 12	@ Georgia 0
October 23	Sewanee 32	@ Georgia Tech 0
October 28	Sewanee 46	Tennessee 0
November 3	Sewanee 54	Southwestern 0
November 9	Sewanee 12	@ Texas 0
November 10	Sewanee 10	@ Texas A&M 0
November 11	Sewanee 23	@ Tulane 0
November 13	Sewanee 34	@ LSU 0
November 14	Sewanee 12	@ Ole Miss 0
November 20	Sewanee 71	Cumberland 0
November 30	Sewanee 11	@ Auburn 10
December 2	Sewanee 5	@ North Carolina 0

Sewanee never won a game in eight seasons in the Southeastern Conference, but the Tigers were a powerhouse in 1899. Sewanee won 12 games and outscored their opponents 322 to 10. In November, they won road games against Texas, Texas A&M, Tulane, LSU, and Ole Miss in a span of six days.

A Vandy Man For Life

In the locker room, prior to Vanderbilt's home game against undefeated and heavily favored Michigan in 1922, Vanderbilt coach Dan McGugin pointed in the direction of a military cemetery near the Vanderbilt football field and told his players, "In that cemetery sleep your grandfathers."

Then McGugin pointed in direction of the Michigan players and said, "And down on that field are the grandsons of the damn Yankees who put them there."

McGugin never mentioned that his father had been an officer in the Union army, but apparently he got his point across. The game ended in a scoreless tie.

Although he was born and raised in Iowa and played football at the University of Michigan, where he also earned a law degree, McGugin left an indelible mark on Southern football. Fred Russell, longtime sportswriter for the *Nashville Banner* and notable historian of Southern football, wrote of McGugin: "sensationally successful, winning glorious intersectional victories . . . responsible, more than any other man, for Southern football gaining national recognition."

McGugin came to Vanderbilt in 1904 and retired in 1934, missing only the 1918 season because of World War I. During that time, his Vanderbilt teams won 13 championships and 197 games with 55 losses and 19 ties. Four of McGugin's teams went undefeated and 11 more lost only one game.

His Commodores outscored opponents 6,812 to 1,692, an all-time average score of 25.1 to 6.2 per game. In the first game under McGugin, Vanderbilt defeated Mississippi State 61-0. The Commodores went on to win the next two games by at least 60 points as well. McGugin remains the only coach in NCAA history to win each of his first three games by 60 or more points. Vanderbilt outscored its opponents 452-4 during the 1904 season and led the nation in scoring. In 1915, the "point-a-minute" Commodores scored 514 points in 510 minutes while allowing only 38 points.

But McGugin did more than win. He also helped to shape the game in its early years. When he arrived at Vanderbilt, five of the more prominent Southern cities, including Nashville, had attracted a combined attendance of 35,000 fans on one Saturday. That seemed like quite an achievement, until Vanderbilt started bringing in more than 35,000 by itself on a single Saturday.

In his thirty seasons as the Vanderbilt football coach, Dan McGugin (seen here standing behind his players during practice) set the standard for Southern football coaches. His first team went 9-0, and he went on to coach four unbeaten teams. Vanderbilt's intersectional games against schools like Harvard, Yale, Michigan, and Ohio State helped to forward the cause of football in the South.

Before he became a successful head coach at Clemson and Rice, Jess Neely (right) played end and halfback at Vanderbilt and was captain of the Commodores in 1922. He earned a place in the College Football Hall of Fame, primarily for his 40 years as a coach.

In 1923, Vanderbilt end Lynn "The Blond Bear" Bomar became one of the first Southern football players to earn a spot on Walter Camp's All-America Team. Although a head injury ended his career five games into his senior season, Bomar was inducted into the College Football Hall of Fame in 1956, the first Commodore player to be so honored.

At 225 pounds, Josh Cody was a big lineman for his era and a big reason for Vanderbilt's success from 1914 to 1916, as well as his final season in 1919, following World War I. With Cody often leading the way as a blocker, Vandy scored 1,099 points in 35 games during Cody's career. Cody was inducted into the College Football Hall of Fame in 1970.

McGugin also secured significant intersectional games against schools such as Harvard, Yale, Chicago, Michigan, and Ohio State, and he led the drive for the construction of the South's first legitimate football stadium in 1922. He also mentored players who went on to become some of the game's most successful coaches, including Red Sanders, Jess Neely, Josh Cody, and Ray Morrison.

In the book *Fifty Years of Vanderbilt Football*, Fred Russell wrote: "In his first year as coach, McGugin developed a team that created a sensation in the South. From that first year until 1908 he was unscored on by a Southern team. For years he ruled supreme in Dixie, and his teams won many glorious intersectional victories."

Russell credits McGugin with doing more to advance the progress of Southern football than any other man. He revolutionized the use of the onside kick, and he was one of the first coaches to bring out guards to block downfield for the backs.

When McGugin retired in 1934, he had the longest single-institution tenure of service of any college football coach. "If ever a coach gave his life to the college he served," Russell wrote, "Dan McGugin gave his to Vanderbilt. His name will never die."

McGugin died of a heart attack in 1936, but his legacy lives on in the name of the Vanderbilt athletics office building, the McGugin Center.

Rise of the Ramblin' Wreck

Which SEC team hired John Heisman, won the most lopsided game in college football history, and won a Rose Bowl with the help of a wrong-way run?

Although Georgia Tech is no longer a member of the SEC, there's no doubt that the Yellow Jackets had a considerable impact on the early ascent of the conference as a national force.

It started with Heisman. After coaching at Auburn from 1895 to 1900, and then Clemson from 1900 to 1903, Heisman took over a Georgia Tech team that had won 13 games in its first 11 years. Tech won eight games in its first season under Heisman, and his Yellow Jackets went on to post four undefeated seasons, capture a national championship in 1917, mount a 33-game undefeated streak between 1915 and 1918, and amass a 102-29-7 record in 16 seasons.

Along the way, Heisman was an innovator. He introduced the hidden-ball trick, developed one of the first shifts to move players around before the snap and create last-second confusion for the defense, and was the first to pull both guards to lead the blocking interference on sweep plays. He also helped push the legalization of the forward pass, which was first allowed in 1906. His centers were the first to snap the ball to the backfield, instead of rolling or kicking it.

When he wasn't coaching football, Heisman served as president of the Atlanta Crackers baseball team and managed a summer stock theater company, spending his off seasons traveling around the country for performances.

While he is most famous for the trophy that bears his name, he is more infamous for his role in a 220-0 victory over Cumberland University in 1916.

History says that Heisman ran up the score as revenge for Cumberland University stocking its baseball team with semi-pro players and running up a 22-0 victory over Tech the previous year. It also claims that Heisman wanted to prove a point to sportswriters who were more concerned with statistics than skills.

In truth, the situation is a bit more complicated. While those factors remain part of the story, it's also true that Cumberland had discontinued its football program before the season, but Heisman refused to cancel the previously scheduled game. Because the contract required Cumberland

On October 7, 1916, Georgia Tech and Cumberland College played the most one-sided game in the history of college football. Tech led 63-0 after the first quarter, 126-0 at halftime, and went on to win 222-0.

John Heisman—whose legendary status is recognized by the naming of the annual award for most outstanding college football player, the Heisman Memorial Trophy—was one of the game's most important innovators. Heisman played his college ball at Brown and Penn and coached at eight different institutions, with his longest tenure at Georgia Tech. He posted a career coaching record of 185-70-17.

After serving as John Heisman's assistant, William "Bill" Alexander took over as Georgia Tech's head coach in 1920 and left his own mark on the program. The Yellow Jackets went 134-95-15 in 25 seasons with Alexander as the coach. Under Alexander, Tech also became the first school to appear in all four of the major bowls: Rose in 1929, Orange in 1940, Cotton in 1943, and Sugar in 1944.

to pay an exorbitant price of $3,000 if it failed to play the game, Cumberland student manager George Allen gathered together 14 men for the trip to Atlanta.

After Cumberland received the opening kickoff and punted after failing to make a first down, the Yellow Jackets scored on their very first play. Cumberland then fumbled on their next play from scrimmage, and a Tech player returned the fumble for a touchdown. When the roof caved in, it brought the entire house down. The Yellow Jackets led 63-0 after the first quarter and 126-0 at halftime.

"You're doing all right, team," Heisman told his players at halftime. "We're ahead. But you just can't tell what those Cumberland players have up their sleeves. They may spring a surprise. Be alert, men! Hit 'em clean, but hit 'em hard!"

Tech went on to total 440 rushing yards and 18 touchdown runs, while Cumberland finished with minus 42 rushing yards on 27 attempts. The Yellow Jackets also added 220 yards on punt returns and 220 yards on kick returns and scored 12 special teams and defensive touchdowns.

Sportswriter Grantland Rice witnessed the debacle and reported, "Cumberland's greatest individual play of the game occurred when fullback Allen circled right for a six-yard loss."

In another famous tale from the game, a Cumberland player fumbled and told a teammate, "Pick it up!" The teammate replied, "Pick it up yourself, you dropped it."

Tech lost Heisman in 1919 after he and his wife divorced, and the court agreement specified that the two were not allowed to live in the same city. So, Heisman left for the

Robert Lee "Bobby" Dodd made an impact on Southern football as both a player and a coach. The Tennessee Volunteers went 27-1-2 with Dodd as the quarterback from 1928 to 1930, and Georgia Tech went 165-64-8 under Coach Bobby Dodd from 1945 to 1966. He was elected to the College Football Hall of Fame as a player in 1959 and as a coach in 1993.

University of Pennsylvania, where he coached for three seasons. He continued his coaching career at Washington & Jefferson and then Rice University before retiring in 1927.

In 1920, Tech replaced Heisman with William Alexander, who played under Heisman in 1906 and '07, served as one of his assistants, and also taught math at the university.

Bobby Dodd, a former Tennessee quarterback who served as Alexander's assistant from 1931 to 1944 before taking the job as head coach at Tech, said, "Coach Alex was wonderful to me. He could growl and snap, but when it came to an emergency, he was your guy. He enabled me to purchase the home my family and I lived in so many years. And he did the same thing for our black trainer, Porto Rico.

"The Old Man was a clearing-house for everybody in the Tech family, from toothaches to funerals to household quarrels. He had the storytelling ability of Mark Twain, the accumulated miscellaneous information of John Kieran, and the sympathetic understanding of Dorothea Dix."

Alexander continued Tech's winning tradition. Under Alexander, the Yellow Jackets earned a share of five conference championships and won 134 games in 25 seasons. Alexander was the first coach to place his teams in each of the four major postseason bowl games of the time (Sugar, Cotton, Orange, and Rose).

His best team, nicknamed "The Golden Tornadoes," won the national championship in 1928 and beat the California Golden Bears in the Rose Bowl on January 1, 1929, due in large part to one of the most embarrassing plays in the history of college football.

Georgia Tech's 1928 team was filled with characters, including lineman Bill Fincher, who would pretend to be hurt after a play, covertly pull out his glass eye, look at his opponents, and say, "So that's how you want to play?" Another Tech player, fullback Bob Randolph, brought a bear cub back from Pasadena, spoiled him with Coca-Colas, and kept him as a roommate until he got too big.

None of them, however, can top Cal's Roy Riegels when it comes to fame—or infamy. Midway through the second quarter of the 1929 Rose Bowl, Riegels recovered a fumble by Tech's Jack "Stumpy" Thomason just 30 yards from the Yellow Jackets' end zone. But Riegels got

Although he went on to become a college All-American and a successful businessman, California's Roy Riegels is best known to Georgia Tech fans as "Wrong Way" Riegels for the time he picked up a Tech fumble during the 1929 Rose Bowl and ran 65 yards—toward the wrong end zone. The blunder helped the Yellow Jackets to an 8-7 victory.

spun around as he was hit, and he dashed 65 yards in the wrong direction.

As the fans and players jumped up and down on the bench, Alexander was heard to say, "Sit down. Sit down. He's just running the wrong way. Let's see how far he can go."

Cal quarterback Benny Lom eventually caught up with Riegels at the Bears' 3-yard line and attempted to turn Riegels in the right direction, but by then they were joined by a rush of Tech players, who knocked Riegels down at the 1-yard line. The Bears punted on the next play, but Tech's Vance Maree blocked Lom's punt, and Georgia Tech scored a safety for a 2-0 lead. Tech went on to win 8-7 and secure the school's first bowl victory. Riegels salvaged some portion of his legacy when he went on to become Cal's team captain and an All-American the next season.

"I thought he was running the right way," Randolph said. "We all thought that. Turned out he was running the wrong way."

Years later, when asked by the *Atlanta Journal-Constitution* if he felt sympathy for Riegels, Randolph initially said, "Oh, yeah," before reconsidering. "No, I guess I didn't, I reckon. Roy said that was the best thing that ever happened to him. He made a million dollars in the fertilizer business. He was a real success, and a real nice guy."

The 1929 Rose Bowl was the first of Georgia Tech's three bowl victories under Alexander and capped the school's second national championship. All told, under Heisman and Alexander, Tech won eight SIAA or Southern Conference titles, establishing the Yellow Jackets' place among the elite in Southern college football.

Wade Sets the Standard

When University of Alabama president Dr. George Hutcheson "Mike" Denny decided to do everything in his power to make Alabama a national football power, his first call went to Dan McGugin, the coach who put Vanderbilt on the national football map.

But at that time, in the early 1920s, McGugin was entrenched at Vanderbilt and not interested in hearing other offers. Instead, he recommended a previously unknown assistant named Wallace Wade. After two years coaching the Vandy linemen and helping the Commodores win 16 out of 18 games, the 32-year-old assistant and Brown University graduate was ready to become a head coach.

From 1923 to 1930, Coach Wallace Wade led Alabama to a 61-13-4 record and five Rose Bowl appearances. The 20-19 victory over Washington in the 1926 Rose Bowl helped put the Crimson Tide, and teams from throughout the South, on the national college football map.

Fortunately for Denny and Alabama football, he gave the unproven Wade a chance. Wade went on to compile a 61-13-3 record and three national championships from 1923 to 1930.

Wade inherited a team that had earned a measure of national recognition in 1922 against John Heisman's reputable Pennsylvania team. After Georgia Tech beat Alabama 33-7, then lost to Navy 13-0, followed by Penn's 13-7 victory over Navy, Grantland Rice picked Penn to beat the Crimson Tide by 21 points. Alabama coach Xen Scott, a part-time coach who also covered horse racing for a Cleveland newspaper, relied on his own Northern connections to scout Penn and prepare his team for the game. Alabama's 9-7 victory put the Crimson Tide in the national spotlight for the first time.

That season turned out to be the last for the popular and personable Scott, who soon died of cancer. Wade took over with a no-nonsense approach and much higher expectations for success.

After Wade's first few months on the job, the *Birmingham News* offered an early assessment of the new coach:

> The spirit of Wallace Wade is already an institution around the Crimson stronghold. There has been a change in the football routine in Crimson town. Xen Scott, fine little tutor that he was, was more or less of the easygoing school. Long practices were not the rule under his regime. Firm, yes, but in the milder sense of the word. But Wade is different. And the warriors who were in harness under Scott were but one day finding this out.
>
> The writer strolled out to Denny Field in the early afternoon just to see if there were any changes since the last trip. "Too early yet," ran our thoughts, "for the football boys." It was not yet 2:30.
>
> But instead of just a football field and bleachers, he found almost the entire squad ready on the practice grounds. The coaches were not out yet and didn't show up for almost half an hour. But the Crimson jerseyed lads were hard at it, nonetheless.

Alabama's Fred Sington was successful on the football field, on the baseball diamond, and in the classroom. He was best known as a 6-foot-2, 215-pound lineman for Wallace Wade's Crimson Tide from 1928 to 1930, a career that earned him a place in the College Football Hall of Fame.

Wade's first Crimson Tide team already included plenty of tough, athletic, hard-nosed kids who were willing to pay a high price for success. The coach brought discipline and focus to a team poised to join the ranks of the national collegiate powerhouses.

Wade left Alabama for Duke following the 1930 season, but not before he led the Crimson Tide to a 9-0 finish, a 24-0 victory over Washington State in the 1931 Rose Bowl, and a third national championship in six seasons.

When legendary Alabama coach Paul "Bear" Bryant introduced Wade and the players from Alabama's 1930

national championship team to his own players in 1980, he told them, "Men, I'd like you to meet Coach Wallace Wade, the man who is most responsible for the University of Alabama football tradition. In many ways he is the reason I'm here and the reason you're here."

Alabama's All-American running back John Henry "Flash" Suther described Wade as a "bloodthirsty Army officer." "We all wanted to hate him," Suther says in the book *Bowl Bama Bowl*, "but when it got down to it, we loved him. He was a helluva coach who developed us into an outstanding team."

The Tide Comes In

Despite the early success of Vanderbilt, Sewanee, and Georgia Tech, the teams that would later make up the Southeastern Conference remained something of a mystery to the rest of the nation's sportswriters and fans.

That became obvious late in the 1925 season when an Alabama team led by future College Football Hall of Fame backs Johnny Mack Brown and Pooley Hubert allowed only seven total points in the regular season and rolled to nine consecutive victories, including a 7-0 win over previously undefeated Georgia Tech and a 27-0 victory over Georgia.

When rumors began to mention Alabama as a possible opponent for West Coast power Washington at the Rose Bowl, college football's only bowl game at the time, observers elsewhere in the country were highly skeptical. Between the 2,800-mile distance between Tuscaloosa and Pasadena and the general lack of national respect for Southern football,

From 1930 to 1932, John "Hurry" Cain was a versatile weapon for Alabama who could run, block, punt, and defend. Zipp Newman, longtime sportswriter for the *Birmingham News*, called Cain "the best all-around back I ever saw." Cain joined the College Football Hall of Fame in 1973.

Alabama backfield mates Johnny Mack Brown (left) and Pooley Hubert weren't the rubes that West Coast writers thought they would be when the Crimson Tide arrived for the 1926 Rose Bowl. Brown and Hubert led Alabama to a 20-19 triumph over Washington.

many doubted whether Alabama could even accept an invitation to the Rose Bowl, let alone compete in the game if it managed to get that far.

Reports suggested that the invitation would go to Tulane, Colgate, Dartmouth, or Princeton, but Alabama coach Wallace Wade refused to put much stock in speculation until an official representative of the Tournament of Roses came to Birmingham with a formal invitation for the Crimson Tide to play Washington.

As the Crimson Tide prepared for its westward journey, Alabama wasn't given much of a chance to beat the Huskies

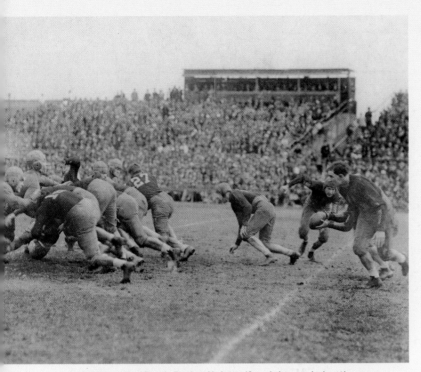

Alabama halfback Pooley Hubert (far right, no helmet) was a rugged runner and blocker, while halfback Johnny Mack Brown (seen here running toward Hubert from the right side of the play) was a swift, elusive runner.

meals in a private hotel dining room and were instructed to avoid the lobby.

Even with Alabama's preparations, the pregame predictions espousing heavily favored Washington looked pretty smart when the Huskies took a 12-0 lead into halftime. Then Alabama charged back in the second half. The Tide scored all 20 of its points during a seven-minute stretch in the third quarter, after knocking Wilson out of the game with an injury.

"I'll never forget coming onto the field and looking up and seeing about 58,000 people at the Rose Bowl," Brown recalled in the book *Talk of the Tide*. "All of the Alabama players were pretty well awestruck by this, and as the game started we fell behind 12-0." Brown credited Pooley Hubert for saving Alabama from an even worse first-half drubbing. Brown recalled that Hubert, who was several years older than most of the other players, made most of the tackles in the early part of the game. "I can still see old Pooley as he made a tackle to save a touchdown and jumped up. His helmet was twisted around, he readjusted it and turned to the ref and said, 'Time out, Mr. Ref!'

"The other ten of us were squatting there looking up at the big crowd and not knowing exactly what to do, and we saw Pooley walking toward us with a very businesslike look on his face. He put his hands on his hips and said, 'Now, just what the hell's going on around here!' That somehow resurrected the Alabama team, and we got together and managed to play pretty well."

Alabama held on for a 20-19 victory that gave the Crimson Tide its first national championship, forever changing the perception of Southern football and putting Alabama on the road to national prominence. "Tuscaloosa, Alabama, which Western fans didn't know was on the map," the *Los Angeles Evening Herald* wrote, "is the abiding place of the Pacific Coast football championship today."

Even if the 1925 national championship failed to convince some that Alabama deserved its place among the best, it was hard to deny when they posted a second consecutive undefeated season in 1926. Alabama went 9-0-1 and allowed a total of 27 points during the season. The Crimson Tide returned to the Rose Bowl, where they tied Stanford, 7-7—good enough to earn them a share of another national championship.

"It was a right pleasant trip going out there, but coming home was the best part about it, because we had been out there representing the South," Hubert said. "We never thought about losing."

and their rugged halfback, George Wilson. Cal coach Andy Smith, following a 7-0 loss to Washington, insisted the Huskies were "one of the greatest football aggregations that I have ever seen, and I believe they are as strong as any team in the country."

Smith had never seen Alabama and didn't know that, during the trip to California, all twenty-two Alabama players were focused on learning all they could about their opponent. As the *Birmingham News* reported, "There isn't a player on the train who can't tell you the name, weight, disposition, and a few other little things about every player eligible on the Washington team." The team's only practice on the trip came after a brief visit to the Grand Canyon, when the Tide stopped in Williams, Arizona, for a workout in rolled-up trousers.

After five days of travel, the team arrived in Pasadena on December 24, 1925—and became immediate celebrities. Over the next four days, the team faced a multitude of distractions, so Wade finally circled the wagons on the 28th and put an end to all outside activities. The players ate their

The 1930s
The Birth of a Conference

On September 30, 1933, in the midst of the Great Depression, the new Southeastern Conference kicked off its first football season in Lexington, Kentucky, with a game between Kentucky and Sewanee.

Only 10 months before, the 13 Southern Conference institutions west and south of the Appalachians met in Knoxville, determined to "form a more compact group of institutions with similar education ideals and regulations in order that they by joint action increase their ability to render services for which they were founded and for which they are maintained, by making athletics a part of the education plan."

With this action, Alabama, Auburn, Florida, Georgia, Georgia Tech, LSU, Ole Miss, Mississippi State, Sewanee, Tennessee, Tulane, and Vanderbilt were able to cast off the cumbersome size, confusing requirements, and often-contentious relationships brought on by the growth and conflicting missions of the Southern Conference.

This new organization planned to reach its goals "by promoting mutual trust and friendly relationships between members." Even today that goal is often difficult to accomplish; the conference occasionally resembles a bickering band of brothers. Like brothers, though, the membership comes together whenever someone from the outside tries to interfere.

That first SEC game featured plenty of defense. Neither team scored through the first three quarters, and it took a 77-yard punt return by Kentucky halfback Pug Bach to finally break the deadlock. The Associated Press report said, "Behind perfect interference, Bach eluded one tackler after another, cut across the entire field and tore down the right side to the Sewanee goal." Bach's touchdown and Ralph Kercheval's extra-point kick were all the points the Wildcats would need in a 7-0 victory.

By the end of the 1933 season, Alabama and its new coach, former Notre Dame standout Frank Thomas, earned the first SEC football championship with a defeat of Vanderbilt 7-0 in Nashville. The Tide finished the season 7-1-1 overall and 5-0-1 in the conference standings. Tennessee's triple-threat standout, Beattie Feathers, became the first SEC Football Most Valuable Player in a vote of coaches surveyed by the *Nashville Banner*.

Robert R. Neyland was known as a stickler for discipline, detail, and precision in his 21 years as Tennessee's head coach—and he was also known to lead his players in song following big victories. The Vols had a lot to celebrate under Neyland, including a national championship in 1951 and shares of the title in 1938, 1940, and 1950. Knute Rockne of Notre Dame called Neyland "football's greatest coach."

Tennessee halfback Beattie "Big Chief" Feathers scored 32 touchdowns in 30 games between 1930 and 1933; the Vols won 25 of those games and tied twice. Beattie was an All-American and SEC Most Valuable Player in 1933 and was inducted into the College Football Hall of Fame in 1955.

The SEC was not content to sit on its early success. In a 1935 decision, which stirred considerable controversy at the time, the conference decided to allow athletes to receive normal student aid, including tuition, books, and room and board. The original firestorm of criticism from the national media and other institutions soon gave way to common sense. With the ongoing Depression, many athletes had to leave school and find work to support themselves. After years of football players being paid under the table and often switching from one school to another under false names and pretenses, grants-in-aid for athletes put more programs on an even playing field under the same rules.

The SEC also remained at the forefront of national football success and popularity, with Alabama becoming the first official conference team to play in a bowl. The Crimson Tide defeated Stanford 29-13 in the 1935 Rose Bowl and finished as the 1934 national champion in five different polls.

The South also refused to allow the Rose Bowl to keep all the postseason fun and prestige to itself. With the popularity of Southern football giving birth to two new bowls, SEC schools immediately became the natural choices for those games. It started when the Sugar Bowl invited Tulane to play in its first game in 1935. (The Green Wave beat Temple 20-14 at Tulane Stadium.) The Sugar Bowl then invited LSU in each of the next three years. When the Orange Bowl played its first game in 1936, it invited Ole Miss, followed by Mississippi State, Auburn, Tennessee and Georgia Tech.

While Ole Miss was losing a 20-19 heartbreaker to Catholic University at the Orange Bowl on January 1, 1936, Auburn was breaking new ground on foreign soil in the Bacardi Bowl in Havana, Cuba. Before the SEC came into existence, LSU (1907), Tulane (1910), Mississippi State (1911), Florida (1912), and Ole Miss (1912) had all participated in the game, but Auburn was the first official SEC team to take part.

The process for selecting national champions might seem complicated in today's era of the Bowl Championship Series, but the BCS is simple arithmetic compared to the process of the 1930s. In those days, national championships were bestowed by a multitude of sources. Many polls that decided the champions in the 1930s have gone the way of the Ford Model A and silent movies, but the Billingsley, Boand, Dunkel, Houlgate, Litkenhous, Poling, Football Research, and Williamson polls meant something to the teams of the era.

LSU won a share of the Williamson national championship in 1935 and 1936, and Tennessee won the national championship in eight separate polls in 1938. The SEC only acknowledges official champions selected by The Associated Press media poll, United Press International (now known as the USA Today coaches poll), and the Football Writers Association of America, but don't try telling the players from the 1930s that they didn't win national championships.

Tennessee certainly presented convincing arguments in 1938 and 1939. In 1938 the Volunteers, coached by then-Major Robert Neyland, finished 11-0, 7-0 in the SEC, and defeated Oklahoma 17-0 in the Orange Bowl, all while outscoring opponents 293-16 and holding eight teams scoreless. The 1939 Vols didn't allow a single point the entire regular season—the only SEC team to ever accomplish this extraordinary feat. Yet Cornell, Southern Cal, and Texas A&M all won shares of the national championship, while Tennessee went on to lose 14-0 to Southern Cal in the Rose Bowl and finished 10-1.

LSU's Gaynell "Gus" Tinsley—seen here, wearing number 24, in action on defense during the 1936 Sugar Bowl—was a record-setting receiver who earned All-America honors in 1935 and 1936. A member of the College Football Hall of Fame, Tinsley later returned to LSU as an assistant coach and served as head coach from 1948 to 1954.

The Vols won 33 consecutive regular-season games between 1937 and 1941. By the time they finally lost on October 4, 1941, Neyland had already returned to active military duty the previous May. Soon the Vols and the rest of the SEC would see the battles fought on Southern football fields superseded by far more furious and monumental battles fought on foreign battlefields.

All-American fullback Bill Hartman was a special-teams standout for Georgia in 1937; he punted for 82 yards against Tulane and returned a kick 93 yards against Georgia Tech. Hartman later coached Georgia's kickers and punters as an unpaid volunteer coach. After the NCAA abolished volunteer assistants, Hartman enrolled in graduate school at age 77 and became a graduate assistant coach. He is a member of the College Football Hall of Fame.

Parker "Bullet" Hall was at his best for Ole Miss in 1938, when the consensus All-American led the nation in scoring, all-purpose running, rushing average, kick-return average, and interceptions. In 11 games, he scored 73 points on 11 touchdowns and 7 extra points and was responsible for 11 more passing touchdowns.

Football on Foreign Soil

Auburn may have not have been the first Southern team to play a bowl on foreign soil, but it was the first official Southeastern Conference team to do so—and under the most unusual and precarious circumstances.

When LSU traveled to Havana, Cuba, in 1907 for the Bacardi Bowl, Cuba was less than 10 years removed from the Spanish-American War and just five years into its status as an independent nation, although still heavily dependent upon the United States government and American business interests.

The weight of American influence made it possible for LSU to play in the bowl, followed by Tulane in 1910, Mississippi State in 1911, Florida in 1912, and Ole Miss in 1921.

The game, also known at various times as the Rhumba Bowl and the Cigar Bowl, was played at La Tropical Stadium only seven times from 1907 to 1946, with the first five taking place between Southern football teams and local Cuban clubs.

The game returned from a 16-year hiatus on January 1, 1937, and for the first time invited two American teams to compete, welcoming Auburn and Villanova into an environment that was far more volatile than anyone realized at the time.

The Tigers had already spent most of the 1936 season on the road, with a schedule that took the team over more than 11,000 miles. This included games against Birmingham-Southern in Montgomery, Tulane in New Orleans, Tennessee in Knoxville, the University of Detroit in Michigan, Georgia Tech in Atlanta, and Florida in Montgomery.

That was not all. The most daring regular-season trip proved to be a road game at Santa Clara, near San Francisco. Auburn played Georgia in Columbus on Saturday, October 24, and boarded a train for California later that day.

Along the way, coach Jack Meagher's team stopped off and practiced in Mobile, San Antonio, Tucson, and Los Angeles before arriving in San Francisco for a game the Tigers lost 12-0.

"Meagher's Marauders" still managed to finish 7-2-1 in the regular season and 4-1-1 in SEC play before receiving its invitation from the Bacardi Bowl to play Villanova, marking the first time two American teams had played on foreign soil.

The game's shaky reputation was evident when Meagher insisted that Auburn sports publicity man Elmer Salter travel to Cuba to collect Auburn's financial share before Meagher would agree to play. According to various accounts, when Salter visited the home of a Cuban sportswriter he was greeted at the door by a shotgun.

When the Auburn travel party reached Cuba, it encountered an island in turmoil. The game was scheduled as part of the Cuban National Sports Festival, the creation of Cuban President Miguel Mariano Gomez y Arias. By late December, heavyweight boxing champion Joe Louis was in Cuba for an exhibition fight, Olympic track star Jesse Owens was there to race a horse, the Columbia University basketball team had arrived to play a Cuban team, and Arias was no longer president, having been deposed just two days before the festival began.

The 1936 Bacardi Bowl nearly ended before it even began. Fulgencio Batista, a dictator of sizeable ego who was ousted by Fidel Castro 22 years later, threatened not to allow the game to be played because his picture was not printed in the game program. A quick reprinting of the program saved the game and Auburn and Villanova played to a 7-7 tie, with Batista and his armed guards in attendance.

Southern Miss played Havana University in 1946 in the last Bacardi Bowl. The next college bowl game played outside the United States was in 1988 when Oklahoma State and Texas Tech played in Japan.

Auburn, in the lighter jerseys, played Villanova to a 7-7 tie in the 1937 Havana Bowl. It was the last college football game played on foreign soil in the twentieth century.

The "Kingfish"

The history of SEC football is filled with fascinating and colorful characters. It's hard to find one more fascinating or colorful than Huey P. Long, the flamboyant and often controversial governor and U.S. senator who ruled Louisiana from 1928 to 1935.

Long's love and devotion for LSU football is legendary. No story better demonstrates this than the time the Barnum & Bailey Circus came to town on the same weekend as an LSU home game against Southern Methodist University.

With ticket sales lagging for the game, Long sent his minions into overdrive. Eventually they found a state law on the books that required the flea-dipping of any animal entering the state, and Governor Long informed the circus that it would have to dip its elephants once it crossed the state line.

The circus, of course, was rescheduled.

Long's time in power often resembled something of a circus, with Long as ringmaster and lion tamer. Long, also known as the "Kingfish," was a populist governor who knew how to push the buttons of the people and make things happen, especially when it came to his beloved LSU, which he often referred to as "my university."

When the Illinois Central Railroad refused to lower fares for LSU students traveling to a football game at Vanderbilt, Long convinced the railroad to rethink its position. He threatened to reassess the value of railroad bridges in Louisville from $100,000 to $4 million. The railroad then allowed LSU students to travel to Nashville and back for six dollars.

Just to make sure those same LSU students could attend the game, Long gave seven dollars to every student who needed it and accepted IOUs in exchange. When he ran out of money he asked for more from LSU President James Smith and got it. Long also brought along his private bodyguards by designating several state troopers as "deputy game wardens."

Huey P. Long's love for his Louisiana State University led to significant improvements in the university and its football program during Long's time as Louisiana's governor (1928–1932) and U.S. senator (1932–1935).

LSU went onto defeat Vanderbilt 29-0, its first-ever victory over the Commodores. After the game, Long rushed on to the field and told anyone who would listen, "We're the greatest team in the world. Anyone who thinks we ain't, we plan to meet 'em."

Of all the things he did to boost the success of LSU football, none made a bigger impact than a major addition to Tiger Stadium. When LSU built the stadium in 1924, it included seating on either side of the field, with open areas beyond each end zone.

When Long decided it was time to add more seats to the stadium, he learned that the state budget had not designated funds for stadium improvements, but it had set aside money for new dormitories. So Long put the dormitories *in* the stadium and added 10,000 seats, closing off the north end to give the stadium a horseshoe shape. Those 1,500 dorm rooms are no longer in use; today Tiger Stadium is completely enclosed and holds 92,400 people.

Long also shared his love of both LSU and music with the marching band. He co-wrote "Touchdown for LSU," a song that is still played before every LSU football game.

Long ruled the state and the university with an iron fist, but he also helped transform what had been considered a poorly run school into a significant Southern university, expanding enrollment from 1,800 students in 1928 to 6,000 in 1936, improving the size and quality of the faculty, initiating a colossal building program, adding a medical school, and ensuring the athletic department had what it needed to field winning teams.

Long was at the height of his popularity when an assassin shot him on September 8, 1935, at the Louisiana State Capitol in Baton Rouge. He died two days later at the age of 42. Depending on which legend people choose to tell, Long's final words were reportedly, "God, don't let me die. I have so much to do," or "I wonder what's going to happen to my poor boys at LSU."

End Gaynell "Gus" Tinsley, along with halfback Abe Mickal, gave LSU a dangerous passing game in the mid 1930s. In 1934, the two hooked up for a 65-yard pass play against Southern Methodist that stood for years as the longest pass in Southern football history.

"Miracle" Abe Mickal had a knack for pulling off big victories and making big pass plays at the most important times as an LSU halfback from 1933 to 1935. During Mickal's 32 games at LSU, the Tigers finished 23-4-5. Mickal is a member of the College Football Hall of Fame.

Howell to Hutson

When Chevrolet commissioned renowned artist Arnold Friberg to paint a series commemorating the one-hundredth anniversary of college football in 1968, Friberg created four paintings representing major turning points in the sport.

One was obvious: the first game between Rutgers and Princeton in 1869. The second took greater care. Friberg wanted to portray the beginning of a new era in the game, an innovation that transformed the game like no other before or since: the forward pass.

Friberg chose not to portray just any forward pass, but the combination of Alabama passer Millard "Dixie" Howell and end Don Hutson. In the painting, titled "The Passing Game: Alabama vs. Tennessee, 1934," Howell is depicted in the far background, having launched a pass downfield over a rushing Tennessee defender; Hutson, in the foreground, is outrunning two Volunteer defenders and reaching back to haul in the pass.

At Alabama, Howell and Hutson teamed up to make the forward pass a dangerous weapon and changed the way the game was played. They also led the Crimson Tide to a 29-13 victory over Stanford in the Rose Bowl on January 1, 1935, and helped secure Alabama's fourth national championship.

Born and raised in Hartford, Alabama, a small town just southwest of Dothan that also produced baseball Hall of Fame pitcher Early Wynn, Howell didn't make much of an impact when he reported to the freshman team as a 150-pound end in 1931. "Physically, he was everything but impressive-looking," Coach Frank Thomas wrote in a 1954 letter to the *Atlanta Constitution*.

After Howell suffered a broken leg during the second week of his freshman year, Thomas moved him from end to left halfback the next spring. Howell didn't play much until injuries to two other left halfbacks opened the door. When Howell finally got his chance to play behind the first-string line, he proved to be a natural at the position, which required him to roll to his right out of the Notre Dame box offense and act as the team's primary passer.

Halfback Millard Filmore "Dixie" Howell teamed up with end Don Huston to give Alabama one of college football's most dynamic passing combinations of the 1930s. Howell, a member of the College Football Hall of Fame, was a true triple-threat who beat opponents with his passing, running, and kicking.

Alabama halfback Dixie Howell scores a touchdown against Stanford in the 1935 Rose Bowl. Howell accounted for 160 yards passing, 79 yards rushing, and 74 yards on kick returns in the game; end Don Hutson caught six passes for 165 yards and two touchdowns. The Crimson Tide won 29-13.

"His mental reactions were the thing to my mind that made him great," Thomas later wrote. "He had the ability to see and realize the situation a split second ahead of the usual player. . . . To me, Howell had something that few athletes possess—a touch of genius in his make-up." The famed sportswriter Grantland Rice dubbed him "The Human Howitzer."

Like Howell, Hutson didn't make much of a first impression at Alabama. Hutson was 6 feet tall and just 150 pounds when he arrived on campus with hopes of competing in baseball and track. He also joined the football team as a walk-on. Hutson spent most of his first three years at Alabama as an outstanding centerfielder and sprinter, but he didn't make much of a contribution to the football team.

That started to change in the fourth game of his senior season in 1934. Hutson, by then weighing in at nearly 180 pounds, caught a 33-yard touchdown pass from Dixie Howell and scored another touchdown on an end-around to lead the Crimson Tide in a 13-6 victory over Tennessee.

By the time Alabama headed to Pasadena for the Rose Bowl on New Year's Day, Hutson was a star—and he proved it on college football's biggest stage. In the game, Hutson caught six passes for 165 yards and two touchdowns. Howell totaled 239 offensive yards and 74 more yards on returns. The duo combined for a 59-yard touchdown pass that put the finishing touch on the win. Bill McGill of the *Atlanta Constitution* wrote, "No team in the history of football, anywhere, anytime, has passed the ball as Alabama passed it today. And no man ever passed as did Dixie Howell, the swift sword of the Crimson attack."

Howell, whom Thomas once called "the greatest player I ever coached," went on to play professional baseball and football. He later became the head football coach at Arizona State and the University of Idaho before entering into successful private business in California.

Hutson went on to transform the passing game in the NFL and rewrite the record books as a member of the Green Bay Packers, dominating his era as no player had done before. He developed pass routes and strategies that are still employed today and set records that stood for decades. Hutson was honored with a spot on the NFL's all-50-year team and its 75th anniversary team, and in 1963 he was enshrined as a charter member of the Pro Football Hall of Fame.

In his playing days, Paul "Bear" Bryant (right) was known as Alabama's "other end." Although Bryant would become one of college football's greatest coaches, Don Hutson (left) was one of the game's all-time best receivers. After an All-American career at Alabama, he became pro football's most accomplished receiver with Green Bay and earned a place on the all-time pro team in 1996.

A Rebel Bruiser

With a nickname like Bruiser it would be easy to picture Frank Kinard as a giant of a man, a behemoth who crushed his opponents with sheer size and brute force.

Instead, at 6-foot-1, 212 pounds, Kinnard was considered rather average in size for a lineman, even in his day. His colorful nickname came from his bruising style of play, an approach that made him one of the best of his era—and one of the best in SEC and pro football history.

The nickname supposedly came from a younger high school teammate who had been flattened by Kinard, picked himself up, and said, "You're a real bruiser."

His aggressive manner came from growing up on a farm as one of seven children in Pelahatchie, Mississippi. Kinard found football during high school in Rolling Fork, Mississippi, and developed into a top high school player. From there he moved on to Central High in Jackson, Mississippi, and then to Ole Miss in 1934.

When he joined the varsity as a 198-pound sophomore, he quickly established himself as a resilient player, capable of playing the entire 60 minutes and utilizing his speed and quickness as a tackler and blocker. In fact, Kinard once played 562 consecutive minutes and 708 minutes out of a possible 720.

He played guard on the Ole Miss basketball team and ran the 440-yard dash for the track team, but Kinard was at his best on the football field. He was the first Ole Miss football player to earn All-SEC honors and All-American status, which he accomplished as a junior and senior in 1936 and 1937. His highest praise, however, came from his coach, Ed Walker, who called Kinard "the best lineman ever to play the game."

He also became the Rebels' first pro football star. After being selected in the second round of the NFL draft by the Brooklyn Dodgers, Kinard earned All-Pro honors in his first season, despite playing for a losing team. Still, Kinard didn't really start hitting his stride until the struggling Dodgers hired University of Pittsburgh coach Dr. John "Jock" Bain Sutherland, whose single-wing offense made the most of Kinard's quickness and rough-and-tumble attack. When Kinard pulled to lead the way for sweeps, opponents either got out of the way or paid the price.

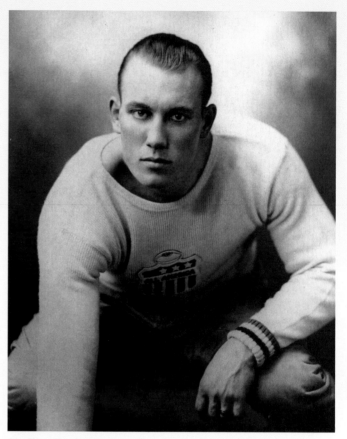

Ole Miss' Frank "Bruiser" Kinard used his size, strength, and quickness to become a devastating lineman and a two-time All-American (1936 and 1937). He was the first collegian from the state of Mississippi to make All-American, the first Ole Miss player selected to the all-Southern team, and the first Ole Miss to earn All-Pro honors.

"Once Bruiser threw the lead block, there was daylight for the ballcarrier," said Joe Stydahar, a Chicago Bears standout and member of the Pro Football Hall of Fame, "and Bruiser never missed throwing that block."

During World War II, Kinard served as a welder in a shipyard and played football with the Dodgers on Sundays from 1942 to 1944. He then joined the Navy in 1946 and played football for a legendary service team, the Fleet City Bluejackets. Kinard's Navy team beat a Marines team in the Los Angeles Coliseum in 1945, in a game that featured several college and pro stars, including future Hall of Famers

Kinard, preparing to throw a block in this 1936 photo, was at his best on offense leading the sweep as a crushing blocker for Ole Miss ball carriers.

Elroy Hirsch and Buddy Young. With a month's pay bet by each side, Young later called it roughest game he ever played.

When the war came to an end, Kinard jumped to the New York Yankees team of the fledgling All-America Football Conference and once again established himself as one of the game's top linemen. He earned All-Pro honors in 1946 and '47 and served as a player-coach in 1947, his final season of pro football.

Kinard retired from pro football and returned to his alma mater in 1948 as a line coach on the staff of legendary Ole Miss coach Johnny Vaught. When Vaught suffered a mild heart attack in 1970, Kinard became the interim coach. When Vaught retired following the season, however, it was Kinard's brother Billy, himself a former Ole Miss player, who replaced Vaught as head coach. Bruiser Kinard then replaced Tad Smith as Ole Miss' athletic director.

Kinard was a true iron man in his college athletic career. In addition to playing an average of 55 minutes per game over 34 games on the football squad, he also started at guard for the Rebels' basketball team, ran the 440-yard dash, and threw the shot put for the track and field team.

The Kinards enjoyed brief success in 1971 with a 10-2 finish. Their stock fell quickly, however, when losses started to add up and their brusque manner began to anger both Ole Miss fans and the press. The Kinards were fired three games into the 1973 season. Vaught came out of retirement to coach the football team and bring the Ole Miss fans back into the fold.

Still, Kinard remains a legendary figure for his playing and coaching success. He served as a team captain from high school all the way through his pro and service career, and he joined the Pro Football Hall of Fame in 1971 in the same class with Vince Lombardi, Jim Brown, Norm Van Brocklin, Y. A. Tittle and Andy Robustelli.

When asked what name he would prefer on his Hall of Fame ring, Kinard said, "Better make it Bruiser. If it said Frank, no one would know it was mine."

When Kinard died at age 70 in 1985, Vaught said, "Bruiser had been sick for a long, long time, but when we knew him and when he was well, he was one of the great, great people in sports."

The next year, the men's athletic dormitory on campus was dedicated as Kinard Hall. In 1992, he was named to the Ole Miss Team of the Century.

Air Kavanaugh

Ken Kavanaugh was a senior end for LSU when the Tigers became one of the first college football teams to fly to a game. It wasn't just any flight, either. It was an 11-hour, four-stop excursion to Worcester, Massachusetts, for a game with Holy Cross, then an Eastern football power.

While others in the travel party were getting sick on the flight, Kavanaugh was just nervous.

"I was trying to figure out how they kept that big machine in the air," Kavanaugh told author Marty Mule in *Game of My Life: Memorable Moments of Tigers Football.*

Kavanaugh eventually figured it out. Not only did he become a master of the air attack as a top-flight receiver in college and pro football, he went on to become a decorated World War II bomber pilot.

Kavanaugh grew up in Little Rock, Arkansas, during the Great Depression. He came to LSU in 1936 and played immediately as a sophomore in 1937, earning All-SEC honors. Kavanaugh eventually earned All-SEC honors three times, but more importantly, he helped transform the game as a record-setting end during a run-oriented era.

As a senior in 1939, Kavanaugh caught 30 passes for 467 yards and eight touchdowns, including four touchdowns against Holy Cross in LSU's 26-7 upset victory. The Tigers finished only 4-5 that season, but Kavanaugh still earned the SEC's Most Valuable Player award, finished seventh in the voting for the Heisman Trophy, and won the Knute Rockne Memorial Trophy as most outstanding lineman.

Even though he played baseball for LSU and minor league baseball for the St. Louis Cardinals, Kavanaugh knew his professional future belonged in football. He proved that point throughout a career as a player, coach, and scout.

As a pro player with the Chicago Bears, Kavanaugh teamed with legendary quarterback Sid Luckman to form a dangerous passing attack on some of coach George Halas' best teams. Kavanaugh became the best of the NFL's deep threats and went on to establish four Bears records that he either still holds or shares: most career touchdown receptions (50), most single-season touchdown receptions (13), most yards per reception in a career (22.4), and most yards per reception in a season (25.6).

In the age of the run-oriented, single-wing offense, LSU's Ken Kavanaugh was a standout receiver. In 1939, he led the nation with 30 catches for 467 yards in nine games and earned the SEC Most Valuable Player award. Kavanaugh is a member of the College Football Hall of Fame.

Who knows how many more records he might still hold if he had not spend three and a half of his prime athletic years serving in World War II? Kavanaugh joined the U.S. Air Force, reached the rank of captain, and faced constant risk by flying B-24s and B-17s on 30 air missions out of England. He received the Distinguished Flying Cross for his service.

Kavanaugh returned to football in 1946 and helped the Bears win the NFL championship that year. He enjoyed his best season in 1947, catching 32 passes for 818 yards and a league-leading 13 touchdowns.

Ken Kavanaugh (left) receives the Knute Rockne Memorial Trophy in January 1940 at the Touchdown Club in Washington, D.C. With him are Iowa's Nile Kinnick (center), winner of the Walter Camp Memorial Trophy, and Texas A&M's John Kimbrough (right).

After his final season in 1950, Kavanaugh went on to coach for the Bears, Boston College, Villanova, and the New York Giants until 1970, when he became a scout for the Giants. Throughout his life, Kavanaugh dabbled in offseason businesses such as cattle ranching in the Sierra Nevada mountains and the lumber and fuel oil businesses in Philadelphia, but he was at his best in football, where he developed a reputation for his keen scout's eye. During his 60 years in professional football, he played a valuable role for six NFL champions, including two Super Bowl winners.

Upon Kavanaugh's death in January of 2007, John Mara, the Giants' president and chief executive officer, said, "Ken Kavanaugh was a revered member of the Giants family. He led an extraordinary life, from his years of service in World War II through his career in the NFL as a player, coach, and scout. He made many important contributions to the Giants over the years and we will miss him very much."

Kavanaugh's extraordinary life is the subject of a book, *The Humility of Greatness*, written by his son Ken Kavanaugh Jr., himself a former LSU receiver.

Neyland's Vols Advance

"Here where the hills are high, Tennessee fans are calling on the Volunteers to give the state its first clear claim to national honors. Knoxville is the perfect example of civil lunacy. Every suburb is a wing of an asylum."

— **Henry McLemore, United Press International, 1939**

As an outsider, it was easy for McLemore to dismiss the fervor of Tennessee fans as "lunacy." To the folks in Knoxville and parts beyond, the passion for Volunteer football was justified by the emergence of one of the most successful eras in the history of Southern football.

In the midst of that era, Robert Neyland and the Vols won 33 consecutive regular-season games between 1937 and 1941, including a mind-boggling 17 consecutive regular-season shutouts from November 5, 1938, to October 12, 1940.

These accomplishments occurred on Neyland's second tour of duty as the Vols' head coach. Neyland was a captain in the United States Army when he led Tennessee to a 76-7-5 record from 1926 to 1934. His run of success was interrupted by a return to military service in Panama in 1934.

But Neyland's impact on the program was just as evident during his absence, as the Vols slipped to 4-5 in 1935 under Neyland assistant W. H. Britton. When Neyland retired from military service and returned to Tennessee in 1936, he immediately set about rebuilding the team into a winner.

After winning only six games each in 1936 and 1937, Neyland's rebuilding project took hold in 1938 when the Vols, led by end and future Tennessee coach Bowden Wyatt, finished 11-0, 7-0 in the SEC, outscored opponents 293-16 and held eight teams scoreless.

With a 17-0 victory over Oklahoma in the Orange Bowl, the Vols shared the national championship with Texas Christian University (TCU) and Notre Dame. While TCU won the Associated Press national title and selection from three other polls, Tennessee was selected the national champions (according to the NCAA) by eight polls: Billingsley, Board, Dunkel, Football Research, Houlgate, Litkenhous, Poling, and Sagarin.

For all the 1938 team accomplished, the 1939 team may have been more impressive. The Vols didn't allow a single point during the entire regular season and still reigns as the only SEC team to ever accomplish this improbable achievement.

Despite their remarkable success, the Vols had to share the SEC championship with Georgia Tech and Tulane when all three finished 6-0 in conference play. While Cornell, Southern Cal, and Texas A&M shared the national championship, Tennessee went on to lose 14-0 to Southern Cal in the Rose Bowl and finished 10-1.

The Vols added another chapter to this legendary era in 1940, winning all 10 regular-season games by recording eight shutouts and outscoring opponents 319-26. However, Tennessee lost 19-13 to Boston College in the 1941 Sugar Bowl. While the Vols finished fourth in the final AP poll behind champion Minnesota, they still earned national championship recognition from the Dunkel and Williamson polls.

Tennessee's streak of regular-season success barely slowed when Neyland was recalled to active duty in the spring of 1941. By the time Tennessee finally lost on October 4, 1941, former Vol player and assistant John Barnhill had stepped in for Neyland. Barnhill led Tennessee to a 32-5-2 record with four second-place SEC finishes in four seasons before World War II put the program on hold in 1943. Still, those successful teams could not match—nor could many SEC teams before or since—the towering standard set by the Vols from 1938 to 1940.

Those teams were known for more than just dominating defense, innovative offense, and military precision. The Vols were also loaded with hard-nosed athletes who fit Neyland's aggressive approach. Rugged linemen Bob Suffridge, Marshall

Under Coach Robert Neyland, the Tennessee Volunteers won 33 consecutive regular-season games between 1937 and 1941, including an extraordinary 17 consecutive shutouts in one stretch.

"Abe" Shires, and Ed Molinski paved the way up front for fleet, feisty backs George "Bad News" Cafego, Johnny Butler, Sam Bartholomew, Bob Foxx, and end Bowden Wyatt—a core described by Allison Danzig of *The New York Times* as "the hardest tackling, blocking and running crew assembled on a gridiron since Knute Rockne's teams were mowing down."

Before the Vols played Southern Cal in the 1940 Rose Bowl, Danzig wrote, "Tennessee is just about the perfectly coached team, outstanding for the savagery of its tackling, the protection it gives its passer, its coverage of its punts, and the strengths of its kicking. . . . If anything said herein indicates an improper lack of respect for the Volunteers, let

it be testified here and now that this department's idea of a sure way to avoid growing old is to get Messrs. Molinski, Suffridge, and Shires fighting mad."

The Vols were more than talented. They could be colorful, too, with an interesting assortment of characters such as Suffridge, Cafego, and Wyatt. Bob Suffridge, a graduate of Knoxville's Central High, won the Knute Rockne Memorial Trophy as the nation's most outstanding collegiate lineman and was named MVP by the Atlanta Touchdown Club. He was described in his College Football Hall of Fame bio as "so quick he once blocked the same point-after-touchdown three times, twice called for offsides when many observers felt he wasn't."

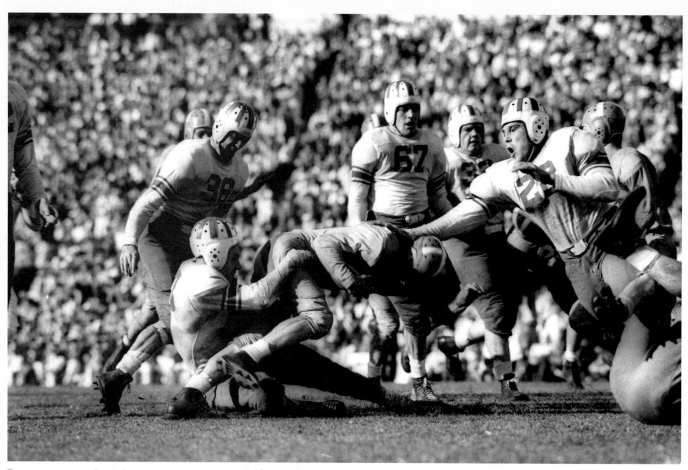

Tennessee quarterback Buist Warren carried the Vols to a 17-0 victory over Oklahoma in the 1939 Orange Bowl. Tennessee completed the season with an 11-0 record (7-0 in SEC play).

In the book *Legends of the Tennessee Vols*, Suffridge's mischief is evident. As a freshman in 1937, he roomed with end Jimmy Coleman, and the two turned out to be too rowdy for their own good. Neyland decided it was time to separate them and told them to find new roommates.

Suffridge agreed, insisting he didn't even like Coleman and telling Neyland it was Coleman who was always getting him into trouble. When Neyland asked weeks later why Suffridge and Coleman had not made arrangements for new roommates, Suffridge said, "Nobody else would room with me and nobody else would room with Coleman."

Neyland responded, "You two remind me of a couple of cadets I knew at West Point." Suffridge couldn't let it go. He had to ask, "Who was the other one, Major?"

For all the headaches he caused Neyland, Suffridge must have been worth it. The Vols lost two games in Suffridge's three years. Suffridge earned a spot on the all-time AP All-America Team, the all-time All-SEC Team (1933–1982), and the Half-Century All-America Team (1950). He also earned membership in the Tennessee Sports Hall of Fame and the Sugar Bowl, Rose Bowl, and Orange Bowl halls of fame.

When asked who his greatest players were, Neyland often refused to name names. Once, however, Neyland admitted, "I'll start a team, but will not attempt to complete it. You'll have to start with Bob Suffridge, the greatest lineman I ever saw, and that's as far as I will go with the line."

Legend says George Cafego earned his nickname from an opponent who thought Cafego was "Bad News." What those opponents probably didn't realize was that Cafego had to be tough to survive a difficult childhood in Scarbro, West Virginia. Cafego never knew his mother, and saw his father

George "Bad News" Cafego was bad news indeed for opponents. Cafego, a member of the College Football Hall of Fame, came from the coal mines of West Virginia and became a two-time All-American back for Tennessee. In 1938 and 1939, Cafego helped lead the Vols to an overall record of 21-1 and a conference record of 13-0.

die of a broken back. He lived with anyone who would take him, whether it was a sister, a coach, or even a boarding house he shared with coal miners.

Mining most likely would have been Cafego's future if not for football, specifically Tennessee football. Cafego tried to generate interest from several schools, including Ohio State, Notre Dame, and West Virginia, but those schools considered him to be too small and Marshall only offered a partial scholarship.

In *Legends of the Tennessee Vols*, Cafego said, "I had nothing. . . . I didn't need a partial scholarship. I needed everything." Cafego arrived in Knoxville with a suitcase held together by a string, and he didn't own a suit until a Tennessee coach bought him one.

Bowden Wyatt presented an interesting dichotomy. On one hand, he was a rough-and-ready country boy from Kingston, Tennessee, who was out fishing on the river when Tennessee freshman coach Hugh Faust came to town. On the other hand, he played the piano and dabbled in theater as a child, with parents who did not allow him to play sports if his grades slipped below a 90 average.

He possessed movie-star good looks and a certain masculine charm, but Wyatt was a football man through and through. He was good enough to earn All-America honors at Tennessee and later returned to his alma mater as head football coach.

As a player, Wyatt was a rugged end who made his impact as a determined tackler, blocker, and competitor. He served as captain in 1938, played a key role on the defensive line, and even kicked a field goal when Tennessee beat Oklahoma 17-0 in the Orange Bowl, the Vols' first official bowl game. It's no wonder Neyland once said Wyatt "is the best looking athlete Tennessee has had in a long time. Apparently he has everything."

Rugged lineman Ed "Big Mo" Molinski was part of the foundation of Tennessee's success from 1938 to 1940, a period in which the Vols won 31 of 33 games and played in the Orange, Rose, and Sugar Bowls. Molinski, a member of the College Football Hall of Fame, made five different All-America teams as a guard in 1939.

Legend has it that Wyatt actually had an offer to take his good looks to Hollywood following his college career. Instead, Wyatt served as an assistant at Mississippi State from 1939 to 1941, served in the Navy from 1942 to 1945, and returned to Mississippi State as an assistant for one season before the University of Wyoming hired him as its head football coach in 1947. Applying the lessons he learned from Neyland, Wyatt spent six seasons at Wyoming and led the Cowboys to national prominence for the first time before he decided it was time to move closer to home.

Wyatt found his opportunity at the University of Arkansas in 1953. He needed only two years to turn the Razorbacks into winners. They beat Texas for the first time in 17 years and won the Southwest Conference championship in 1954. But Neyland was Tennessee's athletic director at that point and when he came calling, Wyatt couldn't say no to his coach and school.

In 1956, his second season on the job, Wyatt's Vols finished 10-0 in the regular season and won the SEC before losing to Baylor in the Sugar Bowl. He never enjoyed that level of success again, and the program fell on tough times. Wyatt lost his job following the 1962 season. He died in 1969 at the age of 51.

Through the years, Wyatt's former players have rallied to his defense, and he remains a popular figure in Tennessee football history. Wyatt was inducted as a player into the College Football Hall of Fame in 1972 and as a coach in 1997.

In 1938, end Bowden Wyatt was the captain of an 11-0 Tennessee team that outscored opponents 283-16 and allowed only one touchdown in 11 games. Wyatt, a two-time All-American, went on to be enshrined in the College Football Hall of Fame as a player in 1972 and as a coach in 1997.

Bob Suffridge was a dominant player on both sides of the ball for a Tennessee team that didn't lose a regular-season game between 1938 and 1940. "Suff" anchored the Vols' dominating line. He has been selected to the College Football Hall of Fame, the all-time AP All-America Team, the all-time All-SEC Team (1933–1982), and the Half-Century All-America Team (1950).

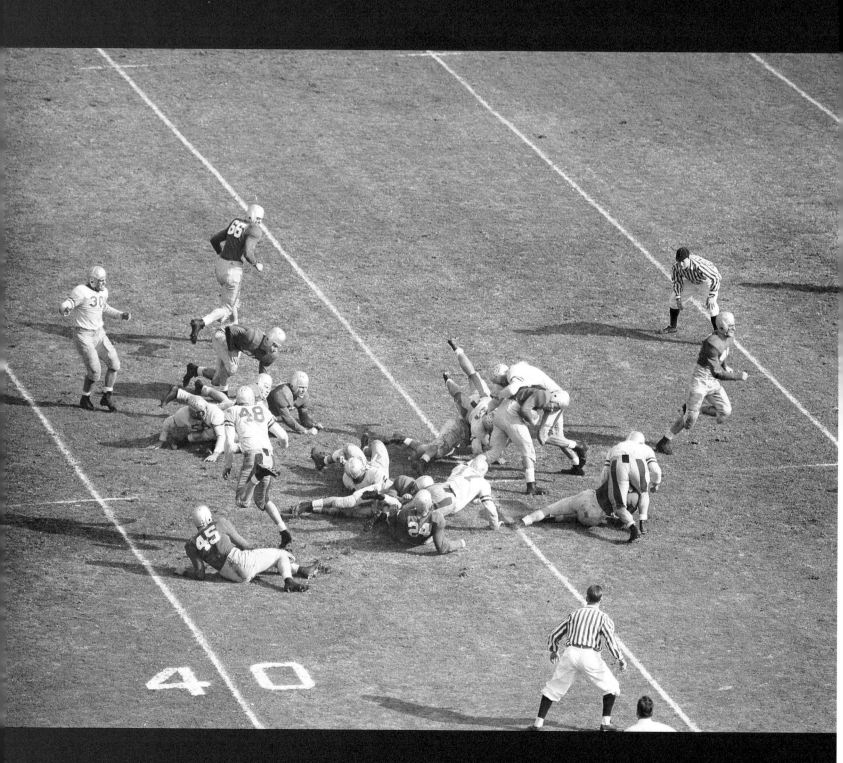

The 1940s

Fields of Glory

A decade that shaped America's "Greatest Generation" started with much promise for the Southeastern Conference. As the Axis powers invaded foreign territories and pushed the world closer to war, on the other side of the globe Tennessee continued to build on what would become a 31-game regular-season winning streak on its way to a 10-1 record, the SEC championship, and a share of the national championship in 1940. By the next spring, Vols coach Robert Neyland, then a major in the U.S. Army, would be recalled to active service in Panama.

The 1940 season also saw a significant change in the administration of the conference, the departure of Sewanee from the SEC, and the emergence of Mississippi State as a force on the football field. With the 1939 arrival of coach Allyn McKeen, who played for Neyland at Tennessee, the Maroons of Mississippi State College improved from 4-6 in 1938 to 8-2 in McKeen's first season. In 1940, the Maroons improved to 9-0-1, finished second to Tennessee in the conference standings, and defeated Georgetown University in the Orange Bowl.

Off the field, the SEC decided it was time to hire a full-time commissioner to oversee the daily operations of the conference and provide a central structure of rules enforcement and communications. When Martin Sennett Conner became the SEC's first commissioner on August 20, 1940, his appointment signified the serious intentions of the conference members' presidents in regard to the business of athletics.

Conner didn't have an extensive athletic background. Rather, he was a successful attorney out of Jackson, Mississippi. In January 1932, at the age of 41, he became the governor of the state at a time "when men are shaken with doubt and fear, and many are wondering if our very civilization is about to crumble," as Conner said at his inauguration.

Conner inherited a bankrupt state treasury and a $13 million deficit, but he put the state back on firm financial footing by the time he completed his term in 1936. Four years later, Conner accepted an annual salary of $7,500 from the SEC and established the first conference office in Jackson.

Georgia halfback Frank Sinkwich barrels through the UCLA defense during the 1943 Rose Bowl. Sinkwich led the Bulldogs to a 9-0 win in the game, a 10-1 record on the season, and a share of the national championship.

Just four months after taking over, Conner accepted Sewanee's withdrawal from the SEC on December 13, 1940. A football program that once ranked among the best in the South had not won an SEC game in 39 tries and decided it was time to move on.

In its letter of resignation, Sewanee admitted, "A small liberal arts college simply cannot compete in football with larger universities. Equal competition in other sports is very difficult."

The SEC and its remaining 12 members turned their attention toward a 1941 season that would see Mississippi State win its first and only conference title in football to date. The Maroons finished 4-0-1 in the SEC and 8-1-1 overall. Despite its success, Mississippi State did not earn a share of the national championship, and the Houlgate poll awarded its title to an 8-2 Alabama team that had lost to the Maroons that season 14-0.

One day after Mississippi State completed its season with an impressive 26-13 victory at San Francisco, Japan launched its sneak attack on Pearl Harbor. Sports quickly took a backseat to more important matters, and able young men shifted their focus from college athletics and studies to joining the war effort.

The SEC, like most college conferences, continued to participate in sports in 1942. Campus leaders at both Georgia and Georgia Tech proposed dropping football in the spring of 1942. Fortunately for Georgia, that proposal failed. Led by coach Wally Butts and an outstanding backfield featuring Frank Sinkwich and Charley Trippi, the Bulldogs finished 10-1. They won the SEC crown, defeated UCLA 9-0 in the Rose Bowl, and earned a share of the national championship in six different polls.

While Sinkwich completed his college career in 1942 by becoming the SEC's first Heisman Trophy winner, Trippi was just getting started. Like so many players of his day, Trippi's career was interrupted by World War II. He returned to play two more seasons for the Bulldogs in 1945 and 1946, and finished second in the Heisman voting in 1946.

In 1943, seven SEC schools cancelled their seasons and the other five played under unusual circumstances. Georgia and LSU played with freshmen and transfers. Vanderbilt played only five games, none against SEC teams. Georgia Tech was able to put together a schedule of 10 games. What made Tech so different? The Tech roster was filled with military officers from the Navy's V-12 program, a training initiative created to produce more college-educated officers. Some of

When former Mississippi governor Martin Sennett Conner was named the SEC's first commissioner in August 1940, it was a sure sign that the conference presidents took the business side of athletics seriously. Conner accepted an annual salary of $7,500 and established the first conference office, in Jackson, Mississippi.

those players happened to be from other top college football programs, including Alabama, Vanderbilt, and Clemson. Georgia's record book doesn't count its losses to Georgia Tech in 1943 and 1944; Tech's counts those games as wins.

All 12 schools fielded teams in 1944, but Vanderbilt played only four games, none against SEC competition, and 9 other teams played fewer than 10 games. Many of those schools relied on freshmen and men who had been declared 4-F (physically unacceptable for military service).

The schools also lost players who never came home. One of the most famous was Georgia Tech's Clint Castleberry, who finished third in the Heisman Trophy voting in 1942—as a freshman. Castleberry enlisted in the Army Air Corps and intended to return to Georgia Tech after the war, but his B-26 Marauder bomber, known as "Dream Girl," never returned from a mission in Africa, and his body was never recovered. Florida standout Walter "Tiger" Mayberry was a decorated Marine pilot who lost his life in battle. Ole Miss star Bill "Greaser" Smith, who played three sports in college and served as president of the student body, was killed in action at Saipan. Georgia lost eight players in all.

Several SEC football players never returned home from fighting in World War II. One of the most famous was Georgia Tech's Clint Castleberry. As a freshman in 1942, Castleberry finished third in the Heisman Trophy voting. During the war, his B-26 Marauder, "Dream Girl," never returned from a bombing mission in Africa. His body was never recovered.

Thanks to World War II and the NCAA's eligibility policies of the time, end Barney Poole played seven years of varsity football at three different schools—three seasons at Ole Miss (1941, 47–48), one at North Carolina (1943) and three at Army (1944–46). He was also a three-time All-American.

The combination of the war and the NCAA's eligibility policies of the era led to some unique playing careers. One of the most interesting careers belonged to George Barney Poole, a three-time All-American end who played seven years of varsity football at three different schools: three seasons at Ole Miss, one at North Carolina, and three at Army.

Poole enrolled at Ole Miss in 1941, played on the freshman team that year, and enlisted in the Marines. He was stationed at the Marines' V-12 Unit at the University of North Carolina, where he played the 1943 season. During a three-year stint at West Point from 1944 to 1946, Poole played with Army legends Glenn Davis and Doc Blanchard. After the war Poole wanted to return to Ole Miss, but Army coach Earl Blaik wouldn't grant him a release. Poole reportedly flunked out of the academy on purpose and returned to Ole Miss for the 1947 and 1948 seasons.

The SEC started to return to relative normalcy in 1945, as every team played at least nine games. The best of the bunch was Alabama's "War Babies," a 37-man team loaded with freshmen and 4-Fs. This was the last Crimson Tide team to play in and win the Rose Bowl. Capped by a 34-14 victory over USC in the Rose Bowl, Alabama finished the season 10-0 with an SEC championship and a share of the national championship in one poll.

Coach Frank Thomas, who led Alabama to a share of three national championships and four SEC championships in 15 seasons, retired due to health problems after the 1946 season. That same year, long-time Tulane athletic director Wilbur Smith resigned after one year as NCAA president, citing personal reasons. Health issues then forced Martin Sennett Conner to resign as SEC commissioner.

While Thomas, Smith, and Conner departed the college football world, former Alabama end Paul "Bear" Bryant left Maryland to become the head coach at Kentucky in 1946. Bryant brought unprecedented football success to a school that had won only one of 20 conference games from 1941 to 1945. After winning only two of ten games overall in 1945, Kentucky won seven games in each of the next two seasons and finished 9-2 and tied for second in the SEC in 1949.

On the field, Georgia finished 10-0 in 1946, shared the SEC championship with Tennessee, and went on to beat North Carolina 20-10 in the Sugar Bowl for a share of the national championship in one poll. Off the field, SEC leaders started earning key positions on NCAA councils and committees and took a more active role in shaping college football.

In 1948, Alabama and Auburn played each other for the first time since 1907, setting aside a 41-year feud that started over per diem money for the players and disagreement over the number of players that could suit up for each team. Even the state legislature failed to bring the teams together. The iron walls finally dropped when the presidents of the two universities, Auburn's Dr. Ralph Draughon and Alabama's Dr. John Gallalee, got together while attending a meeting regarding other matters and decided there was no reason why the teams couldn't play.

That same year, the conference chose former LSU football coach Bernie Moore as its new commissioner. Moore moved the conference offices to Birmingham, a central location for a conference that spread from New Orleans to Gainesville, Florida, and north to Lexington, Kentucky. Moore also set up an information and publicity bureau to publish and distribute statistics and conference communications.

By 1949, the SEC was starting to make money and return it to the members. Even before widespread television and significant bowl-game revenue, the SEC was turning its football success and popularity into profits.

Alabama coach Frank Thomas prepares his team for the 1946 Rose Bowl game against USC. The Crimson Tide won the game 34-14 and earned a share of the national championship.

McKeen's Maroons

By the 1940s, Tennessee and Alabama had established themselves as the conference's best football programs. From 1938 to 1941, no team in all of college football could match Tennessee's success under coach Robert Neyland. In the midst of the Vols' run, though, a different team—one coached by a Neyland protégé—rose from the middle of the SEC pack to challenge Tennessee for the conference championship.

Allyn McKeen led Mississippi State to unprecedented success as its head coach from 1939 to 1942 and 1944 to 1948. In 1940, the Maroons went 9-0-1 and beat Georgetown in the Orange Bowl. In 1941, the school won its only SEC football championship to date. McKeen is a member of the College Football Hall of Fame.

By the second game of the 1941 season, it was impossible for the college football world to ignore Mississippi State. After the Maroons (as they were called at that time) defeated Alabama 14-0 on October 4, sportswriter Grantland Rice took stock of their rise in his national column, writing, "How many recall the fact that Mississippi State, located at a sun-baked citadel known as State College, hasn't lost a football game in 17 starts? Among her victims you find Alabama twice, Georgetown's crack team from last fall, LSU, Mississippi, and several others who can play football."

The primary force behind Mississippi State's emergence was Coach Allyn McKeen. Born in Kentucky and raised in Memphis, McKeen played end for Neyland at Tennessee. In 1926, he scored the first touchdown for Neyland's first Tennessee team. In 1927, he scored 27 points on 21 extra points and two field goals. In his college career, he never missed an extra point and never dropped a pass.

McKeen was at his best as a coach, applying Neyland's principles and innovation to a team that won one SEC game in 1938. In 1939, the Maroons improved to 8-2 overall and 3-2 in conference games. The rest of the SEC took notice on November 11, when McKeen's team defeated LSU 15-12 in Baton Rouge. Bill Keefe of the *New Orleans Times-Picayune* wrote that McKeen and his assistants "brought State from oblivion into the limelight in no time flat."

In 1940, the Maroons took off. They finished 10-0-1, 4-0-1 in the SEC, and beat Georgetown 14-7 in the Orange Bowl. Following that season, the Associated Press reported that Mississippi State "reigns as undisputed king of football in the Deep South."

The Maroons lost many key players from the 1940 team and weren't expected to be as good in 1941, but they still had McKeen and standout J. T. "Blondy" Black. With their early victory over an Alabama team that was expected to win the SEC that year, the Maroons served notice that they weren't going to fade away.

"Alabama was not only beaten, 14 to 0," wrote Grantland Rice, "but was badly outplayed by Coach McKeen's team that now has an excellent chance of going through another unbeaten year and finding again the solace of another bowl party on New Year's Day."

Billy Jefferson scores the winning touchdown for Mississippi State, then known as the Maroons, in a 14-7 victory over Georgetown in the 1941 Orange Bowl, capping MSU's only undefeated season.

Although they finished 8-1-1 and won the SEC championship with a 4-0-1 record, the Maroons did not receive a bowl invitation. With only five bowls at the time, there was no such thing as an automatic bid for the SEC champion. Alabama (8-2) played in the Cotton Bowl and Georgia (8-1-1) played in the Orange Bowl.

That 1941 squad remains the only Mississippi State team to win an SEC football championship.

"It was not a really good football team, but it had desire," McKeen later recalled in the book *The Maroon Bulldogs*. "That team got more out of its ability than any team I coached."

Mississippi State had to settle for a final regular-season game at San Francisco. The Maroons won the game, 26-13, on December 6, 1941. As they celebrated their victory on the train to Los Angeles the next day, however, the team's mood took a serious turn.

"I remember we were playing cards when someone came through and said Pearl Harbor had been bombed," halfback Spook Murphy said in *The Maroon Bulldogs*. "I remember Coach McKeen saying that we would whip them in six months. I believed him."

McKeen completed his coaching career at Mississippi State in 1948 with a 65-19-3 record. He left the game and moved to Montgomery, Alabama, where he owned a sporting goods business.

Sinkwich Finds a Home in the South

Frank Sinkwich was born well above the Mason-Dixon Line, but his heart belonged to Georgia.

Born in McKees Rocks, Pennsylvania, and raised in Youngstown, Ohio, Sinkwich found his fame and fortune in football at the University of Georgia, where he became a two-time consensus All-American halfback and the SEC's first Heisman Trophy winner in 1942.

"I'm from Ohio," Sinkwich said, "but if I'd known when I was two what it was like down South, I would have crawled here on hands and knees."

It took a twist of fate and a low gas tank to bring Sinkwich all the way from Ohio to Georgia. In the summer of 1939, former Georgia assistant Bill Hartman was on a mission to recruit the best back in Youngstown. At the time, however, that back was not Sinkwich.

"We went to contact the best back in Ohio, who was in Youngstown," Hartman told the *Athens Banner-Herald*. "When we got there, the boy had already made up his mind to go to Ohio State. His name was Paul. I forget his last name now, but he went to Ohio State.

"Coming back out of town, we stopped at a filling station to get some gas and got to talking to the filling station attendant. And he said, 'Well, the best back in the state really lives right down the street here, about three or four blocks.' We said, 'Who is that?' And he said, 'Well, that's Frank Sinkwich.'"

Hartman found Sinkwich sitting on the porch of the family home. At 5-foot, 10-inches tall and 185 pounds, Sinkwich didn't make much of an impression, but that changed over the course of the day. Hartman saw enough in the young man to invite him to Georgia for a recruiting visit.

When the coaches saw Sinkwich with a football in his hands, it didn't take long to realize that Hartman had found something special.

"Back at that time, you could do anything you wanted to with high school prospects," Hartman said. "We went out and got a ball and a center and we put [Sinkwich] at wingback first. . . . The center would snap the ball to the tailback and Sinkwich would come around and take it on a wingback reverse. Well, the thing that impressed us almost

"Fireball Frankie" Sinkwich helped put Georgia football on the map in 1942. Sinkwich used his combination of running and passing skills to set a national record with 2,187 yards of total offense.

immediately was how quick he could start. We saw with that quickness that he could be a real good tailback in the single-wing, rather than as a wingback."

After that impressive visit, Sinkwich didn't have to crawl on his hands and knees to reach Georgia, even though he might have been tough enough to pull it off. Born to ethnic Croatian parents who immigrated from Russian Georgia, Sinkwich learned some valuable lessons while growing up on the working-class streets of Youngstown's West Side.

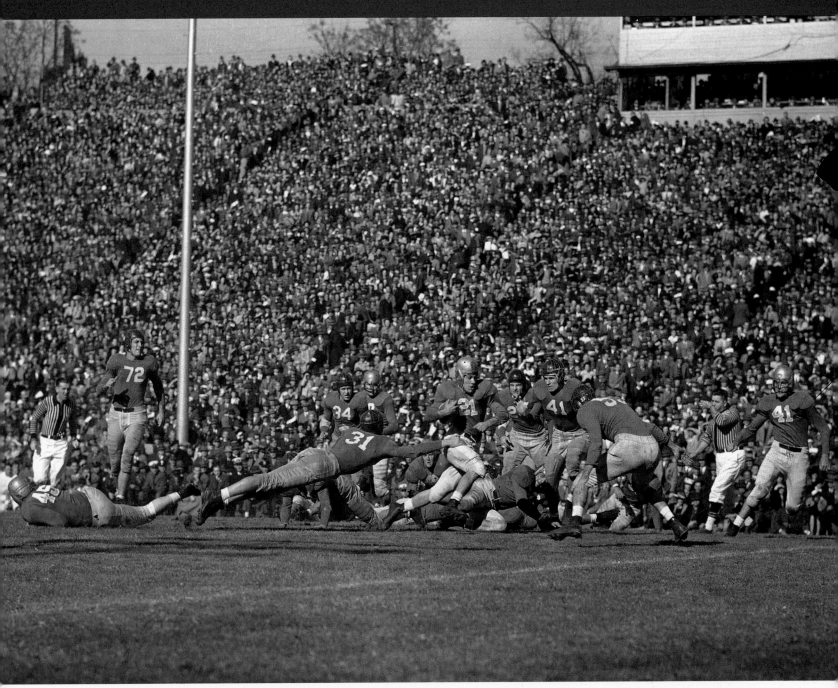

Georgia's Frank Sinkwich—seen here wearing number 21 and running for a first down against Tulane—ran with an awkward, flat-footed style that disguised his combination of speed and power.

"I learned early in neighborhood pickup games that I had the desire to compete," he said. "When people ask why I succeeded in athletics, I always tell them that I didn't want to get beat."

That same toughness was obvious at Georgia, where he was more than just a star back on an outstanding team. In 1941, three weeks after Sinkwich suffered a broken jaw in a game against South Carolina, the Bulldogs traveled to New York to play a formidable Columbia University team. Sinkwich played with his jaw wired shut and held intact with a cumbersome, padded chinstrap. The injury made breathing difficult so Sinkwich made frequent trips to the sideline between plays to receive a few whiffs of oxygen and get his wires tightened with a pair of pliers. He still played the entire game—with no facemask—and scored the game's only touchdown in a 7-3 victory.

Sinkwich wanted to be a fullback so he could run the ball all the time. Georgia Coach Wally Butts (right) had to convince him to play halfback so he could take advantage of Sinkwich's strong arm.

"He can do everything but bite into a steak," said Columbia coach Lou Little.

Sinkwich certainly could do everything as a true triple threat, running, punting, and passing his way to SEC and national recognition. The running and punting came naturally to Sinkwich, but it took some convincing and practice before coach Wally Butts and Hartman could get Sinkwich to include passing in his arsenal.

"He was mainly an effective passer because he could fake the run," Dan Magill, former Georgia sports information director and tennis coach told the *Banner-Herald*. "[Defenses] were so scared of him running that he could detect them if they came in too close and he could find somebody open to complete a pass."

After making his presence known as a sophomore, Sinkwich earned All-America honors and finished fourth in the Heisman voting in 1941. More important, he helped a team that finished 5-4-1 in 1940 improve to 9-1-1 and earn

Georgia its first official postseason berth. In the Orange Bowl, the "Point-a-Minute" Bulldogs beat TCU 40-26. Sinkwich rushed for 139 yards, passed for 243 yards, and scored three touchdowns.

When talented halfback Charlie Trippi joined the varsity team in 1942, Sinkwich moved to fullback—a position that barely resembles the blocking back it has become today. Sinkwich continued to excel as a triple threat, setting an SEC passing record of 1,392 yards and a school record for touchdown responsibility (27) that stands today. He repeated as an All-American, won the Heisman, and led Georgia to a 9-0 Rose Bowl victory over UCLA. It was his final college game, and he played on two sprained ankles. To top it off, Georgia shared the national championship with Ohio State following the 1942 season. In the words of Magill, Sinkwich "put us on the map."

Sinkwich had joined the Marine Corps and he accepted his Heisman Trophy wearing his Marine Corps uniform. He wanted to serve his country, but flat feet and high blood pressure led to an honorable discharge. He spent the 1943 and 1944 seasons with the Detroit Lions and earned All-Pro honors both years and the league's most valuable player award in 1944.

The U.S. Army Air Force finally accepted him after the 1944 season and sent him to play on the Air Force football team in Colorado Springs, but he suffered a serious knee injury that led to two operations. Sinkwich soon retired and returned to his adopted home of Athens to start a family. He eventually became a beer distributor in Northeast Georgia and remained in Athens until his death on October 22, 1990.

Upon Sinkwich's death, longtime Georgia coach and athletic director Vince Dooley said, "We've lost one of the great legends in football history. He was not only a great player but a wonderful person and citizen of Athens."

Opposite: The SEC's first Heisman Trophy winner, halfback Frank Sinkwich, accepts his award in his Marine uniform, just days after entering the Corps. Flat feet and high blood pressure led to an honorable discharge, but Sinkwich later served in the Air Force.

From Rockne to Tuscaloosa

When Wallace Wade announced his resignation as Alabama's head coach in April 1930, he agreed to honor the final year of his contact to give the school time to find a new football coach. Wade also offered President George H. "Mike" Denny some advice.

"There is a young backfield coach at Georgia who should become one of the greatest coaches in the country," Wade wrote to Denny. "He played football under [Knute] Rockne at Notre Dame. Rock called him one of the smartest players he ever coached. He is Frank Thomas, and I don't believe you could pick a better man."

Thomas made good on Wade's recommendation. Thomas inherited a winning program from Wade in 1931 and perpetuated Alabama's success by winning the first SEC championship in 1933. His teams went on to win two national championships and four conference titles. Alabama posted a 115-24-7 record in fifteen seasons under Thomas, during which the team never had a losing season. During the Thomas era, the Crimson Tide also played in the Rose Bowl three times and earned trips to the Cotton, Orange, and Sugar bowls.

Thomas grew up in Chicago, the son of Welsh immigrants. His father was an ironworker, but Thomas' high school coach, Floyd Murphy, convinced him to go to college. He started at Kalamazoo College (1919) and ended up at Notre Dame (1920–1922), where he once roomed with George Gipp, the Fighting Irish star immortalized in Rockne's "Win One for the Gipper" speech in the movie, *Knute Rockne, All-American.*

Rockne saw something special in Thomas. "It's amazing the amount of football sense that Thomas kid has," Rockne remarked. "He can't help becoming a great coach some day." When Thomas arrived at Alabama, he replaced Wade's single-wing offense with Rockne's Notre Dame box offense. In his first three seasons, Thomas' teams finished 9-1 in 1931, 8-2 in 1932, and 7-1-1 in 1933. The 1934 squad went 10-0 and beat Stanford in the Rose Bowl for the Crimson Tide's fourth national championship. That 1934 team included the lethal combination of Millard "Dixie" Howell and Don Hutson as well as a hard-nosed end from Morrow Bottom, Arkansas, named Paul Bryant.

Thomas' teams were fast and tough. Three games into the 1935 season, Bryant suffered a broken leg in the first quarter, yet he returned in the third quarter and finished the game. Bryant ended up in a cast and on crutches, but only missed one game before returning to play in a 25-0

Frank Thomas played quarterback for Coach Knute Rockne at Notre Dame from 1920 to 1922 and went on to coach at Alabama from 1931 to 1946. (Alabama had no team in 1943.) The Crimson Tide went 108-20-7 during Thomas' tenure and won a share of three national championships.

Alabama sophomore Johnny August bounds through the Boston College defense during the 1943 Orange Bowl. The Crimson Tide came from behind in the game to win 37-21. Alabama was 5-1 in six bowl games under Coach Frank Thomas.

victory at Tennessee. In the 1938 Rose Bowl, All-American guard Leroy Monsky played with 14 stitches and a drain on his eye after colliding with a teammate during a stopover practice on the way to California. Monsky refused to wear a face bar on his helmet and paid the price in the first quarter while tackling 224-pound Cal quarterback Johnny Meek. The hit knocked him out and tore his face open again, but Monsky returned in the second quarter and played the rest of the game.

Alabama won a share of another national championship in 1941 before World War II called most able young men to military service. When the Crimson Tide joined most college football programs in canceling the 1943 season, Thomas devoted his time to leading War Bond drives and serving as the president of the Tuscaloosa Exchange Club. When Alabama decided to restart its football program in 1944, Thomas filled the roster with 17- and 18-year-old freshmen and players who were unable to serve in the military for medical reasons, including Harry Gilmer, a 155-pound halfback from Birmingham's Woodlawn High School, and Vaughn Mancha, who spent two years in the Merchant Navy because vision problems from a childhood injury prevented him from serving in the military.

With Gilmer and Mancha leading the charge, the team Thomas called his "War Babies" won five games, lost one, and tied two. They earned an invitation to play in the Sugar Bowl against a Duke team loaded with naval officers in training. Despite the gap in age and experience, the Tide held its own in a 29-26 loss.

"I've never been so proud of any team I've coached," Thomas said.

In 1945 the Crimson Tide welcomed back several players returning from the war. The team set a school record with 430 points scored and won all nine of its regular-season games, good enough to earn an invitation to play in the Rose Bowl.

Above: Lineman Leroy Monsky was the captain of Alabama's 1937 team and one of Coach Thomas' favorites. Thomas said his own practice philosophy was, "Keep the players high and make practice a pleasure but not a lark. Be a disciplinarian, but not a slave-driver."

"Haven't my War Babies grown up?" Thomas told his wife before the bowl. "These are the greatest kids I've ever coached. I'm sure they'll do just as fine a job against Southern California as my 1935 team did against Stanford."

The Crimson Tide defeated USC 34-14. Sadly, it was Thomas' last complete season at Alabama. Thomas started to experience increasing fatigue and high blood pressure. He tried changing his diet, foregoing cigarettes, and resting more frequently, and he spent the summer visiting medical specialists in North Carolina. However, he spent most of the 1946 season in bed, rising only to conduct practices while riding in a trailer because he could no longer stand for long periods of time.

After a 7-4 finish, Thomas resigned following the season and agreed to become Alabama's athletic director. His deteriorating health eventually forced him to leave that job as well. In 1951, he became a charter member of the College Football Hall of Fame. He died in 1954.

"We knew Coach Thomas was not well, but he was not the kind of man to complain or quit," Hal Self, Alabama's quarterback from 1954 to 1956, said in *Bowl Bama Bowl.* "He was some fellow. Even when he was sick, he worked hard until he could work no more. We all loved him for it, too."

Tackle Don Whitmire played two years at Alabama (1941 and '42) before transferring to the Naval Academy, where he won the Rockne Trophy as the nation's best lineman. He was elected to the College Football Hall of Fame in 1956 and became a rear admiral in the U.S. Navy.

Thomas stands in a Pasadena train station with two of his star players, halfback Harry Gilmer (left) and center Vaughn Mancha (right), as the Crimson Tide arrives for the 1946 Rose Bowl. Alabama defeated USC 34-14.

Alabama's "War Babies"

Harry Gilmer was a sub during his sophomore and junior seasons at Birmingham's Woodlawn High School, and he didn't throw a pass in a game until his senior year. Even after colleges started to notice him, he figured he'd follow his father into the carpentry business. That is, until an Alabama assistant coach convinced Gilmer to give college a try.

Gilmer showed up on campus in 1944 in time to join Alabama's first team following a one-year hiatus for World War II. Gilmer was part of a group of freshmen and 4-Fs who provided the nucleus of the 1944 team. He arrived at Alabama weighing only 155 pounds and suffering from a stomach ulcer. Doctors put him on a strict diet of milk, cereals, and strained vegetables, and he was not allowed to eat any meat.

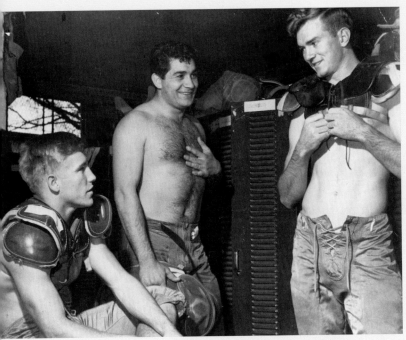

Lowell Tew, Vaughn Mancha, and Harry Gilmer all played valuable roles for Coach Frank Thomas' "War Babies" at Alabama in the 1940s.

Because of the diet, Gilmer wasn't able to add to his thin frame. What he was able to do was make an immediate impact as an 18-year-old freshman, starting as the left halfback and primary passer in coach Frank Thomas' Notre Dame box offense.

"There weren't any upperclassmen there to be ahead of me," Gilmer said. "We only had about 35 players on the whole squad. I didn't know any better. I was the one who was there to do that job and I worked at doing it. I liked it. I loved it, really. I really enjoyed playing football."

Gilmer's teammate, center and defensive lineman Vaughn Mancha, tried to join the military in the spring of 1942, but none of the four primary services was willing to give him a chance, even in the reserves. Instead, he joined

the Merchant Navy, moved to California, and worked repairing destroyers for two years. Having spent his teenage years toiling through the Depression as a boilermaker, Mancha knew how to work. He also knew how to overcome the vision problems that kept him out of the military.

Mancha was six years old and living in Sugar Valley, Georgia, when a child playing with a bow and arrow shot him directly in the middle of his left eye. The injury left him with decent peripheral vision but blurred straight-ahead vision. The injury didn't keep him from becoming a high school star or from making plans to play at Alabama in 1941. The war delayed his plans, but it didn't change them. When UCLA attempted to recruit him, Mancha barely gave the Bruins the time of day. "All I could think of was wanting to get back to Alabama," Mancha says.

Mancha was older, bigger, stronger, and more mature than the freshmen he played with and against, and it showed. "I was 240 (pounds) with good speed," Mancha said, "and that helped."

Alabama was one of the relatively few schools able to field a full team in 1944, filling the roster with 17- and 18-year-olds and 4-Fs. Led by Gilmer and Mancha, the Crimson Tide—Thomas' "War Babies"—played an eight-game schedule and finished 5-1-2. That led to an invitation to the Sugar Bowl to play against a veteran Duke team loaded with Navy trainees.

Despite the differences in age, experience, and depth, the Crimson Tide gave the Blue Devils all they could handle before losing 29-26. After the game, Grantland Rice called Gilmer "the most amazing back that football can show today."

Duke star Tom Davis agreed and told Rice, "[Gilmer] is no 158-pounder. He must have nailed me 10 times today and I thought he was going to tear me apart."

Rice also observed that Gilmer wasn't the only talent that Coach Frank Thomas had to work with. "Mancha, one of the best centers in football, heads a strong, fast charging line."

Opposite: Because of Alabama's depleted roster during World War II, halfback Harry Gilmer started for the Crimson Tide as a 155-pound freshman. He developed into a star passer and runner for Alabama from 1944 to 1947. His distinctive jumping style of throwing is on display in this photo.

A childhood eye injury kept Vaughn Mancha from fighting in World War II, but it didn't prevent him from becoming a standout lineman for Alabama.

Coach Thomas was especially proud of his "War Babies," including halfback Harry Gilmer (left) and lineman Vaughn Mancha (right). Both players were selected by pro teams in the 1948 NFL draft, and both are members of the College Football Hall of Fame.

While the Tide did earn a share of the national championship from the National Championship Foundation in 1945, the wartime climate meant Alabama had no chance in the voting against a strong and popular Army team.

Gilmer has never been bitter about the results of that vote. In fact, he's always been quick to point out Alabama's distinct advantage that season.

"It was a close-knit team because nearly everyone was in the same boat," Gilmer said. "Most of us were freshmen. A few guys had been in the service and were already out, and some were 4-F." Gilmer pointed out that other teams had just restarted their programs in 1945, whereas Alabama had already played the year before. "We were playing a lot of teams that were in the position we were in [in 1944]. The times were not normal, and we hit it just right and we had a good team."

The Best Bulldog?

Strong arguments can be made for Herschel Walker or Frank Sinkwich as the greatest overall athlete in University of Georgia history. Most longtime Georgia and SEC observers would insist, however, that Charley Trippi is indisputably the Bulldogs' all-time best.

Trippi earned All-America honors as a halfback, finished second in the Heisman Trophy voting as a senior in 1946, and was the first player selected in the 1947 NFL draft. He was also a standout college baseball player who played two years of Class AA baseball for the Atlanta Crackers and turned down offers from the Yankees, Red Sox, Braves, Phillies, and Athletics because he didn't want to be away from his family for so many months each year.

The decision turned out to be a smart one for Trippi. Longtime Georgia assistant coach Bill Hartman called Trippi the best defensive back ever to play at Georgia. Alabama coach Bear Bryant insisted Trippi was the greatest college football player ever. Georgia Tech coach Bobby Dodd once called Trippi "the best safety man the South ever had."

Fred Russell, who covered college football for 68 years for the *Nashville Banner*, wrote, "The best all-purpose back of his era was Charley Trippi of Georgia. In his prime, he removed the ceiling of what one man could mean to a football team."

It's likely Trippi would have soared to such heights wherever he played his college football. Georgia fans have the late Harold "War Eagle" Ketron to thank for recognizing Trippi's talent and sending him to Georgia.

Trippi grew up in Pittston, Pennsylvania, the son of a coal miner. Ketron had played for Georgia in the early 1900s before moving north. He operated Coca-Cola bottling plants in western Pennsylvania and scouted prospective Bulldogs.

Trippi was just a skinny 160-pounder when he caught Ketron's eye. Several northern schools took a look at Trippi but decided not to offer him a scholarship. Ketron, however, provided Trippi with a scholarship—which was allowed in those days.

"I was very fortunate to get a scholarship offer. I wanted to get out of that area," Trippi told the *Athens Banner-Herald*. "I couldn't visualize mining coal eight hours a day for the rest of my life."

After an outstanding sophomore season in 1942 Charley Trippi served in World War II. When he returned in 1945, he took up where he left off and earned consensus All-America honors as a senior in 1946.

Charley Trippi pounds the Georgia Tech defense for a big gain in 1945. The Bulldogs whipped their in-state rivals 33-0 that day.

Trippi was honest enough with himself to know he needed a little more time to prepare for the college game, so he spent a year at LaSalle (N.Y.) Military Academy gaining weight, maturity, and confidence. This time several schools came calling—including national powers such as Notre Dame and Fordham—but Trippi remained loyal to Ketron and the school that wanted him in the first place.

"I had dozens of offers and a lot of pressure to go to other schools," Trippi said. "But I'm a man of my word. I had told Mr. Ketron that I was going to Georgia, and I was not changing my mind."

Trippi was an immediate star for the freshman team in 1941. He made such a strong impression as a sophomore that coach Wally Butts moved All-American Sinkwich from halfback to fullback to free up the position for Trippi.

"We really had an awesome offense," Trippi said. "Frank's quickness off the ball was so devastating that you could not imagine a more effective inside runner. And his running opened up the outside lanes for me."

With plenty of help from his Georgia teammates, Charley Trippi takes off for the end zone against Tulsa in the 1946 Oil Bowl. The Bulldogs won 20-6.

Trippi finished the season with 1,239 total yards, as the Bulldogs won the SEC championship and earned a trip to the Rose Bowl. With Sinkwich limited by two sprained ankles, Trippi rushed for 130 yards in the game and earned MVP honors in the 9-0 victory over UCLA. Georgia shared the national championship with Ohio State.

Like so many college football players of the time, Trippi joined a military reserve unit. He played football for the Air Force from 1943 to 1945, but he was discharged in time to join the Bulldogs for the final six games of the 1945 season. When Trippi returned he found Butts had switched from the single wing to the T-formation, a popular move made by most college football programs in that era. Trippi said it took him two or three games to learn the new offense. When he finally found his way in the T, he discovered that it fit his passing talents more effectively than the single wing had.

That was evident in the final regular-season game against Georgia Tech, when Trippi set an SEC single-game record with 323 passing yards and 384 total yards. In a 20-6 victory over Tulsa in the Oil Bowl, Trippi completed a 47-yard touchdown pass in the fourth quarter and then returned a punt 68 yards for a touchdown. He reversed field from one sideline to the other in a play that longtime Georgia fans still discuss

"I ran on instinct," Trippi said. "Occasionally, I would reverse my field or go against the grain because it came natural to me."

The next season, as a senior captain, Trippi led the SEC with 84 points while rushing for 744 yards and passing for 622 yards. Georgia finished 11-0 in 1946, including a victory over North Carolina in the Sugar Bowl. Trippi played the entire 60 minutes and completed a 67-yard go-ahead touchdown pass.

Georgia halfback Charley Trippi receives the Most Valuable Player trophy following the 1945 All-Star Game. Minnesota coach Bernie Bierman, right, coached Trippi's all-star squad.

It was a tough year in the polls for Trippi and the Bulldogs. Trippi won the Maxwell Award, but Army's Glenn Davis won the Heisman. The Bulldogs finished on top of only one national poll, while eleven polls chose Notre Dame and five selected Army.

Trippi was disappointed, but he said, "The big deal to me was winning. If you win, you don't worry about ratings or making All-America teams or anything like that. Those things just fall in line if you win."

After his Georgia career, Trippi took advantage of the competition between the NFL and the rival All-America Football Conference. The NFL's Chicago Cardinals made him the first overall choice in the 1944 draft, ahead of future NFL stars Elroy "Crazylegs" Hirsch and Tom Fears. The Cardinals still held his rights when the New York Yankees selected Trippi in the 1947 AAFC draft. That put Trippi in an excellent negotiating position. The Yankees were so sure they had their man that they called a news conference, only to learn that Cardinals owner Charles W. Bidwill Sr. had

signed Trippi for the then-unheard sum of $100,000 over four years.

Trippi was the final piece in Bidwill's quest for a "Dream Backfield." With Paul Christman, Pat Harder, and Marshall Goldberg, the Cardinals won the NFL championship in Trippi's rookie season. Against the Eagles in the championship game, Trippi wore basketball shoes for better traction on an icy field. He gained 206 yards with two touchdowns, one on a 44-yard touchdown run and another on a 75-yard punt return.

Trippi starred for nine seasons with Chicago as a halfback, quarterback, safety, and punter, and he spent five years as a backfield coach. His success led to induction in the Pro Football Hall of Fame and the College Football Hall of Fame. He also had a 2000 Kentucky Derby entrant named after him.

Trippi, one of four players in Georgia football history to have his jersey retired, continues to live an active life in Athens.

"Life has been good to me because of sports," Trippi said. "I feel very fortunate that my dreams came true."

The Georgia Bulldogs posted an 11-0 record in 1946 but won only a share of the national championship in one poll. Trippi finished second in the Heisman voting. In postwar America, no one was more popular than national champion Army and its Heisman winner, Glenn Davis.

Charley Trippi (left) and Frank Sinkwich (right) spent one season together in the Georgia backfield. They led the Bulldogs to a 10-1 record and a share of the national championship in 1942.

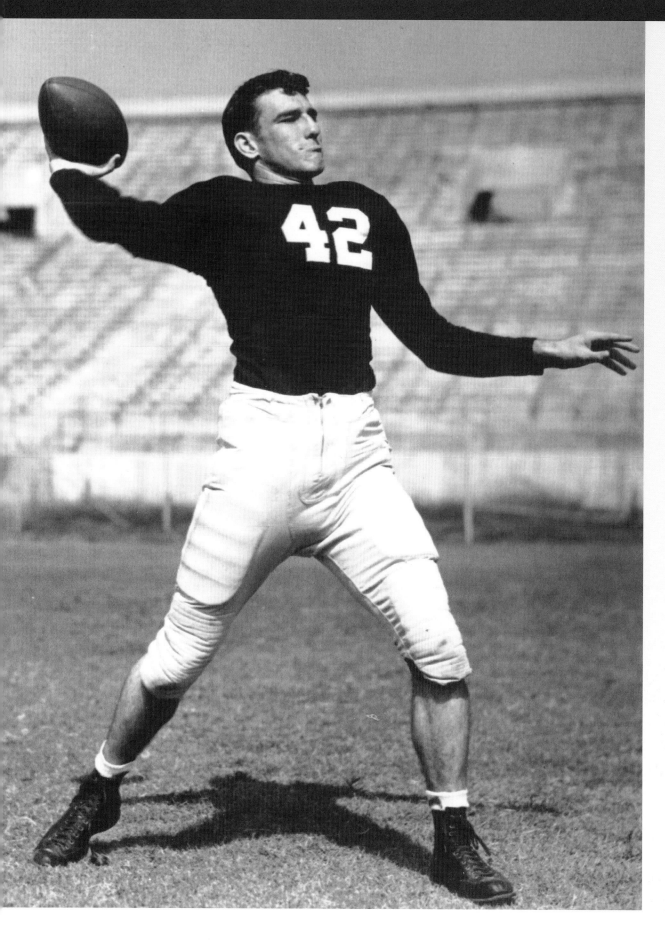

In 1947 "Chunkin' Charlie" Conerly led the nation with 133 pass completions, while also passing for 18 touchdowns and running for 9. For his efforts, he earned consensus All-America honors and was named the national Player of the Year by the Helms Foundation.

Chunkin' Charlie

Ole Miss' legendary coach Johnny Vaught had a reputation for developing outstanding quarterbacks. On a list that includes Jake Gibbs, Eagle Day, Ray Brown, Bobby Franklin, and Glynn Griffin—among others— the most famous was Archie Manning. The most dynamic, however, was Charlie Conerly, Vaught's first quarterback.

Stats and accolades don't tell the complete story of Conerly's value to the Rebels, although he produced plenty of both. Conerly's most important assets were his leadership and his ability to turn nothing into something on the football field.

In the book *Southeastern Conference Football: America's Most Competitive Conference*, John McCallum wrote of Conerly, "Though critics said he ran like a duck and had less foot speed than a pregnant woodchuck, he left no doubt in the huddles who was in command and that he was there to win. When desperation demanded it, he could get a pass off with a man on his neck and slip it through an opening no larger than a porthole."

"All American Chunkin' Charlie" was born and raised in Clarksdale, Mississippi. He came to Ole Miss in 1942 but joined the Marines and saw action in the Pacific. He returned in 1946, and the time away actually proved to be beneficial for Conerly. Vaught, who saw something special in Conerly and end Barney Poole, soon became the new head coach.

After one season of varsity football for Ole Miss in 1942, Chuck Conerly served as a combat Marine in the South Pacific during World War II. His return signaled a revival for the Rebels. After a 2-6 finish for the team in 1946, Conerly captained Ole Miss to a 9-2 record and its first SEC football championship.

In Harold "Red" Drew's lone campaign as the Ole Miss coach in 1946, the team finished 2-7, and Drew jumped at the chance to coach at Alabama after the season. Ole Miss promoted Vaught from line coach to head coach for 1947.

Vaught made the most of his team's passing game. He personally preferred the T-formation, but instead he adapted Drew's version of the Notre Dame box shift to allow Conerly to remain at tailback, no matter which direction the backfield shifted.

The result was a national record of 133 completions, including 18 touchdowns, for Conerly, and another national record for Poole with 52 receptions (44 of them from Conerly). Conerly earned All-America honors and finished fourth in the Heisman Trophy voting. Even more important, his combination of leadership, savvy, and toughness helped the Rebels finish 9-2 and win their first SEC championship.

"Charlie was always able to fire up our kids," Vaught said, "and he sure made life miserable for our opponents."

Conerly went on to do more of the same in the NFL, earning Rookie of the Year honors in 1948, the Most Valuable Player award in 1959, and All-Pro selection twice as a quarterback in a 14-year career with the New York Giants. Just as in his college career, Conerly's real value was his leadership: The Giants won three NFL Championship games in four seasons (1956, 1958, and 1959).

Off the field, Conerly portrayed the Marlboro Man in commercials, and his wife, Perian, wrote a book called *Backseat Quarterback*, an account of pro football in the 1950s.

Conerly is a member of the National Football Foundation Hall of Fame, College Football Hall of Fame, the Mississippi Sports Hall of Fame, the Ole Miss Sports Hall of Fame, and the Ole Miss Team of the Century. The only thing missing is the Pro Football Hall of Fame, an affront that still irks his Giants teammates. Giants co-owner Wellington Mara often commented that Conerly was the best player not enshrined in the hall of fame in Canton, Ohio. Mara said Conerly "has better numbers than some quarterbacks who are there."

Conerly died in 1996 but his legacy lives on, appropriately enough, with the Conerly Trophy, awarded annually to the top college player in the state of Mississippi.

The 1950s
Dramatic Change, Dynamic Success

In the fifth year of his five-year plan, Paul "Bear" Bryant finally had the Kentucky program on top in the Southeastern Conference in 1950. Through relentless recruiting and a demanding training and practice regime, Bryant molded the Wildcats into SEC champions with 10 consecutive wins heading into their final regular-season game at Tennessee.

For all he could do as a coach, Bryant couldn't control the weather, and a freak blizzard left Knoxville buried under a thick blanket of snow. The weather slowed down the Kentucky offense, and General Robert Neyland's Volunteers were able to topple the undefeated Wildcats. Tennessee beat Kentucky 7-0 in a game that still stands out in college football lore.

A flurry of changes took place in college football in the 1950s. The SEC would see its way through this time of transition, as 10 different teams from the conference would win a share of the national championship between 1950 and 1959, including three Associated Press championships.

Off the field, one-platoon football and limited substitution, in which players played both offense and defense, finally gave way to two-platoon football and the use of more players in the mid-1940s. Rule changes in 1947 and 1948 made nearly unlimited substitution possible. In 1953, a return to a preference for smaller, quicker players who could play the entire game, rather than larger players who could not last the entire game, brought single-platoon football back into favor. Two-platoon football did not return in full until 1965. More minor changes came later in the 1950s, such as the institution of the two-point conversion option after a touchdown beginning in 1958, and in 1959, an increase in the distance between the goal posts by nearly five feet.

At the beginning of the decade, a more significant development in the game of college football occurred when nearly 50 schools dropped their football programs in 1951 due to the rising costs of competition, dwindling interest and attendance at private institutions such as Georgetown and Fordham, and a national crackdown on illicit recruiting practices by the NCAA. The Ivy League's eight institutions chose to de-emphasize football in 1954, eliminating spring practice, football scholarships, and postseason games. Institutions throughout the nation debated whether they should follow the Ivy.

Coach Paul "Bear" Bryant and his staff led the Kentucky Wildcats to unprecedented success from 1946 to 1953. Bryant (lower right) is pictured with (back row, left to right) Clarence Underwood, Frank Moseley, and George Chapman; (front row, left to right) Bill McCubbin and Carney Laslie.

That debate even existed within the SEC, but the conference moved forward with its commitment to big-time football. And big-time it was, especially when Bryant's powerhouse Kentucky team followed its loss at Tennessee with a victory over then-undefeated Oklahoma in the 1951 Sugar Bowl. Oklahoma had already won the AP national championship, but the combination of quarterback Babe Parilli's passing and Bryant's innovative plan to counter the Sooners' split-T formation with four defensive tackles led the Wildcats to a 13-7 victory.

At Ole Miss, halfback Arnold "Showboat" Boykin played a game for the ages by scoring seven touchdowns in a 1951 game against Mississippi State.

At Tennessee, Neyland faced criticism that he was no longer an effective coach, and he countered by digging in even deeper. The result was an 11-1 finish and a share of the national championship in five polls in 1950, followed by a 10-1 record, an SEC championship, and the AP national championship in 1951. At the end of an 8-2-1 regular season in 1952, poor health forced Neyland to give up coaching and focus solely on his role as athletic director. He retired from coaching with his legend intact; at Neyland's retirement banquet, Bryant quipped, "Thank God the old guy finally quit."

Georgia Tech took its place on the national stage in 1952. The Yellow Jackets were impressive enough in 1951,

Long before he coached Pittsburgh to the national championship and then returned to his alma mater as head coach, Johnny Majors was an outstanding all-purpose back for Tennessee. Now a member of the College Football Hall of Fame, Majors won the SEC MVP awards in 1955 and 1956, and as a senior he finished second in the Heisman Trophy voting.

During a decade in which the SEC continued to raise its national profile, LSU back Billy Cannon did his part by winning the Heisman Trophy in 1959. He was LSU's first and only Heisman winner.

Following some lean seasons in the late 1940s, critics insisted the game had passed General Robert Neyland by. The coach responded by leading Tennessee to 21 combined wins in 1950 and 1951 and a national championship in 1951.

going 11-0-1, sharing the SEC championship with Tennessee, and winning the Orange Bowl, but they were even better in '52. They had a 12-0 record, won another conference title, and won the Sugar Bowl for a share of the national title. It was the third national championship in Tech history and the first under coach Bobby Dodd.

Dodd relied on a two-platoon system throughout the season so that none of his players had to play offense and defense in the same game. Dodd called it the greatest team he had seen at Tech since becoming an assistant to Bill Alexander in 1931. No opponent scored a touchdown pass against the Yellow Jackets during the entire 1952 season.

By 1953, Bryant was growing frustrated that his football program always took a backseat to Kentucky basketball under Coach Adolph Rupp. Bryant left Kentucky midway through a 12-year contract to become the head coach at Texas A&M.

The 1953 SEC season ended on one of the strangest plays in the history of college football. With the Rice Owls leading Alabama 7-6 in the 1954 Cotton Bowl, Owl back Dickey Maegle raced down the sideline en route to an apparent 95-yard touchdown run. Alabama fullback Tommy Lewis flew off the bench without his helmet and tackled Maegle at midfield. The officials awarded the touchdown to Rice, and Lewis entered the ranks of college football infamy.

"I'm too emotional," Lewis said after the game. "I kept telling myself, 'I didn't do it. I didn't do it.' But I knew I had. I'm just too full of 'Bama. He just ran too close. I know I'll be hearing about this the rest of my life."

As the Ivy League and other schools moved to downplay their athletic programs, the SEC's focus on winning football was evident. In 1954, the conference sent three teams—Ole Miss, Georgia Tech, and Auburn—to bowl games. That same year, Mississippi State took a chance on a 30-year-old head coach named Darrell Royal (who would leave after two seasons and go on to win three national championships at Texas). Tennessee finished 4-6, prompting Neyland to fire his successor, Harvey Robinson. Neyland called it "the hardest thing I've ever had to do."

The 1955 season brought plenty of change to the SEC. New coaches came on board at three of the schools. Bowden Wyatt, a former Neyland player, returned to Tennessee as head coach. Paul Dietzel, an assistant under Bryant at Kentucky, got his first head-coaching job when he was hired by LSU. Georgia assistant J. B. "Ears" Whitworth took over at Alabama.

The season closed with Vanderbilt playing in its first bowl—a bowl that almost didn't happen for the Commodores. When Vanderbilt was offered a chance to play Auburn in the Gator Bowl, coach Art Guepe told his players to decide whether they wanted to accept or reject the invitation. However, Vanderbilt Chancellor Dr. Harvey Branscomb was concerned that playing in a bowl game would detract from the school's academic reputation. The response from the players was forceful.

"Chancellor Branscomb, you can talk until you're blue in the face but we've talked it over and we have made our decision," guard Larry Haynes said. "We want to go. We're going to go." The Commodores made the most of their opportunity. Despite an injured throwing arm, quarterback Don Orr led Vandy to a 25-13 victory in the Gator Bowl.

Georgia Tech line coach Ray Graves poses with his linemen before the 1955 Cotton Bowl. Georgia Tech emerged as a national contender under Coach Bobby Dodd during the decade. Graves went on to become the head coach at Florida.

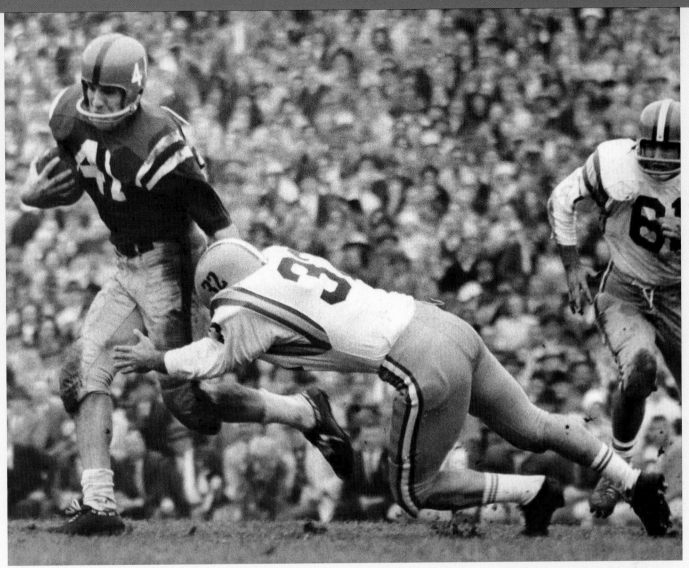

Ole Miss produced several outstanding quarterbacks under coach Johnny Vaught, but fullback Charlie Flowers was an excellent all-around back who could beat opponents as a runner, blocker, receiver, kick returner, and punter. The Arkansas native was inducted into the College Football Hall of Fame in 1997.

While Harvey Robinson had failed to follow Neyland with any success for Tennessee, Robinson's successor, Wyatt, made his mark quickly. The Vols closed out the 1956 regular season with a 10-0 record and earned Tennessee its first SEC championship since 1951. Johnny Majors, the single-wing, pass-run tailback, finished second to Notre Dame's Paul Hornung in the Heisman Trophy voting.

By 1957, the NCAA had placed 10 collegiate programs on probation and issued numerous sanctions for recruiting violations. One of those programs was Auburn. The NCAA prohibited the Tigers from playing in a bowl, but that didn't stop them from making the most of their season. Led by coach Ralph "Shug" Jordan, quarterback Lloyd Nix, All-American

end Jimmy "Red" Phillips, and guard Zeke Smith (the 1958 Outland Trophy winner), the Tigers outscored their opponents 207-28. They finished the season with a 10-0 record and the conference championship. In those days, the AP voting took place before the bowl games, and Auburn was selected as the 1957 national champions by the Associated Press.

When the Tigers closed out the season with a 40-0 victory over Alabama, it paved the way for a seismic shift in the state as well as the entire SEC. Alabama fired Whitworth after three seasons and a 4-24-2 record. For a replacement, the school went directly after Bryant, a former Crimson Tide player and assistant coach. Asked about his return to Alabama, Bryant stated simply, "Mama called."

No one picked Auburn to win the national championship in 1957 once the Tigers lost two key players before the start of the season. That didn't prevent the Tigers from holding opponents to just 28 points on the way to a 10-0 finish and the AP national title.

While Bryant went to work rebuilding the Alabama program, its cross-state rival continued its success. Auburn won 9 of 10 games in 1958, and were it not for a 7-7 tie against Georgia Tech in the fourth game of the season, the Auburn Tigers might have captured another national championship. Instead, the Tigers of LSU rode big-play halfback Billy Cannon and a unique three-team platoon defense to an 11-0 record. LSU featured only three seniors on its 55-man roster, but the team was able to keep its defense fresh with its three units, including the legendary "Chinese Bandits." LSU won both the conference championship and the AP national championship.

Cannon was back in 1959 to run, pass, and return punts in a Heisman Trophy–winning season. His legendary 89-yard fourth-quarter punt return on Halloween night gave the

Tigers a 7-3 victory over No. 3 ranked Ole Miss. LSU had opened the season ranked first in the nation in both polls and stayed there until one week after the Ole Miss win, when they lost 14-13 to Tennessee.

That opened the door for Ole Miss, and the Rebels responded by beating Tennessee 37-7 and Mississippi State 42-0. The loss to LSU was the team's only defeat of the season, and Ole Miss' 10-1 record was good enough to earn them a share of the national championship with Syracuse. The Rebels then got their revenge against LSU at the Sugar Bowl, dominating the Tigers 21-0.

The victory closed out a decade in which the SEC further established its place as an elite conference and set the stage for another decade of great college football in the South.

The General's Legacy

In the beginning there were Amos Alonzo Stagg, Pop Warner, Bob Zuppke, and Knute Rockne. These men were college football's original innovators, the men who helped shape and popularize the game.

Robert Reese Neyland stands side-by-side with those coaches for his impact on the game as Tennessee's head coach.

"The things he taught are still the basis of what coaches teach today," says Vince Dooley, who participated in SEC football as a player and assistant coach at Auburn and as head coach and athletic director at Georgia. "He was ahead of his time."

His record is impressive enough. In his three stints as coach (1926–1934, 1936–1940, 1946–1952), Neyland won 173 games, six SEC championships, and four national championships. In Neyland's 213 games as Tennessee's coach, the Vols recorded an astonishing 113 shutouts. His 1939 team finished the regular season without losing a game or even allowing a point, something that likely will never happen again. In 1940, he became the first coach in history to take a team to the three consecutive major bowls.

His bearing on Tennessee football is also manifest in steel and concrete. Tennessee's stadium had 3,200 seats in 1925. Today, Neyland Stadium seats 102,037 and ranks as college football's third-largest stadium.

Neyland's influence is still evident in today's strategy, particularly in terms of defense and the kicking game. His philosophy of winning football is best expressed in Neyland's "Seven Maxims of Football."

1. The team that makes the fewest mistakes will win.
2. Play for and make the breaks and when one comes your way—score.
3. If at first the game or the breaks go against you, don't let up—put on more steam.
4. Protect our kickers, our QB, our lead, and our ball game.
5. Ball, oskie, cover, block, cut and slice, pursue, and gang tackle—for this is the winning edge.
6. Press the kicking game. Here is where the breaks are made.
7. Carry the fight to our opponent and keep it there for 60 minutes.

After returning to Tennessee to national prominence in 1950 through 1952, Robert Neyland retired as the Vols coach with 173 wins, six SEC championships, and at least a share of four national championships in 21 seasons.

Neyland's devotion to precision and disciplined football found its roots in his childhood and took shape in the military. Born in 1892 and raised in Greenville, Texas, Neyland studied engineering and played baseball and football at Texas A&M for one year before he won a competitive appointment to the U.S. Military Academy at West Point. He excelled as a football end, a baseball pitcher, and a boxer before graduating and serving in France during World War I.

A New Orleans native, halfback Hank Lauricella came to Tennessee in 1947 because Coach Neyland was still using the single-wing offense at a time when most coaches were running the T-formation. In Lauricella's senior season of 1951, Tennessee won the national championship, and Lauricella was a unanimous All-America selection. He is a member of the College Football Hall of Fame.

Guard John Michels was another fixture in Tennessee's success from 1950 to 1952. Michels, a member of the College Football Hall of Fame, earned consensus All-America honors in 1952 and won the Jacobs Trophy as the SEC's best blocker.

After returning to West Point in 1921 as an assistant coach in football, baseball, and basketball and an aide-de-camp to Academy Superintendent General Douglas MacArthur, he faced a critical juncture in his life. MacArthur wanted him to continue in the Army, but Neyland wanted to coach. He found his solution at Tennessee, where he could coach football and teach military science.

He had some idea of what he was getting into at Tennessee, because he had seen the outmanned Volunteers lose 41-0 at Army in 1923. He came to Tennessee as an assis-tant in 1925 and took over for one week that season when head coach M. B. Banks fell ill. The Vols upset Georgia 12-7 and when Banks moved on after the season, Neyland was the logical choice.

Nathan W. Dougherty, engineering professor, chairman of the University of Tennessee athletic association, and a Tennessee player from 1906 to 1909, hired Neyland and gave him one primary mission: Beat Vanderbilt. Before Neyland arrived, Tennessee was 2-17-2 against Vandy. Under Neyland, the Vols went 16-3-2 against the Commodores.

Doug Atkins came to Tennessee to play basketball, but the 6-foot-8-inch, 245-pound tackle was a big asset for the Volunteers football team. He earned All-America honors as a senior in 1952, when Tennessee led the nation in total defense. Atkins is a member of both the Pro Football Hall of Fame and the College Football Hall of Fame.

As a head coach, he applied the principles of discipline and precision he learned at Army. As an engineer accustomed to applying a logical, thorough process, he played an innovative role in the development of the single-wing offense, which was designed to outnumber the defense at the point of attack. But Neyland was at his best teaching defense and special teams, focusing on field-position football and forcing the other team to make mistakes.

His coaching put the Vols on the path to a 70-2-6 record from 1926 to 1932, Tennessee's final eight years in the Southern Conference. In the first two seasons after Tennessee became a charter member of the Southeastern Conference, Neyland's Vols finished a combined 15-5 overall and 10-3 in conference play. Then, in 1935, the Army sent Captain Neyland to the Panama Canal Zone. When Tennessee finished with a 4-5 record under W. H. Britton that season, the university asked Neyland to return. Neyland realized he missed football more than he had anticipated.

The next year, then-Major Neyland retired from active service and returned to Tennessee as head football coach. He immediately set about building a team that would put together a run of three seasons that rivals any in college football history. From 1938 to 1940, the Vols went 31-2 overall and 18-0 in SEC play, and played in the Orange, Rose, and Sugar Bowls.

The only thing that would slow Neyland down was World War II. He left Tennessee in the spring of 1941 to return to active military service and didn't return until 1946. During that time he served as one of the top commanders in the India-Burma Theater of Operations, helping to keep critical supply lines open and running. A brochure published by the University of Tennessee claimed, "China would have become a conquered nation in 1943 without the campaign conducted by Neyland." Neyland rose to the rank of brigadier general and was awarded the Legion of Merit with two clusters and the Distinguished Service Medal from the United States, as well as the Chinese Cloud and Banner and the British Knight Commander.

When Neyland retired from the Army for good in 1946, he returned to Tennessee with more than winning on his mind. He set out to add seats to the football stadium and designed its expansion. He also focused on his goal of preparing his players and assistants for head coaching jobs. At one point seven Neyland disciples were head coaches at major programs, including four Hall of Fame coaches who coached in the SEC: Bobby Dodd (Georgia Tech), Bowden Wyatt (Tennessee), Murray Warmath (Mississippi State), and Bob Woodruff (Florida).

Wallace Wade, who coached against Neyland at Alabama and Duke, once called Neyland "one of the very greatest coaches of all time. He had a tremendous impact. He coached in all phases of the game better than any other coach."

That was easy for many Tennessee fans to forget when the Vols slipped to 5-5 in 1947 and 4-4-2 in '48. Neyland had inherited a team low on talent, but critics were convinced that the game had passed the coach by. Neyland responded with two of his best recruiting classes. He brought in players such as multitalented single-wing tailback Hank Lauricella and dominating linemen Doug Atkins and John Michels.

After posting a 7-2-1 record in 1949, Tennessee improved to 11-1 in 1950 and won a share of the national championship in five polls. The Vols peaked in 1951, when they finished 10-1 overall, went 5-0 in the SEC, and won the consensus (Associated Press and UPI) national championship.

With his health in decline, Neyland started preparing for the future and resigned following an 8-2-1 season in 1952. He stayed on at the university as athletic director and continued to command a high degree of respect and fear from his former players and coaches.

In one famous story, Woodruff was coaching practice at Florida and visiting with Phil Dickens, the Indiana coach and a former Tennessee player under Neyland. Woodruff was smoking a cigarette when he noticed a visitor walking toward the practice field. When Woodruff realized it was Neyland, he immediately dropped the cigarette and stepped on it. Dickens said, "You don't have to do that—you don't play for him anymore." Woodruff replied, "You know that, and I know that, but I don't think the General knows that."

Neyland was inducted into the College Football Hall of Fame in 1956. He remained athletic director until his death on March 28, 1962.

Neyland Stadium is another sign of General Robert Neyland's legacy at the University of Tennessee. Tennessee's football stadium had 3,200 seats in 1925. Today, Neyland Stadium seats 102,037 and ranks as college football's third-largest stadium.

His legacy is both profound and enduring. In addition to Neyland Stadium, the University of Tennessee awards the Robert R. Neyland Scholarship to non-athletes based on academic merit and leadership. The road behind the stadium's south end is called Neyland Drive, and the Vols' football complex is named the Neyland-Thompson Sports Center.

Bluegrass Bear

By 1945 Kentucky was well on its way to establishing itself as a national basketball power under coach Adolph Rupp. Kentucky football, however, had yet to finish with a winning record in SEC play. The program finally hit bottom in 1945 when the Wildcats finished 2-8 and lost all five conference games.

Then Paul "Bear" Bryant came to Kentucky.

After finishing 6-2-1 as the coach at Maryland in 1945, Bryant decided that university president Harry C. Byrd was too meddlesome for Bryant's tastes. He left and took the job in Lexington.

Bear Bryant was still an unproven head coach when Kentucky students and faculty welcomed his arrival in Lexington in January 1946. Bryant would go on to win 60 games in eight seasons at Kentucky.

As soon as Bryant arrived at Kentucky, the players knew things were about to change.

Asked about his time in Bryant's presence, Kentucky quarterback George Blanda once said, "I thought, 'This must be what God looks like.'"

Holding to his "Be good or be gone" motto, Bryant quickly put his imprint on the program. He worked the players like they had never been worked before and demanded more than they thought was possible. The result was consecutive 7-3 finishes in 1946 and 1947.

In 1949, Bryant's Wildcats finished with a 9-3 overall record, a 4-1 conference record, and earned a trip to the Orange Bowl. Kentucky lost the bowl game to Santa Clara 21-13, but the new coach boosted the Wildcats to where they had never been: in contention for the conference championship.

The 1950 season would be the best in Kentucky football history. With Bryant's program fully entrenched and players such as quarterback Vito "Babe" Parilli and linemen Bob Gain and Walt Yaworsky emerging as stars, the Wildcats won their first 10 games and found themselves on the brink of a perfect regular season. The offense averaged 38 points a game and the defense was ranked second in the nation.

It took a freak winter storm and the Tennessee Vols to finally slow down the Wildcats. It was difficult enough just to travel through the mountains on the train trip from Lexington to Knoxville, but when the game started the Wildcats couldn't get any offense going. With Parilli's passing game grounded by the snow, Kentucky lost 7-0. Despite the loss, the Wildcats still won their first SEC football championship.

Later that same day, Bryant convinced Sugar Bowl representatives to invite the Wildcats by promising that his team would beat Oklahoma. Bryant and Oklahoma coach Bud Wilkinson traveled together on a speaking tour for more than a week in December. By the time Bryant returned to Lexington, he had decided to counter Oklahoma's split-T formation with a four-tackle scheme on the defensive line. With the corners up tight on the outside, the Wildcats would show a nine-man front.

Bryant poured everything he had into the 1951 Sugar Bowl. The Wildcats took a 13-0 halftime lead behind the four-tackle defense, Dom Fucci's punting, and Parilli's 13

One of Coach Bear Bryant's first big recruits, College Hall of Famer Bob Gain played four years at Kentucky, started on both sides of the ball as a tackle (as well as the place kicker), and played a major role in the Wildcats' success from 1947 to 1950. As a senior in 1950, Gain helped lead Kentucky to a 10-1 regular-season record, its first SEC title, and a win in the Sugar Bowl. He won the 1950 Outland Trophy.

Vito "Babe" Parilli drove Kentucky's T-formation offense with his passing and his sleight-of-hand ball fakes. Defenders who chased would-be ball carriers often realized too late that Parilli still had the ball. In 1950, Parilli broke numerous SEC passing records, won first-team All-America honors, and led Kentucky to the SEC title.

for 15, two-touchdown performance. From there, Bryant put the game on the shoulders of his defense.

"Coach Bryant told me we would handle them on defense," Parilli said. "I threw one pass in the second half."

Kentucky held on for a 13-7 victory. The *Louisville Courier-Journal* described it as "Kentucky's greatest football triumph since it took up the game in 1881."

Unfortunately for the Wildcats, the victory came too late to change the national polls.

"We didn't talk about it much at the time, because that was just how the system worked. The bowl games weren't included as part of picking the national champion," John Griggs, a sophomore offensive lineman, told the Associated Press. "We believed we had the best team in the country that year, and we've often said what a shame it was that we couldn't be listed as national champs."

Despite Bryant's success, basketball still ruled at Kentucky. There is a popular story about a banquet in which Rupp received a Cadillac from boosters while Bryant received a cigarette lighter, although Bryant told *Sports Illustrated* in 1966 that it was just a funny story to tell at speaking engagements. In truth, university President Dr. Herman Donovan told Bryant that Rupp was going to retire the following year, in 1952, in the wake of a basketball point-shaving scandal and NCAA rules violations. Instead, Rupp

Although Kentucky won only 15 games during his career (1955–1957), tackle Lou Michaels earned All-America honors twice and was named the SEC Most Valuable Player in 1957. In the first 50 years of the award (initiated in 1933), Michaels was the only tackle to win conference MVP. Michaels, a member of the College Football Hall of Fame, also finished fourth in the Heisman Trophy voting in 1957.

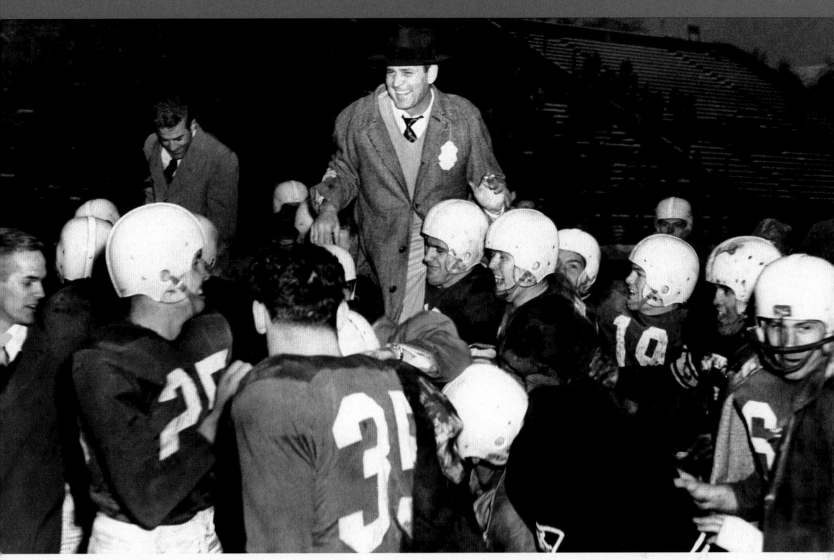

Coach Bear Bryant is carried off the field on the shoulders of his players after Kentucky scored twice in the final five minutes to tie favored Tennessee 14-14 in 1952.

received a new contract and Bryant quickly realized he would never be the top dog at Kentucky.

In his autobiography, *Bear*, Bryant wrote about his relationship with Rupp: "The trouble was we were too much alike and he wanted basketball No. 1 and I wanted football No. 1. In an environment like that, one or the other has to go."

Following a 7-2-1 finish in 1953, Bryant left Kentucky for Texas A&M.

In eight seasons at Kentucky, Bryant's teams went 60-23-5 and earned four bowl berths. He would go on to establish Alabama as one of the premier programs in college football and become major college football's winningest coach.

Kentucky has not won an outright SEC football title since Bryant's departure.

Vandy Dandy

Playing for Vanderbilt was a natural choice for Bill Wade, a quarterback born and raised on Commodore football.

Wade was born on October 4, 1930, at Vanderbilt Hospital. He was the son of William Wade Sr., Vanderbilt's football captain in 1921. As a child, Bill Jr. accompanied his father to numerous Vanderbilt football games.

His athletic career began at Woodmont Grammar School in Nashville, where the coaches played him on the line. One of Wade's childhood thrills came when his Woodmont team played at the halftime of a Commodore game at Vanderbilt's Dudley Field.

Vanderbilt won a total of only 18 games from 1949 to 1951, but quarterback Bill Wade (right) set numerous school passing records on his way to being named SEC Player of the Year and second-team AP All-American in 1951.

While playing high school football at Nashville's Montgomery Bell Academy, Wade played more tailback than quarterback. Wade's passing didn't make a big impression until someone spotted him throwing and kicking a football on one of his almost daily trips to Dudley Field. Between his ability to throw the ball 60 yards and his talent as a pitcher on the MBA baseball team, someone had to notice.

Word spread to Vanderbilt coach Red Sanders, and Sanders quickly offered Wade a scholarship. Wade was just as quick to accept.

Wade made such an impression playing quarterback for Vanderbilt's freshman team in 1948 that when his sophomore season began he was pictured on the cover of *Look* magazine's 1949 "Football Forecast," posing with two Vanderbilt co-eds. Grantland Rice, himself a Vanderbilt graduate, wrote the story. He picked Vanderbilt third in the nation in his preseason poll and proclaimed Wade a player to watch that season.

While Vanderbilt fell short of Rice's predictions that fall, Wade proved to be worth watching throughout his college career. The Commodores finished with mediocre records (5-5, 7-4, and 6-5) during Wade's three seasons from 1949 to 1951, but Wade set numerous school passing records on his way to earning SEC Player of the Year and second-team Associated Press All-America honors in 1951.

The Los Angeles Rams selected Wade with their first pick in the 1951 NFL draft. After serving two years as an officer in the Navy, Wade joined the Rams for the 1954 season and went on to play 14 years in the NFL with the Rams and the Chicago Bears. In the 1963 NFL Championship game, Wade scored both of Chicago's touchdowns in a 14-10 victory over the New York Giants.

"He was tough. He was a good quarterback, and he was a winner," said Doug Atkins, a Pro Football Hall of Fame defensive end who played for the Tennessee Vols in college and the Bears in the NFL. "He could run the ball, and when he ran the ball, he never slid. He'd try and run over you, and he did. He was as tough as nails. In that championship game, he did a fine, fine job. He was our leader."

In 1966 Wade retired to Nashville, where he lives today.

Two of the SEC's best quarterbacks of their era, Vanderbilt's Bill Wade (left) and Kentucky's Babe Parilli (right), pose with Georgia Tech coach Bobby Dodd before the college all-stars faced the NFL's Los Angeles Rams in August 1952.

Ol' Spaghetti Legs

Jackie Parker spent most of his life following a unique path, with and without the ball. This path took him from East Tennessee, to a Mississippi junior college, to Mississippi State, to the Canadian Football League and a long life in Edmonton, Alberta.

On the football field, his unusual flat-footed, pigeon-toed, spindly-legged running style earned him the nickname "Ol' Spaghetti Legs" and brought him considerable success in college and pro football.

He nearly died from a ruptured appendix as a child and almost lost one of his feet to a virus. Later, Parker was usually bored at Young High School in his hometown of Knoxville, Tennessee, but he made the Dean's list. He hardly played organized sports until he reached high school. When he did participate, he didn't play much football until some other players got hurt. At that point, he became an overnight sensation.

Because Parker got married in high school, most college football programs didn't want him. So, he ended up at Jones County Junior College in Ellisville, Mississippi. When new Mississippi State coach Murray Warmath found himself in dire need of players in 1952, assistant coach Billy Murphy tried to convince him to give Parker a chance. Warmath had a rule forbidding married players, but Mississippi State's baseball coach Doc Patty didn't, so Parker received a baseball scholarship.

Parker turned out to be an outstanding shortstop and even received an offer from the Cincinnati Reds, but he rejected it simply because he liked football better. Parker started out as a halfback and didn't make much of a first impression at State—until the coaches grew desperate for a quarterback for the team's new split-T offense. They weren't impressed with Parker's wobbly passes until the final scrimmage before the first game, where Parker threw for seven touchdowns.

His coaches didn't know what to do with him when he arrived at Mississippi State, and his teammates called him "Ol' Spaghetti Legs" because of unusual flat-footed, pigeon-toed, spindly-legged running style, but Jackie Parker had a knack for making big plays.

Parker went on to earn SEC player of the year honors in 1952 and 1953. He set an SEC single-season record and led the nation by scoring 120 points in 1952, despite playing for a 5-4 team. In 1953 he received All-American recognition. Through it all he maintained a fascinating dichotomy. He was "aw-shucks" humble and reserved off the field, casual in practice to the point of frustrating his coach, yet fully confident and fiercely competitive on the field.

"He was the greatest clutch player I ever saw," Warmath said in *The Maroon Bulldogs*. "When it had to be done, he would do it."

Darrell Royal, who was Parker's quarterback coach at State before he went on to win three national championships as the head coach at Texas, said, "In my whole career Jackie Parker would be right at the top—in a top, select group of all-time athletes."

Parker was drafted by both the CFL's Edmonton Eskimos and the NFL's New York Giants. Back in those days, the CFL was a viable alternative for players. Although Giants owner Wellington Mara offered him nearly twice as much to sign, Parker chose the CFL, in part because Royal had become the Eskimos head coach.

Royal left Edmonton after one season to return to Mississippi State as head coach in 1954, but Parker and his wife Peggy liked what they saw in Canada and decided to stay. They never left.

"The Fast Freight from Mississippi State" played 14 years at quarterback, halfback, and defensive back for three CFL teams. He played on three Grey Cup winners with Edmonton, won the Schenley Award as the CFL's top player three times, and earned All-Star honors eight consecutive seasons.

"If we were in trouble we didn't even worry," Edmonton tackle Bob Dean said. "We were convinced it was only a matter of time before Jackie was going to pull us out. And 99 percent of the time, he did."

Jackie Parker was a multi-talented star quarterback for Mississippi State in 1952 and 1953. He earned All-SEC and All-America honors in both seasons. Parker went on to become one of the legends of the Canadian Football League and is a member of both the CFL and the College Football Halls of Fame.

When he wasn't beating his teammates in golf or cards, he constantly kept them on their toes. One time he got up during dinner with his teammates at a fine Toronto hotel, went outside, rounded up some street people, and brought them in for dinner. When the bill came, he signed the name of the team's general manager.

While Parker often defied the norm in his life and career, he met the highest standard on several levels as a member of the College Football Hall of Fame, the National Junior College Athletic Association Hall of Fame, and similar halls in Canada, Mississippi, and Tennessee. Even though he only played two seasons at Mississippi State, he is still widely regarded as the best quarterback in school history.

Parker died on November 7, 2006, in Edmonton, of course, where Jackie Parker Park is named in his honor.

Go, Billy! Go!

It's been nearly 50 years since Billy Cannon caught that punt on a bounce and took off through the ethereal mist on Halloween night, 1959, breaking seven tackles on his way to a game-winning touchdown against Ole Miss.

Billy Cannon (right) was a reckless young man in need of direction when he arrived at LSU. Coach Paul Dietzel was able to channel some of that energy to success on the playing field.

The record book says Cannon's punt return covered 89 yards. In the hearts and minds of longtime LSU fans, Cannon never stopped running, and he never will.

Over time, Cannon and his legendary return have taken on an almost mythological status that remains alive and well on grainy black-and-white film. LSU has produced its share of outstanding teams, players, games, and moments, but none carry the magic of Cannon and that night in Baton Rouge.

Beyond the folklore, Cannon was an excellent all-around football player, a natural athlete with a rare mix of size and speed at 6-foot-1, 216 pounds. Cannon ran a 9.4-second 100-yard dash and could claim a 54-foot shot put and a 435-pound bench press.

"I've never seen that combination of speed and strength in anyone else, including Bo Jackson," Boots Garland, longtime LSU track coach told *The New York Times*.

Born in Philadelphia, Mississippi, in 1937 and raised in Baton Rouge, Cannon arrived at Istrouma High School as a tall, skinny, and awkward kid and left as one of the nation's top recruits. He could have played anywhere, but he chose to stay at home and play for LSU. He twice earned All-America honors (1958 and 1959) and won the 1959 Heisman Trophy. He finished his career with 1,867 rushing yards and an average of 5.2 yards per carry; he also had 19 rushing touchdowns, as well as two touchdown catches and one touchdown each by punt return, kickoff return, and interception return.

Those numbers come nowhere close to explaining Cannon's impact. In the big picture, the Tigers went 24-7 during Cannon's three seasons at LSU, including 19 straight victories from the end of the 1957 season to the eighth game of the 1959 season. In between, and most importantly, the Tigers won the school's first Associated Press national championship in 1958 with an 11-0 record.

For all he accomplished, no statistic, award, or feat stands out more than his performance against Ole Miss on October 31, 1959. On a thick, humid night with fog rolling in off the Mississippi River, the Tigers trailed the Rebels 3-0 in the fourth quarter when Ole Miss elected to punt.

Ole Miss standout Jake Gibbs (who went on to play baseball for the New York Yankees and coach the Ole Miss

Billy Cannon's dramatic 89-yard punt return against Ole Miss on Halloween night in 1959 remains one of the most legendary plays in the 75-year history of SEC football. Cannon also made a key tackle late in LSU's 7-3 win over the Rebels.

baseball team) was supposed to avoid Cannon and kick the ball out of bounds. Instead, his 47-yard punt stayed just inside LSU's right sideline and hit the ground near the Tigers' 16-yard line. The ball bounced to the waiting Cannon on the 11-yard line. He took off upfield, stumbled momentarily around the 18-yard line, and immediately met a swell of Ole Miss players around the 20-yard line. Just as suddenly as he reached his attackers he surged through them, breaking six tackles. He then pulled away from Gibbs and raced down the sideline to the end zone, and into history. What is often forgotten is how, on defense, Cannon helped

to stop Ole Miss at the 1-yard line in the final minute to secure a 7-3 victory.

"I watched the ball bounce down by the 10, and I kept saying, 'No, Billy, no!' Then it became 'Go, Billy, go!'" said Paul Dietzel, Cannon's coach at LSU. "You have to understand it was a hot, muggy night and late in the game. The players on both teams were exhausted, but not Billy. He was so strong, so fast, he basically ran through the whole team. It was one of the greatest runs in college football. I have a film clip of it. I still watch it more than I'd like to admit."

LSU star Billy Cannon possessed a unique combination of gifts. At 6-foot-1 and 216 pounds, he had the speed of a sprinter and the strength of most linemen.

Some LSU fans named children after Cannon. When one of Cannon's children was born during his college career, someone ran a diaper bearing his No. 20 up the flagpole at Tiger Stadium.

Forty-four years later, Cannon attended an LSU homecoming game and stood on the field while the stadium's video board played his celebrated run. Fans not only stood to applaud Cannon, but the players, all born long after his playing days, raised their helmets in salute to Cannon. As LSU athletic director Skip Bertman commented to *The New York Times* that day, "He's still an icon, isn't he?"

He remains an icon, despite injuries that prevented his pro career from meeting expectations and a two-and-a-half-year prison term for counterfeiting. Cannon served his time quietly and upon release asked for little more than forgive-

ness. He also put his skill and experience as an orthodontist to good use by returning to prison to run a dental clinic for prisoners.

Time heals some wounds, and the forgiveness accorded Cannon is evident in the way he is still revered by LSU fans. His No. 20 remains LSU's only retired jersey and his life curiously resembles the main character of Frank Deford's novel *Everybody's All-American*, even though Deford has denied this.

Midway through the 2007 season, with LSU ranked No. 1 in the national polls, Cannon signed hundreds of autographs during a pregame promotion.

"This is extremely nice," Cannon said. "Me and a bunch of other kids played almost 50 years ago, and to still be remembered like this, on a day when there's so much else going on, is just so nice for an old man."

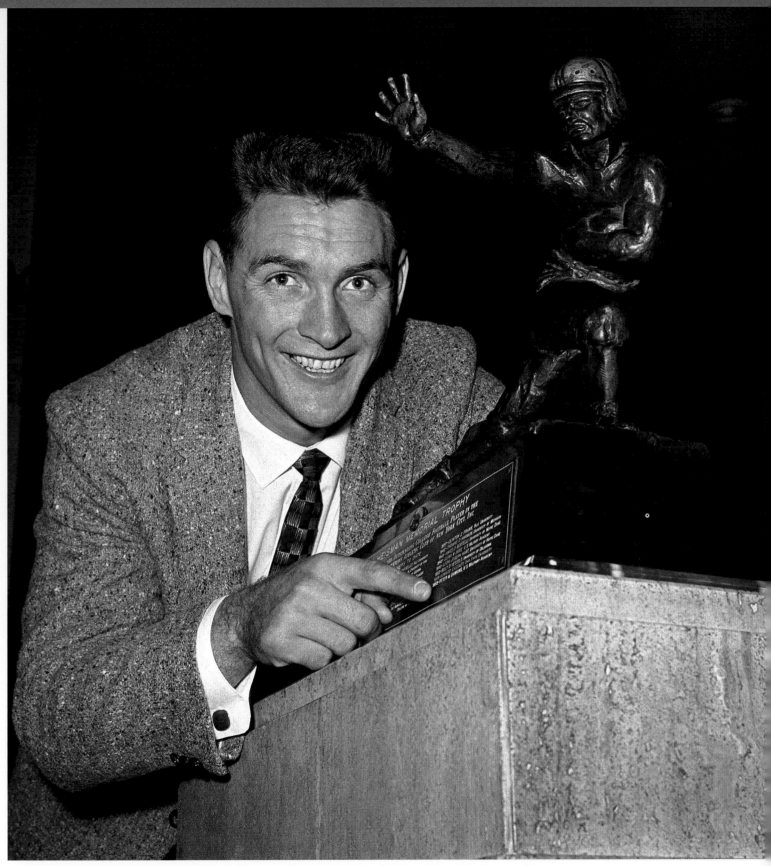

In 1958, Cannon became the second Heisman Trophy winner in SEC history. He was also selected as an All-American and was named "Back of the Year" by the Associated Press.

The Chinese Bandits

Even before LSU's game against Ole Miss in 1956, Paul Dietzel was concerned about his team's lack of size, strength, and depth. When the Rebels beat his Tigers 46-17 in Baton Rouge, Dietzel and his coaches knew they had to do something to counter their weaknesses.

"That's what got us going," Dietzel said in the book, *Greatest Moments in LSU Football History.* "We could not play both ways with just one team. They just wore us out. Our first team could play them to a standstill, but got tired. We just didn't have enough depth."

What LSU did have in reserve were a number of tough little guys willing to play hard and hit harder. Dietzel knew that if he put them on the field for an entire game, they wouldn't have won many games in the Southeastern Conference. But if he played them in a more limited role, they had a chance to make the entire team better.

Dietzel had a tough time creating two teams of equal strength. Instead, he created a three-platoon system. The best 11 players would be the White team, (so named because of the Tigers' white home jerseys), and they would play both sides of the ball during the first half of every quarter. For the other half of the quarter, Dietzel had a team of offensive specialists (originally called the "Gold" team and eventually shortened to the "Go" team) and a team of defensive specialists. "Naturally the defensive team had to be the Chinese Bandits," Dietzel said in *Tales from the LSU Sideline.*

They were neither Chinese nor bandits, but they were fierce and effective. The name came from an old "Terry and the Pirates" comic strip that referred to Chinese bandits as the "most vicious people in the world." Dietzel started using the term when he was the line coach under legendary coach Sid Gillman at the University of Cincinnati.

The LSU defensemen who made up the Chinese Bandits weren't very big or fast, but according to Coach Paul Dietzel, "they all arrived in a bad frame of mind."

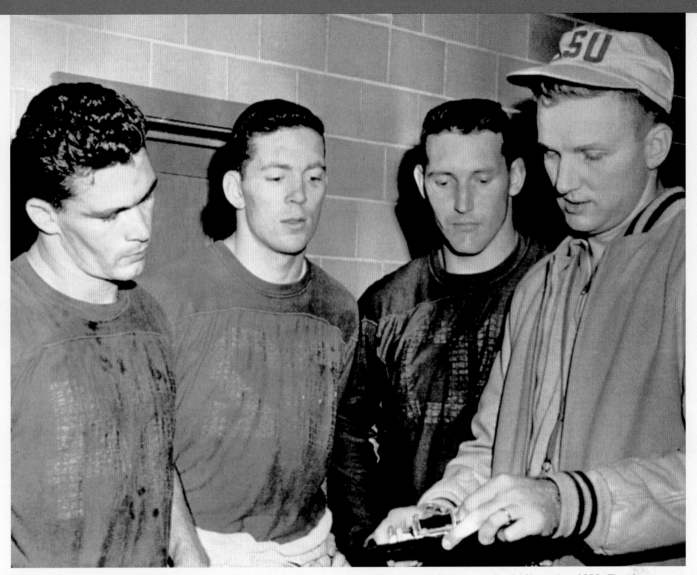

Coach Dietzel works with (left to right) Andy Bourgeois, John Langan, and Mel Branch during practice in November 1958. The three members of the Chinese Bandits played a central role in LSU's national championship that season.

It's not a term that works well in today's world, but the unit got the job done, despite its shortcomings. LSU rode its three-platoon system to 19 straight wins from 1957 to 1959 and the 1958 Associated Press national championship.

"That [system] wouldn't work anymore, I don't think," Dietzel said. "The Chinese Bandits, they weren't very big. They were slow. But they proved to me what gang-tackling was. Because they were so slow, they all got [to the ball] at the same time."

Dietzel and his staff would grade the athletes on every play. If somebody wasn't within a yard of the ball when it was ruled down, that player got a grade of zero for the play. "So," the coach recalled, "they all arrived [at the ball] in a bad frame of mind."

LSU's starting defense in 1958 allowed just less than 3 yards per carry. The Chinese Bandits, always fresh and alert because they didn't have to play the entire game, allowed less than one yard per carry.

"It proved to me that it's morale over material three to one every time, just as Napoleon said," Dietzel said. "One of the greatest thrills I ever had in the coaching business was the Chinese Bandits."

The Chinese Bandits were disbanded when Dietzel left to coach at Army after the 1961 season.

Even today the Chinese Bandits are honored each time the LSU defense stalls an opponent's drive, as the LSU band plays the "Bandit" song and the entire stadium bows to the defense.

The 1960s
Opening, Closing, and Knocking Down Doors

Like the world around it, the Southeastern Conference in the 1960s moved from a simpler time to an era of dynamic change. Among the dramatic transformations undertaken by the conference, the SEC opened the door to African-American athletes, closed the door to two original members, and busted down the doors of the college football world to claim a share of the national championship in eight of ten seasons.

On the gridiron, the decade opened with Ole Miss on top. The rebuilding job that Coach Johnny Vaught undertook in 1947 stood on firm footing by the time the Rebels won nine games in both 1957 and 1958. The Rebels closed out the 1950s with its best team to date. The 1959 squad lost only one game during the regular season and topped it off with a bowl victory and a share of the national championship in four polls. While many remember Billy Cannon's legendary 89-yard punt return to give LSU a 7-3 victory over Ole Miss on Halloween night, it is often forgotten that the Rebels dominated that same LSU team in a 21-0 victory two months later in the Sugar Bowl.

In 1960, Vaught fielded another strong team led by quarterback Jake Gibbs and receiver Bobby Crespino. Except for a 10-7 victory over Arkansas and a 6-6 tie with LSU, the Rebels rode roughshod over their opponents and closed out the season with a 10-0-1 record, a 14-6 Sugar Bowl win over Rice, and a share of another national championship in seven polls.

When Coach Paul "Bear" Bryant arrived at Alabama in 1958, he told his first recruiting class that if they did everything he told them and believed in him and his way of doing things, they would win a national championship by the time they were seniors. In 1961 those seniors fulfilled that destiny by finishing 11-0 and defeating Arkansas 10-3 in the Sugar Bowl. It was good enough to earn the Crimson Tide the consensus national championship.

Auburn's Tucker Frederickson (number 20) was one of the last true two-way football stars. He played halfback on offense and safety on defense at a time when most players were playing just one side of the ball. Coach Shug Jordan called Frederickson the "most complete football player" he had ever seen. Frederickson was the conference Most Valuable Player and an All-American in 1964 and is a member of the College Football Hall of Fame.

While USC was named the 1962 national champion by the AP and UPI polls, Ole Miss, Alabama, and LSU all received national-champion recognition from other polls. The Rebels claimed the SEC championship in both 1962 and 1963.

A three-year period of success began in 1964, when Bryant would cement his reputation among the nation's best football coaches of his era. The Crimson Tide would win the AP and UPI national championships in 1964 and the AP national title in 1965.

The 1965 season has long been regarded as the most competitive season in SEC history. Although a convincing argument could be made on behalf of the conference's great successes in the first decade of the twenty-first century, seven SEC schools finished in the top 18 in the UPI coaches' poll in 1965. In addition to No. 4 Alabama, the UPI's final poll included No. 7 Tennessee, No. 12 Florida, No. 14 LSU, No. 15 Georgia, No. 17 Ole Miss, and No. 18 Kentucky.

Jake Gibbs, seen here carrying the ball on a bootleg play, was one of several outstanding quarterbacks who played for Coach Johnny Vaught at Ole Miss. In his junior year, Gibbs was tops in the conference in total offense and was named All-SEC quarterback for 1959. In 1960, he led Ole Miss to a 10-0-1 record and a share of the national championship.

Tennessee's rise in 1965 came during Doug Dickey's second season as the Vols' coach, but it didn't come without tragedy. Tennessee had slipped considerably since the days of Robert Neyland, but Dickey and his staff pushed their team back to the upper tier of the SEC in 1965 with an 8-1-2 record, which included an emotional 7-7 tie against Alabama that felt more like a victory. The celebration didn't last long. Early the next morning, a train struck the car carrying coaches Bill Majors, Bob Jones, and Charley Rash, who were on their way to work. Majors and Jones died that day. Rash died five days later. The heartbreaking loss left three wives, seven sons, and a football team to pick up the pieces. To their credit, coaches and players responded by pulling together. They went on to win six of their next seven games.

In 1966, Alabama fielded what Bryant considered to be his best Crimson Tide team to that point. The Tide's shot at a third straight national title disappeared when Notre Dame and Michigan State played to a safe, cautious 10-10 tie on November 19, leaving both teams undefeated at the end of the regular season. Alabama also finished the regular season undefeated and untied, but Notre Dame and Michigan State shared the national title while the Crimson Tide was left out of the title picture in all but one poll. The 1966 national title is still a source of controversy. Notre Dame did not accept bowl bids at the time, and the Big Ten did not allow the same team to play in the Rose Bowl in consecutive years, so Michigan State also missed out on a bowl. Meanwhile, Alabama overwhelmed Nebraska 34-7 in the Sugar Bowl.

Tennessee captured a share of the national title in 1967 and Georgia followed with its own share in 1968.

While the SEC continued to grow in stature on the field throughout the 1960s, it declined in numbers off the field when two of its founding members, Georgia Tech and Tulane, left the conference. Georgia Tech made its official announcement in June 1964, provoked by coach Bobby Dodd's belief that the Yellow Jackets could become a national independent power, similar to Notre Dame, Penn State, Pittsburgh, and the service academies. The final straw came when Tech was unsuccessful in its attempt to convince the rest of the SEC to raise its limit of 140 football and basketball scholarships.

Tech's departure left the SEC with an odd number (11) of schools, but that problem would be solved on June 1, 1966, when Tulane followed Tech out of the SEC, but not

When Coach Bear Bryant arrived at Alabama in 1958, he immediately set about building a championship program. The first of his six national championships came in 1961.

for the same reasons. Some believed that Tulane also intended to pursue its own national schedule, but the truth had more to do with university cutbacks that reduced the number of players Tulane could afford to field. After enduring its ninth consecutive losing season in 1965, Tulane officials decided it was time to move on.

The conference leadership also underwent a change with the retirement of Commissioner Bernie Moore and the hiring of new Commissioner A. M. "Tonto" Coleman in April 1966. Within this transition period, the SEC decided not to pursue new members to replace Tech and Tulane.

Under Coleman's watch, the SEC took a major step toward righting a wrong and opening up athletic participation to African-American athletes.

In a decade that saw Florida quarterback Steve Spurrier become the SEC's third Heisman Trophy winner in 1966 and the emergence of other outstanding quarterbacks such as Ole Miss' Jake Gibbs, Georgia's Fran Tarkenton, Alabama's Joe Namath, and Ole Miss' Archie Manning in the national spotlight, the most significant football players of the era may have been Kentucky's Nat Northington and Greg Page, the first African-American athletes to receive football scholarships in the SEC.

The seeds of change were planted before the arrival of Northington and Page. In 1963, Mississippi State basketball coach Babe McCarthy defied Governor Ross Barnett's orders not to play against integrated teams when the Bulldogs faced Loyola of Chicago in the NCAA basketball tournament. The reality of integration in athletics hit home in the spring of

Linebacker D. D. Lewis played on three losing teams at Mississippi State, but he didn't let that stop him from becoming a two-time All-SEC selection (1966 and 1967) and an All-American in 1967. Alabama coach Bear Bryant called him, "no doubt about it, the best linebacker in the country." Lewis was voted into the College Football Hall of Fame in 2001.

Tennessee's middle guard Steve DeLong was so good from 1962 to 1964 that he was voted the SEC's defensive lineman of the year in all three seasons. He also won the Outland Trophy in 1964, despite playing on a losing team. In 1968 he was named to the all-time SEC team, in 1990 he was selected to Tennessee's all-time team, and in 1993 he was inducted into the College Football Hall of Fame.

1966, when a Texas Western basketball team started five African-American players and defeated all-white Kentucky for the national championship.

Syracuse's Ernie Davis had won the Heisman Trophy in 1961, and USC's Mike Garrett won the award in 1965. In 1966, Kentucky coach Charlie Bradshaw took the then-

bold step of signing Northington and Page. That fall Northington became the first African-American player to participate in an SEC football game.

In 1968, Lester McClain became the first African American to play for Tennessee, in the same year that Tennessee introduced artificial turf to the SEC. On November 16,

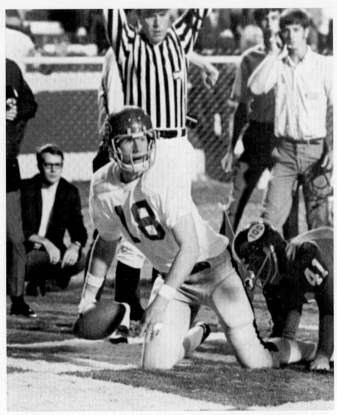

Ole Miss quarterback Archie Manning scores a touchdown against Alabama in one of the most dramatic games in SEC history. On October 3, 1969, Manning produced an SEC-record 540 total yards of offense, but Alabama quarterback Scott Hunter completed 22 of 29 passes for 300 yards in the Crimson Tide's 33-32 victory.

Alabama defeated Miami 14-6 in a nationally televised night game from the Orange Bowl Stadium, which was the first regular-season collegiate game televised in prime time.

The following autumn, Alabama hosted Ole Miss in Birmingham on October 3 in the first-ever prime-time telecast of an SEC football game. College football celebrated its 100th anniversary in 1969 and both teams wore a "100" insignia on their helmets. Most importantly, they played a game for the ages. Ole Miss' Manning produced a conference-record 540 total offensive yards and Alabama quarterback Scott Hunter completed 22 of 29 passes for 300 yards in a 33-32 victory for the Rebels.

Florida was still working to establish itself as a championship contender in the SEC when Jack Youngblood emerged as one of the conference's all-time best ends. Youngblood, a member of the College Football Hall of Fame, achieved All-American status as a senior in 1970 and was chosen to the All-SEC 25-year team for 1950 to 1974.

Crossing the Racial Divide

Most colleges and universities had already begun to integrate their football teams by the 1960s, and many of them found success on and off the field. The Southeastern Conference needed someone to step forward and light the spark for this necessary and inevitable change.

One such person was Edward T. "Ned" Breathitt, who served as governor of Kentucky from 1963 to 1967, as well as chairman of the University of Kentucky board of trustees. As governor, Breathitt had put his full weight behind strong civil rights and anti-discrimination legislation. In his role at the university, Breathitt met with university President John Oswald. Noting that the University of Louisville and Western Kentucky University had already integrated, Breathitt convinced Oswald to spearhead the drive to bring black athletes to Kentucky.

"Not only will it help the image of the state," Breathitt said, "but it is the right thing to do."

Breathitt took a personal interest in the recruitment of two of the state's best high school football players. He called Louisville's Nat Northington and Middlesboro's Greg Page and helped convince them to give Kentucky a chance. Breathitt was even present at Northington's home when Northington signed his letter of intent in December 1965 and became the first African American to sign up to play football in the Southeastern Conference.

There was only so much that Breathitt could do from there. The rest was up to Northington and Page. The two arrived at Kentucky at a time when head coach Charlie Bradshaw and his assistants were trying to resurrect a once-competitive program, and they often used brutal tactics to get results. Bradshaw inherited 88 players from the previous coach, Blanton Collier, in 1962, but Bradshaw and his staff managed to run off 58 players during the course of the first year. Some of those tactics were still in use when Northington and Page first put on their pads for the Wildcats in August 1966.

Northington and Page endured a difficult first year at Kentucky. No one could or would protect them from threats, insults, and isolation, but it didn't keep them from excelling for the freshman team. Page averaged 12.5 tackles per game as a freshman.

Kentucky Coach Charlie Bradshaw and his coaches were often accused of using brutal tactics with their players, but Bradshaw broke new ground when he signed the SEC's first African-American players, Nat Northington and Greg Page.

Northington and Page both seemed headed for bigger, better things at Kentucky until tragedy struck in August of 1967. During an afternoon practice, Kentucky ran a pursuit drill in which 11 defensive players were ordered to converge on a single ballcarrier and bring him to the ground. When Page's turn came to be the carrier, he didn't get up after the tackle. Page was paralyzed from the nose down.

Page's health deteriorated over the next month. He died on September 29, 38 days after that fateful practice. The next day Northington, who had been Page's roommate, became the first African-American athlete to participate in an SEC football game. He played several minutes at wide receiver in Kentucky's 26-13 loss to Ole Miss in

Kentucky's Nat Northington was the first African-American player to participate in an SEC game. He entered the game as wide receiver during Kentucky's 26-13 loss to Ole Miss in Lexington on September 30, 1967.

Linebacker Wilbur Hackett became the first African-American athlete to start for any sport's team at Kentucky. In 1969, he was the first to be chosen a team captain. He is now a referee for SEC football.

Lexington. Northington appeared in three more games that season before leaving the team late one night, distraught over his friend's death.

"Nat said he'd just sit in his room and talk to the bricks in the wall," Wilbur Hackett, an African-American linebacker on the freshman team in 1967, told *Sports Illustrated*. "Nat didn't feel close enough to anyone else, and nobody came to him. And the only reason I was at the school was because of Nat and Greg."

To his credit, Northington convinced Hackett and another African-American freshman, Houston Hogg, to stay at Kentucky. They went on to earn varsity letters, Hackett from 1968 to 1970 and Hogg in 1969 and 1970. Hackett's reputation for playing hard on every snap earned him the respect of teammates who voted him defensive captain in 1969 and 1970. Hackett was the first African-American co-captain in the SEC.

"It was tough," said Hackett, who is now an SEC football referee. "Houston and I packed our bags more than once. . . . I felt if I didn't [play hard], I wouldn't make it," he says. "And with Greg and Nat gone, I had to make it."

Fifty years later, Northington has never responded to requests for interviews and maintains his silence. Page was honored in 1979 when the University of Kentucky named a campus apartment complex in his memory, making Page the first African American to have his name on a University of Kentucky building.

On the athletic department questionnaire Page filled out before his arrival at Kentucky, he addressed the question "Why did you choose UK?" by responding: "I wanted to play football for UK and to help open the way for more Negro athletes to play ball here."

Sadly, Page never played in a varsity game for the Wildcats. Fortunately for the SEC, he met the greater of his goals. By 1972, every SEC football team had integrated.

Opposite: Lester McClain was the first African American to play football for the University of Tennessee. A Nashville native, McClain was a receiver from 1968 to 1970. He later served as an alumni member of the university's athletic board.

Bryant Builds a Dynasty

When new Alabama coach Paul "Bear" Bryant met with his first class of freshmen, he laid out a vision for the program that left no doubt of his intentions.

"Look around at the guys sitting next to you," Bryant said. "Chances are, four years from now, there's probably going to be no more than a double handful of you left. But if you work hard and do the things I ask you to do, you can be national champions by the time you're seniors."

Bryant did not return to his alma mater just to win football games. He came to win championships, and no one in college football did it better than Bryant in the 1960s. Yet for all he accomplished, Bryant never seemed to waver far from his basic beliefs and roots.

"I'm just a simple plow hand from Arkansas," Bryant said, "but I have learned over the years how to hold a team together, how to lift some men up, how to calm others down, until finally they've got one heartbeat, together, a team."

Bryant was born the youngest boy in a family of 12 (three died in infancy) on September 11, 1913, in rural Moro Bottom, Arkansas. His father, William Monroe Bryant, tried to farm but was often ill. His mother, Ida Kilgore Bryant, held the family together and maintained a special place in her son's heart; as Bryant often said, "I was a mama's boy."

As a 14 year old, Bryant wrestled a bear at a carnival and earned the nickname that became both a symbol and moniker throughout his life. A hard-nosed player at Alabama under Coach Frank Thomas, Bryant once played with a broken leg against Tennessee during his senior season. All-American end Don Hutson may have been the player who got the glory on that Crimson Tide team, but Bryant, at 6 feet, 3 inches and 210 pounds, was a tough cuss who knew how to block, tackle, and win.

Those qualities helped Bryant move through the coaching ranks. He started at Union College in Jackson, Tennessee, came back to Alabama to work as an assistant to Thomas, and then moved to Vanderbilt in 1939 for a chance to take on more responsibility under coach Red Sanders. After two seasons at Vanderbilt, the 28-year-old Bryant was offered the head coaching job at Arkansas, but World War II got in the way and Bryant went to serve his country.

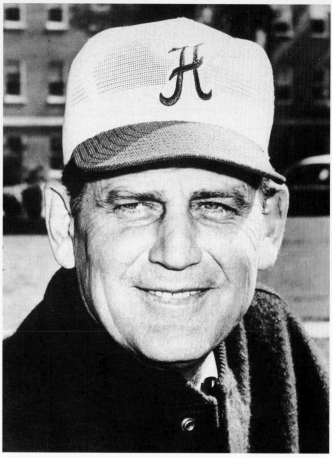

Asked why he left Texas A&M for the opportunity to coach at his alma mater, the University of Alabama, Bear Bryant told reporters, "Mama called." It wasn't long before his decision paid off for him and the university.

After serving in the Navy, Bryant became the head coach at Maryland in 1945. He stayed for one season and then moved to Kentucky, where he turned a moribund program into a winner during his eight seasons there. He moved on to Texas A&M in 1954.

Bryant took his first Aggies team off to a dusty old Army base near the remote town of Junction, Texas, for a severe preseason challenge that reduced the roster from 100 to 29. The group that returned formed the core of a program that finished 9-0-1 in 1956, including a 34-21 victory over arch-rival Texas, and won the Southwest Conference title. The next

Bear Bryant told his first Alabama recruiting class that if they worked hard and did what he told them to do, they would be national champions by the time they were seniors. Of the more than 100 recruits that came to Alabama, the players pictured here are the only ones who were around as seniors when the Crimson Tide won the national championship in 1961.

year, Alabama offered him the chance to return to his alma mater as football coach.

Alabama had won just four of thirty games in three seasons under J. B. "Ears" Whitworth and needed a major turnaround. It started with that first freshman class under Bryant.

Lineman Dave Sington recalled that, in Bryant's first meeting with the team in 1958, he told them, "I'm not worried about whether I'm going to win or lose. I know I'm going to win. I know that. And I'm not worried about my assistant coaches. I know they're winners. And I'm not worried about whether Alabama is going to win. I know that.

The only thing I don't know is how many of you in this room are winners, and how many of you will be with us."

In 1961, what was left of that class led Alabama to an 11-0 record and the national championship. "In 1961, we had the best team in college football," Bryant said. "We had 16 or 17 players, the nut of the team, and all 16 or 17 were leaders."

There was nothing inherently special about those recruits. Most of them never made it through the full four years. Those who persevered and bought in to Bryant's demands found themselves in position to turn Bryant's vision into reality in 1961.

Linebacker Lee Roy Jordan was a big factor in Alabama's turn-around under Bryant. In Jordan's three seasons, the Crimson Tide won 29 games and a national championship. Bryant called Jordan "one of the finest football players the world has ever seen. If runners stayed between the sidelines, he tackled them."

Billy Neighbors was a cornerstone of Alabama's 1961 national championship team. The tough, powerful lineman earned All-America honors as a senior and was voted the SEC's top lineman in 1961. In 2003, he became a member of the College Football Hall of Fame.

"We worked like hell for the first two years," lineman Billy Neighbors said. "I think there were something like 118 of us who came in as freshman and eight of us were left after four years. But by the time we were juniors he had us where he wanted us: He had us all well trained, we knew how to run his system, and we could beat people in the fourth quarter by being in better shape. He taught us that if we were in better shape than the other team we would win sooner or later."

Neighbors described how Bryant had "something special about him" that got the players fired up to play and the coaches ready to coach. "You'd do anything he told you to do," he said.

Five games into the 1961 season, Bryant had his team convinced of just how far they could go.

"We beat Tennessee 34-3 in Birmingham and after that game he came on the bus and told us we had a great football team," Neighbors said. "Three or four weeks before that he had told us we wouldn't win a game, that we were sorry as hell."

Led by a defense that allowed only 25 points all season, and by senior quarterback Pat Trammell—who brought the toughness, leadership, and intelligence Bryant sought in a quarterback—Alabama went 11-0. The Tide beat Arkansas in the Sugar Bowl and finished first in both the AP and UPI final polls.

Quarterback Joe Namath (number 12) was a star in the making in 1964, and he had plenty of help from his teammates, including: (front row, from left) right end Wayne Cook, right tackle Frank McClendon, right guard Jim Fuller, center Gaylon McCollough, left guard Ken Mitchell, left tackle Ron Durby, and left end Tommy Tolleson; (back row, from left) flanker Ray Ogden, fullback Larry Wall, Namath, and fullback Steve Bowman.

Alabama went a combined 19-3 in 1962 and 1963 and finished in the AP top 10 in both seasons as it built toward the 1964 season and another run at the national title. Senior quarterback Joe Namath spent most of 1964 playing through a knee injury, but he and junior quarterback Steve Sloan combined with another stout defense to go 10-1. Alabama's only loss, 21-17 to Texas in the Orange Bowl, came after the AP and UPI had already selected the Crimson Tide as their national champion. Alabama's loss remained a point of controversy after Namath emerged from a pile on a fourth-and-goal quarterback sneak with the goal-line chalk across his chest, only to have the officials rule he had not scored.

Alabama's dynasty during this span was defined by how it responded to adversity. The 1965 season provided its share of difficulty, starting with its season opener at Georgia.

The Crimson Tide led 17-10 and the Bulldogs faced a steep hill at their own 30-yard line with two minutes and eight seconds to play. On second and eight, Georgia quarterback Kirby Moore passed to Pat Hodgson, who then tossed a lateral on a "hook-and-ladder" play to Bob Taylor, who ran for a 73-yard touchdown. Rather than play to tie, second-year Georgia coach Vince Dooley threw caution to the wind and opted to go for the two-point conversion. The Bulldogs succeeded on the conversion and won the game 18-17.

Alabama halfback Les Kelley follows his blockers through the heart of the Nebraska defense in the 1966 Orange Bowl. The Crimson Tide won the game 39-28 and captured the 1965 AP national championship.

The touchdown play remains a subject of debate for Tide supporters, who insist that Hodgson's knee hit the ground before his lateral. The game films appear to support this claim, but Bryant didn't waste any time looking back, saying, "You don't win games in the movies on Monday."

On October 2, the Tide rallied from a 16-7 fourth-quarter deficit to beat Ole Miss 17-16. On October 16 against Tennessee, with the score tied 7-7 and the clock ticking down to the final seconds, quarterback Kenny Stabler drove to the Volunteers' four-yard line. The scoreboard showed it was third down, so Stabler threw the ball away to stop the clock for a potential game-winning field goal. Unfortunately for Stabler and Alabama, it was actually fourth down and the Tide had to settle for a painful tie.

Alabama went on to win its five remaining regular-season games and beat Nebraska 39-28 in the Orange Bowl. With the UPI poll picked before the bowls that season, the Tide finished fourth in the final rankings. However, the AP voted after the bowls that season and when No. 1 Michigan State lost the Rose Bowl, No. 2 Arkansas lost the Cotton Bowl, and Alabama beat No. 3 Nebraska, the Crimson Tide jumped to the top of the final AP poll for a second straight national title.

Most of Alabama's biggest challenges in 1966 came off the field. Integration had become a hot-button issue in college football, and Alabama was an easy target for the national media. To his credit, Bryant had welcomed the opportunity to play integrated teams in bowl games, and he had referred

several talented African-American players to coaches at Northern schools. He was also exploring how to integrate his own team within the climate of intense resistance to desegregation. Segregationist Governor George Wallace played to the base fears of voters, and Bryant's hands were effectively tied by politics. The Crimson Tide paid the price.

After being picked No. 1 in the preseason polls, Alabama quickly slipped back to No. 3 after the first week of the season and to No. 4 three weeks later—without losing a single game. Over the course of the season, the media pushed Notre Dame to the top; the Fighting Irish had only one African-American player. When No. 1 Notre Dame and No. 2 Michigan State met in a battle of undefeated teams in November, the score was tied 10-10 in the final quarter. In the waning minutes of the game, Notre Dame coach Ara Parseghian chose to run out the clock rather than attempt a potential game-winning field goal and risk a turnover.

Parseghian had played for the tie in order to protect his team's ranking, and he admitted as much. Alabama coaches and players, angry and perplexed by Parseghian's tactics, thought the result would lead voters to pick the Tide No. 1.

"Everything we do at Alabama is based on winning," Bryant said. "If I directed our team to go for a tie late, I believe they would be disappointed in me. I would not be practicing what I preach."

Bryant believed his team had done all it could do. "They said our boys were No. 1 before the season, and we haven't lost."

The AP had decided in the offseason to move its final poll back to the end of the regular season. Notre Dame won both the AP and UPI polls, and Alabama finished third behind Michigan State.

Bryant and his team took the high road in public, but the slight motivated the Tide to prove its point in a rematch with Nebraska in the Sugar Bowl. At the time Notre Dame did not accept bowl invitations and Michigan State could not play in the Rose Bowl because of a Big Ten rule that prohibited back-to-back Rose Bowl appearances. The Tide, meanwhile, made its case with a 34-7 victory over the Cornhuskers.

"Alabama is several touchdowns better than the team that beat us last year," Nebraska coach Bob Devaney said. "Alabama is the best football team I have ever seen."

Alabama players carry Coach Bryant off the field following their victory over Nebraska in the 1966 Orange Bowl. The victory gave the Crimson Tide its third national championship of the decade.

He got no argument from Bryant. The coaches and players from the 1966 team—the subject of *The Missing Ring: How Bear Bryant and the 1966 Alabama Crimson Tide Were Denied College Football's Most Elusive Prize* by Keith Dunnavant—will always contend they were cheated out of a third straight national championship.

"It is the greatest college team I've ever seen, too," Bryant said, "and they proved it today."

Butts and the Bulldogs

When future SEC commissioner Bernie Moore became the head football coach at Mercer University in 1925 and met his new players, most of them offered a friendly welcome. When Moore reached a round-faced player with a determined expression on his face, the player simply said, "I'm your right end."

That player was James Wallace Butts Jr., better known as Wally. Butts would go on to be the football coach at the University of Georgia from 1939 to 1960, where he led the Bulldogs to four Southeastern Conference titles, one undefeated season, a share of two national championships, and eight bowl games.

Legendary Notre Dame coach Frank Leahy called Butts "football's finest passing coach." One of Butts' best players, NFL Hall of Fame quarterback Fran Tarkenton, said Butts "knew more football than any other man I ever met." The highest praise, however, may have come from Butts' 1942 Heisman Trophy winner, halfback Frank Sinkwich, who said, "He made a man of me."

Butts was born and raised in Milledgeville, Georgia, and attended high school at Georgia Military before enrolling at Mercer, where he competed in football, basketball, baseball, boxing, and wrestling. Butts, a stocky 5-foot-6, stood out in football, where Moore called him "the best blocking end I ever coached."

After graduating from Mercer in 1928, Butts spent 10 years coaching at the high school level before Georgia head coach Joel Hunt hired him as an assistant coach in 1938. When Hunt left to become the head coach at Wyoming after the 1938 season, Butts suddenly found himself as the Bulldogs' head coach.

Butts proved to be a good choice, coaching a team led by Sinkwich and multi-talented fullback Charley Trippi to an 11-1 record, an Orange Bowl victory, and a share of the national title in just his fourth year on the job. When Trippi returned from World War II, the Bulldogs finished 9-2 in 1945 and then 11-0 with a share of the national title in 1946.

Wally Butts' football coach at Mercer University, Bernie Moore, called Butts (above) "the best blocking end I ever coached." Butts' greatest impact in college football was as Georgia's coach from 1939 to 1960. His teams won 140 games, four SEC championships, and a share of the 1942 national championship—a legacy that earned him a place in the College Football Hall of Fame.

In an era when the running game ruled college football, Georgia's Wally Butts was an innovator in the passing game. He coached talented passers such as Frank Sinkwich, Charlie Trippi, John Rauch, Zeke Bratkowski, and Fran Tarkenton. Notre Dame coach Frank Leahy called Butts "football's finest passing coach."

In an era when many coaches failed to master the intricacies of the passing game because they had no intentions of relying on it, Butts took a more innovative approach to passing. Trippi called Butts "a master at the passing game." Trippi recalled, "We would hide the blackboard from Coach Butts because he would draw a new passing play every time he saw the board."

Butts earned the nickname "Weeping Wally," both for the way he poor-mouthed his teams to the press and for his emotional motivational speeches. In 1946 against Furman, Georgia led 28-7 at halftime but Butts was not satisfied with his team's performance. He made certain they knew of his displeasure during his halftime speech. Butts kicked a pot-bellied stove, busting the pipe connecting the stove to the wall and sending a cloud of soot through the room.

The years from 1947 to 1958 were filled with ups and downs. Butts appeared to be on his way out after winning just three games each in 1956 and 1957 and four games in '58. Instead, Butts responded with a renewed commitment and one of his best teams. In January 1959 he was elected president of the American Football Coaches Association. That fall, led by Tarkenton in the backfield and future Auburn coach Pat Dye on the line, Georgia finished 10-1 and beat Missouri 14-0 in the Orange Bowl.

When the Bulldogs finished 6-4 the next year, Butts resigned as coach and became Georgia's full-time athletic director. Butts' darkest day was yet to come, however. In 1964, the *Saturday Evening Post* published a story that accused Butts and Alabama coach Bear Bryant of fixing the 1962 Georgia-Alabama game, which the Crimson Tide won 35-0. After careful investigation and film study, Butts and Bryant were cleared of all charges. Both coaches successfully sued the *Post* for libel and Butts was awarded a $3.06 million settlement, at the time one of the largest amounts ever awarded to a libel plaintiff.

Unfortunately for Butts, the amount was later reduced to $460,000, and his reputation had been damaged by the accusations and by scurrilous unrelated rumors. This dark cloud over his name made it easy for a group of Georgia power brokers to force Butts out as athletic director.

Butts died on December 17, 1973. Over the years the legacy of his accomplishments as coach and athletic director has outshone any doubt cast by the *Post* case. His career record of 140-86-9 at Georgia is second only to Vince Dooley in total wins. He is a member of the College Football Hall of Fame and the Georgia Sports Hall of Fame.

The Georgia players still wear the "silver britches" that Butts first put on his Bulldogs in 1939. The football program is housed in Butts-Mehre Heritage Hall, honoring him and another coaching legend, Harry Mehre.

Above: Wherever Fran Tarkenton played, success followed. He led Athens High School to the Georgia state championship, the University of Georgia to the SEC title, and the Minnesota Vikings to three Super Bowls in the NFL. Tarkenton, a renowned scrambler who played 18 years in the pros, is a member of both the College and Pro Football Halls of Fame.

Left: Quarterback Fran Tarkenton was a good fit for Coach Butts' passing game at Georgia from 1958 to 1960. Tarkenton said Butts "knew more football than any other man I ever met."

From 'Bama to Broadway

No one but Alabama coach Bear Bryant ever climbed the tower Bryant used to oversee the Crimson Tide practice fields. So when Bryant called for a visiting prospect to join him for a private chat in the tower during practice one day, Alabama coaches and players took notice.

One of the witnesses was Mal Moore, a former Crimson Tide quarterback and assistant coach and current Alabama athletic director. "He goes up on that tower and we were all kind of watching out of the corner of our eyes," Moore said. "We knew for that to happen Coach Bryant must have thought he was pretty special."

Joe Namath was definitely someone special. The history of the SEC is filled with legendary coaches and players and colorful characters—and in the annals of SEC football, it's difficult to find someone who became more of a cultural icon than Namath.

As a gunslinging quarterback for the AFL's New York Jets, Namath turned the pro football world and popular culture upside down with his white football cleats, long hair, sideburns, and flashy lifestyle. Like Babe Ruth, Joe DiMaggio, and Muhammad Ali, "Broadway Joe" Namath personified an era with a reputation that went far beyond his accomplishments on the field.

Before he stepped on to the national stage in New York, Namath was a tough, confident quarterback who grew up in western Pennsylvania and helped lead Alabama to the 1964 national championship.

Born in 1943 in Beaver Falls, a blue-collar town 30 miles outside Pittsburgh, Namath excelled at football, basketball, and baseball. His father, John, was a Hungarian immigrant who worked in coal and steel. Namath's family wanted more for Joe and convinced him to attend college instead of signing one of several pro baseball offers.

Alabama caught Namath's attention in part because Bryant had recruited Namath's older brother Frank at Kentucky and because another western Pennsylvania quarterback, Vito "Babe" Parilli, played at Kentucky for Bryant. When Bryant sent assistant coach Howard Schnellenberger to Beaver Falls, he spent a week winning the approval of Namath's mother, Rose.

Alabama quarterback Joe Namath was a quick study. Coach Bryant often said that once he told Namath how to do something, he never had to tell him again.

"When Howard came to the house my mother took a real liking to him and my mother decided that's where I was going," Namath said.

Namath made a strong first impression on the freshman team and made an immediate impact on the varsity as a sophomore in 1962. Namath stepped into the ominous shadow of Pat Trammell, who had quarterbacked Alabama to the 1961 national championship. Namath set his own mark, however, leading the Tide to a 29-4 record in his three seasons as quarterback.

Namath was off to a strong start as a senior in 1964 when he suffered a knee injury during the fourth game of the season, against North Carolina State. Namath, whom Bryant called "the greatest athlete I've ever coached," had

Before knee injuries took their toll, Joe Namath was both a dynamic passer and runner. Bear Bryant called Namath the greatest athlete he ever coached.

been both a dynamic runner and passer until his injury. After that, he struggled with chronic knee problems throughout his career. Namath shared the starting job with Steve Sloan the rest of the season, but it was Namath who often came in to spark game-winning rallies. Alabama finished 10-0 in 1964 and won the AP national championship.

In his final college game, the 1965 Orange Bowl, Namath came off the bench to pass for 255 yards and two touchdowns. He brought the Tide to the brink of victory, inches away from Texas' goal line. On a fourth-and-goal quarterback sneak, Namath emerged from the pile with goal-line chalk across his chest. Every Alabama player, coach, and fan—especially Namath—was convinced he had scored. The officials, however, ruled Namath had come up short, and Texas won 21-17.

Bad knee and all, Namath turned down the establishment NFL and the St. Louis Cardinals for a record-breaking deal with the New York Jets of the renegade AFL. Namath's status as pro football's first real "bonus baby," along with his flashy lifestyle, made him an easy target for criticism.

Namath says that he wasn't widely accepted in the pro ranks early on, but he was accepted by his fellow players and by coaches because he had played for Bryant at Alabama. "A lot of veterans didn't like the idea of a rookie making so much money," Namath says, "but they knew I had played for Coach Bryant and that was my ace in the hole."

Namath played that ace as part of his best hand in 1968. That season he became the first quarterback to pass for more than 4,000 yards and earned AFL Player of the Year honors. He helped carry the Jets to Super Bowl III in January 1969 and boldly guaranteed a victory over the NFL's Baltimore Colts. Namath led the underdog Jets to a shocking 16-7 win for the AFL's first Super Bowl triumph. In the process, Namath earned himself a permanent place in sports history.

Through all his fame and success, Namath never left Alabama very far behind. During his Pro Football Hall of Fame induction speech in 1985, Namath broke down when he mentioned Bryant. He continues to help Alabama with various fundraising efforts and maintains close relationships with many of his former teammates and coaches. The very idea that Alabama people still regard him as one of their own still humbles Namath.

As was typical of the time, Coach Bryant focused his offense more on the running game than on passing. That changed when Joe Namath came along. Bryant adjusted his coaching staff and coaching philosophy to make better use of Namath's passing ability.

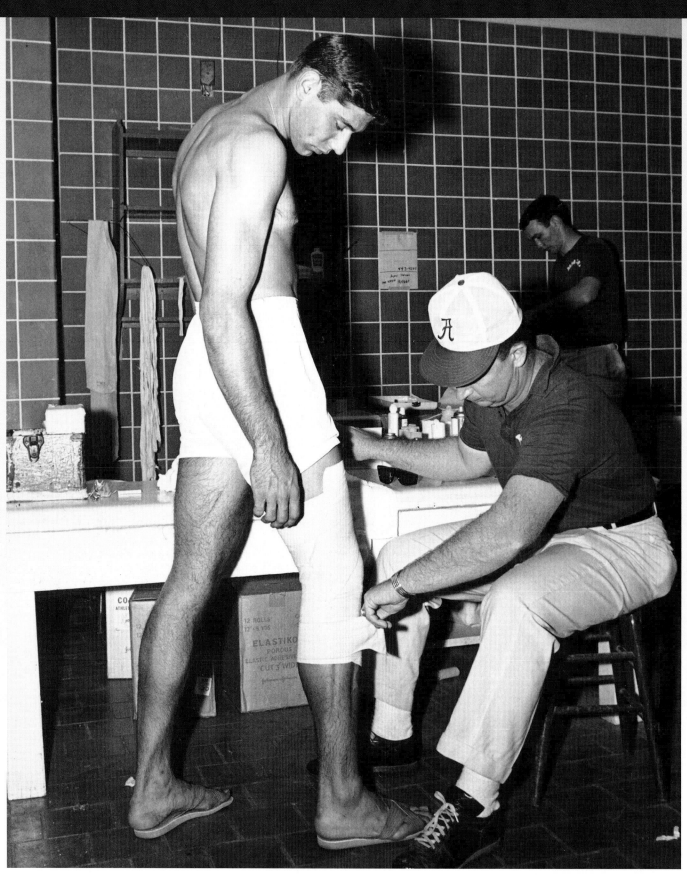

Joe Namath suffered a knee injury early in his senior season at Alabama, and he struggled with knee problems throughout his career. Here, longtime Alabama trainer Jim Goosetree wraps Namath's knee.

"To be considered a legend by Alabama people . . . I think, first of all, that I'm not worthy," Namath says. "Second, I think it's mainly because of my association with Coach Bryant and some great coaches and teammates. I gladly accept that love because I love life and people, but I know it's not just Joe. I know I reflect Coach Bryant to the people I've been around, and I think that's basically why people care about me.

"Winning championships and being part of a championship, even when I was a freshman in 1961, that's special, but when I think of what Alabama means to me, Coach Bryant comes first, and then the people and friends I met at Alabama. That's been lasting. That's part of me. It's always been with me and it's still with me today."

Namath's relationship with Alabama took another memorable turn in December 2007, when he graduated with a bachelor of arts in interdisciplinary studies from the UA external studies program at age 64—forty-two years after he left the university to start his pro football career.

"This is an Alabama family," Namath said. "I feel more part of it today than I ever have. But I didn't do anything any other student wouldn't do. It just took me a lot longer. This was a team effort, and I'm just lucky to be able to join up. Don't let anyone tell you it's too late."

Joe Namath returned to the University of Alabama in December 2007 to complete his degree—42 years after he left the school to pursue a pro football career with the New York Jets.

Steve Superior

On October 29, 1966, with two minutes and twelve seconds left in a tie game between Florida and Auburn, the Gators faced a critical fourth down and a 40-yard field goal attempt. Most everyone at Florida Field that day expected Coach Ray Graves to send in place kicker Wayne Barfield for the potential game-winning kick.

Everyone, it seemed, but Florida senior quarterback Steve Spurrier. Before Barfield could leave the sideline, Spurrier pointed to himself and looked directly at Graves. The coach understood Spurrier's message: He wanted to kick the field goal himself.

Even though he knew full well that Spurrier didn't spend much time practicing his kicks, Graves put his trust in his confident quarterback.

To Graves and the Gator team, Spurrier wasn't just a quarterback. He had that special something that separates the merely talented from the winners. That quality was quickly apparent in young Steven Orr Spurrier. Spurrier clung to his passion for sports as his family moved frequently to follow his father John Graham Spurrier's vocation as a Presbyterian minister. The elder preacher pushed his son to succeed and often coached his youth sports teams. According to one popular story, Rev. Spurrier once asked if his players believed the adage, "It's not whether you win or lose, but how you play the game." Those players who raised their hands received a stern lecture on the value of winning.

By the time Spurrier reached Science Hill High School in Johnson City, Tennessee, he was a multitalented athlete who earned all-state honors in football, basketball, and baseball. Football was his true love and his success on the gridiron led to a long list of offers from college football's major powers.

Spurrier seriously considered Tennessee, Alabama, and Florida, but the Vols still ran the single wing and Spurrier wanted to throw the ball. Alabama had Joe Namath, Steve Sloan, and Kenny Stabler, and Spurrier didn't want to spend his whole college career waiting for a shot. Florida offered Spurrier the opportunity to compete for the starting job as soon as he became eligible for varsity as a sophomore.

Until Graves took over in 1960, Florida had spent most of its time in the SEC as an also-ran, never winning more

Auburn's Coach Shug Jordan unintentionally added to the lore surrounding quarterback Steve Spurrier when he called him "Steve Superior." Spurrier waved off the regular kicker and kicked the game-winning field goal himself in a 30-27 win over Auburn in 1966.

than seven games a season and playing in just two bowls. Graves, who played for Robert Neyland at Tennessee and coached under Bobby Dodd at Georgia Tech, changed the Gators' fortunes by establishing a winning attitude and the work ethic to pull it off.

Spurrier brought plenty of attitude, with an air of confidence often mistaken as cockiness. The self-assurance was in

Steve Spurrier's Florida Gators didn't play a single game on television during his senior season in 1966, but his accomplishments didn't go unnoticed. He won the Heisman Trophy and was a unanimous All-America selection in 1966.

evidence against Auburn that day when he slipped on his square-toed right shoe and kicked the game-winning field goal. In a quote that has now become part of Spurrier lore, Auburn center Forrest Blue said, "I think if there had been no goal posts and the official had said, 'Steve, you'll have to kick it through my upraised arms,' Steve would have done that."

If Spurrier's Heisman candidacy needed one final push, that was it. After having led the Gators to consecutive seven-win seasons in his first two years as a starter, Spurrier entered his senior year as one of the top candidates for the Heisman, along with UCLA's Gary Beban and Purdue's Bob Griese.

Longtime Florida sports publicist Norm Carlson ran one of the first national Heisman campaigns with help from Florida's Department of Tourism. They played off of Auburn coach Shug Jordan's "Steve Superior" malapropism and worked to keep the most influential national writers informed of Spurrier's latest accomplishments. Florida didn't play a single game on national television that year, but Carlson still

managed to convince *The New York Times* to send reporter Joseph Durso to cover the Auburn game—just one week before Heisman ballots were due. In addition to Spurrier's clutch kick, Durso also saw him complete 27 of 40 passes for 259 yards and a touchdown, run for another score, and punt five times for an average of 46.9 yards per kick.

One week later, Carlson answered a phone call from the office of University of Florida President Dr. J. Wayne Reitz, telling him to find Spurrier and bring him over right away. The news was in: Spurrier had won the Heisman. After accepting the trophy at New York's Downtown Athletic Club, Spurrier immediately handed it over to Reitz, saying the trophy belonged to the university.

Fortunately for Spurrier, Florida's student body pulled together the proper funding and convinced the Downtown Athletic Club to issue another trophy for Spurrier. Because of Spurrier's gesture, the club now presents two Heisman Trophies each year—one for the athlete and the other for the school.

The 1970s

Power in Numbers

As the turbulent 1960s gave way to the "me" decade of the 1970s, the Southeastern Conference put the "we" before "me" and continued to grow as a single entity, capable of providing for all 10 members.

On the field, Alabama claimed three national championships and eight conference titles, and Georgia, Auburn, LSU, Florida, and Kentucky all experienced their share of success.

Off the field, the SEC established itself as a true power conference and experienced unprecedented growth through the impact of integration, the addition of women's sports, progressive television deals, rising game attendance, and unparalleled financial growth.

In 1972, Commissioner Tonto Coleman retired and gave way to Dr. H. Boyd McWhorter, dean of arts and sciences at the University of Georgia and secretary of the SEC since 1967. In McWhorter's first full year on the job, the SEC distributed $1.57 million in revenue to its member institutions. In his final year, 1986, the conference distributed $15 million.

Under McWhorter's watch, the SEC made significant progress in racial and gender diversity, equality, and opportunity. Other innovations instituted by McWhorter included the SEC's first conference baseball tournament and, in 1979, the return of the SEC basketball tournament.

The televised Alabama-Auburn game on November 27, 1971, drew the highest rating ever for an SEC game, with nearly 50 million viewers. In 1973, LSU hosted undefeated Alabama at Tiger Stadium in the first prime-time college football game on Thanksgiving night.

On New Year's Eve 1974, Florida played Nebraska in the last Sugar Bowl played in Tulane Stadium. One year later, Alabama played Penn State in the first Sugar Bowl played in the Louisiana Superdome. Two years later, the SEC and the Sugar Bowl officially became long-term partners and agreed that the SEC champion would receive an invitation to the game each year. It was the SEC's first such agreement with a bowl game.

On November 5, 1977, ABC televised a national doubleheader featuring Florida versus Georgia in Jacksonville, and Alabama at LSU. It was the first time a network televised a doubleheader featuring four teams from one conference. The SEC received a record payoff of $1 million for the doubleheader. The next year Georgia Tech attempted to gain re-entry into the SEC but failed in a vote of the conference's presidents.

After Alabama won only six games in each of the 1969 and 1970 seasons, critics insisted that Bear Bryant had lost his touch and was no longer an effective coach. Bryant responded by leading the Crimson Tide to three national championships in the 1970s.

On New Year's Eve 1974, Florida played Nebraska in the final Sugar Bowl held at Tulane Stadium. The game had been played there every year since 1935, until the bowl was relocated to the Louisiana Superdome in 1975. Although the SEC did not have a formal agreement to send the conference champion to the Sugar Bowl until 1976, SEC teams were regular participants in Tulane Stadium's annual bowl game.

On October 20, 1979, the SEC took a chance on an upstart cable television network when it allowed the Entertainment and Sports Programming Network (ESPN) to televise its first SEC game. The game, between Alabama and Tennessee at Legion Field in Birmingham, was broadcast on a delayed basis.

One of the most significant events of the decade is often clouded by more fiction than fact. On September 12, 1970, an integrated USC team came to Legion Field and beat Alabama 42-21. USC's sophomore tailback Sam "Bam"

Cunningham rushed for 135 yards in the game and scored two touchdowns. One of the myths that surround this game has Coach Bryant bringing Cunningham, who happened to be African American, into the Alabama locker room and telling his players, "Gentlemen, this is what a football player looks like." Another tale has Bryant conspiring to set up an Alabama loss and then thanking USC Coach John McKay after the game for making it possible for the Crimson Tide to finally integrate its football program.

In truth, five African Americans had joined the Crimson

Tide as walk-ons in the spring of 1967. By the time Alabama played USC three years later, Bryant had already signed two African-American players, John Mitchell and Wilbur Mitchell. Years later, Cunningham told sportswriter Roy S. Johnson that he had received a recruiting letter from Alabama two years before the historic game.

Still, the USC loss left an indelible fingerprint on football at Alabama—and throughout the South. As Alabama assistant Jerry Clairborne said, "That game did more for integration in 60 minutes than had been done in 50 years." Only two years later, Tennessee sophomore Condredge Holloway became the SEC's first African-American starting quarterback.

Tommy Casanova was more than just an All-American defensive back for LSU in 1970 and 1971. A future Hall of Famer, Casanova played both ways as a sophomore and junior and was a dangerous punt and kick returner for the Tigers.

Halfback Johnny Musso's running and blocking was well suited to Alabama's wishbone offense in the early 1970s. The halfback led the SEC in rushing and scoring in 1971 and set a school record with 34 rushing touchdowns, a record that stood for 28 years. Musso was inducted into the College Football Hall of Fame in 2000.

Charles McClendon played under Bear Bryant at Kentucky but is best known for his 18-year stint as LSU's head football coach (1962–1979). "Cholly Mac" finished his coaching career with a record of 137-59-7 and 13 bowl appearances.

The game itself also was slowly changing. Auburn became the first SEC team to lead the nation in passing offense in 1970, behind the combination of quarterback Pat Sullivan and receiver Terry Beasley. One year later, Sullivan became the conference's fourth Heisman Trophy winner and the first player to win the award at a school where John Heisman had coached.

Major coaching moves shaped the SEC landscape in the 1970s. None was more significant than the retirement of Johnny Vaught on January 13, 1971, after 24 seasons as the head coach at Ole Miss. When Ole Miss fired his replacement three games into the 1973 season, Vaught returned to pick up the pieces and coached the Rebels to five wins in eight games before retiring for good. Ken Cooper became the Rebel coach in 1974, and in 1977 he pulled off one of the biggest upsets in SEC history by beating No. 3 Notre Dame 20-13 in Jackson. Notre Dame would go on to win the national championship. Ole Miss would go on to fire Cooper at the end of the season and replace him with Steve Sloan.

Leaving one SEC school for another was unusual for a head coach, but Doug Dickey did it in 1970. After rejuvenating the Tennessee program and winning SEC championships in 1967 and 1969, Dickey left to become the head coach at Florida, his alma mater. Tennessee replaced him with 28-year-old Vols assistant Bill Battle, a former Alabama player under Bryant. Battle went 31-5 in his first three seasons on the job and started out 5-0 in 1973 before the program started to slide bit by bit. After a 6-5 finish in 1976, Battle resigned. He was replaced by former Vols star Johnny Majors, who had just led Pittsburgh to the national title.

At Auburn, Shug Jordan had hoped to coach one final season in 1975 before making his intended retirement official. When word of his decision started to leak out in the spring of that year, however, Jordan announced on April 9 that the upcoming season would be his last.

In 1978, former Alabama player Charley Pell resigned as the head coach at Clemson to take over at Florida, replacing Doug Dickey. Though Pell's tenure at Florida would be marked by NCAA rules violations, he helped to lay the foundation for the Gators' future success.

At Georgia, a 5-6 finish in 1977 proved to be nothing more than a hurdle on the path to bigger, better things. Coach Vince Dooley and his staff started putting together the pieces that would put the Bulldogs on top of the college football world.

In the meantime, Bryant added more achievements to his legacy. In addition to the 1973 national championship, Alabama added two more in 1978 and 1979.

Johnny Rebel

When Johnny Vaught continued, well into his 90s, to play golf three times a week and hit 400 to 500 golf balls at haystacks at his ranch outside Oxford, Mississippi, his former Ole Miss players weren't a bit surprised.

As his star quarterback Archie Manning once said of Vaught, "Coach just flat-out hated to lose."

Vaught won a lot more than he lost throughout his 24 seasons as Ole Miss' head coach, taking the Rebels to unprecedented heights and giving them a place on the national college football landscape.

Under Vaught, the Rebels won a share of three national championships (1959, 1960, and 1962) and six Southeastern Conference championships. His teams played in 18 bowl games, including 14 straight from 1957 to 1970. Ole Miss has never won an outright SEC title under any other coach. Before Vaught arrived, the Rebels had been to only one bowl game, and they didn't play in another for another 10 years following his final retirement in 1973.

"What Vaught did at Ole Miss," wrote long-time *Atlanta Journal-Constitution* columnist Furman Bisher, "was establish a football kingdom."

No coach before or since has matched Johnny Vaught's success at Ole Miss. Under Vaught, the Rebels won a share of three national championships and won six conference titles.

Johnny Vaught originally retired as the head coach of Ole Miss following the 1970 season, but he returned to Oxford to lead the team through the final eight games of the 1973 season.

Vaught had been an All-American lineman as a player at Texas Christian University. He first came to Ole Miss as an assistant under Red Drew in 1946. One year later, Drew left for Alabama, and Ole Miss smartly made Vaught its head coach. In one season, Ole Miss went from 2-7 under Drew to 9-2 and the Delta Bowl under Vaught.

Vaught established a reputation for himself as an innovator. He was the first Southern coach to install a split-T formation offense and became the master of the sprint-out offense. He also coached a long line of standout quarterbacks. His first quarterback, Charlie Conerly, described Vaught as "years and years ahead of most other coaches. He was so organized, so detailed."

Vaught's best team may have been the 1959 Rebels, who recorded seven shutouts and outscored opponents 329-21 on the way to 10-1 record. Their 21-0 victory over LSU in the Sugar Bowl on January 1, 1960, brought revenge for LSU's 7-3 upset of Ole Miss on Halloween night in Baton Rouge.

Vaught's favorite team, however, was the 1962 team that became a rallying point for a state and a campus in turmoil during violent racial unrest. In the autumn of 1962, a mob of segregationists attempted to block the admission of Ole Miss' first African-American student, James Meredith. In the wake of riots that left two people dead and hundreds injured, U.S. Attorney General Robert Kennedy asked Vaught to help quell the violence. Vaught opened his practices to the public and the National Guard soldiers sent to protect Meredith, and those practices became an acceptable diversion. The Rebels went on to finish 10-0 that season and beat Arkansas 17-13 in the Sugar Bowl.

After suffering chest pains during the 1970 season and missing two games, Vaught retired at age 61 on the advice of his doctors. But when Ole Miss needed him three years later, Vaught was ready to serve.

Vaught had recommended assistant coach Bob Tyler as his successor, but the university instead hired former Ole Miss player Billy Kinard. After Kinard went 10-2 in his first season, he slipped to 5-5 in 1972 and discontent set in among boosters. After a 17-13 loss to Memphis State three games into the 1973 season, Kinard was forced to resign and Ole Miss called on Vaught for help.

Vaught accepted, saying, "I love Ole Miss and I would do anything for it once." His final team won five of its eight remaining games before Vaught retired for good and took the position of athletic director. Vaught ended up with a career record of 190-61-12.

While Vaught never integrated his program, he made it clear that his decision was mainly due to his concerns about how African-American players would be treated under the circumstances of the day. By the time Vaught returned as head coach, Kinard had already brought in African-American players, starting with All-American defensive tackle Ben Williams. Vaught not only played the African-American players he inherited, but established a lifelong friendship with Williams. Before he retired as athletic director in 1978, he oversaw the integration of all Ole Miss athletics.

Vaught remained close to the football program for the rest of his life and was always ready to help in any way he could.

Coach Vaught earned a reputation for developing one outstanding quarterback after another. Two of his best were Archie Manning (left) and Charlie Conerly (right). All three are honored in the College Football Hall of Fame.

When Ole Miss coach David Cutcliffe had to be hospitalized before the 1998 Independence Bowl, Vaught stopped by athletic director John Shafer's office to see how he could help.

"I told Coach Vaught, in jest, that I might have to get him to coach the team if David doesn't get better," Shafer told the *Biloxi Sun-Herald*. "He was as serious as he could be. He said, 'John, it wouldn't be a problem. A lot of my coaches are still in Oxford.' I told him I was kidding, but I have no doubt that he was ready."

Vaught was inducted into the College Football Hall of Fame in 1979. In 1982, Ole Miss added his name to Vaught-Hemingway Stadium. On February 3, 2006, Vaught died at the age of 96 in Oxford.

Upon Vaught's death, Manning said, "We all would love to have such a rich life, with so many friends, but we all would like to be able to influence that many people, too. Coach Vaught is gone, physically, but he lives on, in each one of us, and in this university."

Ole Miss' Favorite Son

Even today, in his late fifties, Archie Manning seems to have it all. He's still youthful enough to remind observers of those rollout passes he threw for the Ole Miss Rebels. He married the Ole Miss homecoming queen. On the Ole Miss campus the speed limit is 18 miles per hour, in honor of his jersey number. Each of his three sons earned scholarships to play college football. Two sons have quarterbacked their teams to the Super Bowl victories; the other is a successful businessman.

Not everything has always seemed so perfect for Elisha Archie Manning. He was born and raised in Drew, a small farm town in northwest Mississippi, the son of Sis and Buddy Manning. They never had much money from Buddy's job as manager of a farm machinery dealership, but Archie Manning was too busy playing sports year-round to notice.

Manning was a tall, skinny kid by the time he reached his senior season at Drew High School. Having sustained a broken ankle as an eighth grader, a broken right arm as a freshman, and a broken left arm as a junior, besides playing for a small school, Manning was lightly recruited and his only scholarship offers came from Ole Miss, Mississippi State, and Tulane.

In Manning, Ole Miss assistant Tom Swayze saw raw athletic ability, the potential to fill out his lanky frame, and the intangibles to be a successful quarterback for the Rebels. In Ole Miss, Manning saw the opportunity to play for the legendary Johnny Vaught in a program that had produced quarterbacks such as Charlie Conerly and Jake Gibbs.

Manning won the starting job in the spring of his freshman year at Ole Miss and started for the next three seasons (1968–70). When he passed for 436 yards and ran for 104 as a junior in a 33-32 loss to Alabama on national television, Manning established himself as one of the nation's best

During his college career at Ole Miss (1968–1970), Archie Manning passed for 4,753 yards, threw 56 touchdown passes, and ran for 824 yards. He earned All-SEC honors in 1969 and 1970 and was the SEC Most Valuable Player in 1970. Although he never won the Heisman Trophy, he finished fourth in the voting in 1969 and third in 1970.

quarterbacks. He finished the season with All-SEC honors, won the Walter Camp Award, and finished fourth in the Heisman Trophy race. Even better, Manning met his future wife, Olivia, that year.

Archie Manning was often at his best when on the run. Alabama coach Bear Bryant said of Manning, "He could hurt you in more ways than any other quarterback I've seen—sprinting out, dropping back, throwing while scrambling, and running. His most important assets were leadership and the ability to win close games by the force of his personality and talents."

What many did not know is that Manning's junior season was also clouded in heartache. In August, Manning came home from a wedding to find that his father had committed suicide. Manning initially wanted to stay home and work to support his mother and sister, but his mother convinced him to return to Ole Miss.

Manning opened his senior season as a leading Heisman candidate. He was off to a strong start through the first four games until suffering a groin pull that contributed to a loss to Southern Miss. After Vaught missed two midseason games due to heart trouble, Manning suffered a broken left arm and missed the next two games. He played the last two games of his Ole Miss career with his arm encased in heavy padding.

After a 35-28 loss to Auburn in the Gator Bowl, Manning said, "The way things worked out there wasn't too much to shout about at the end." He downplayed the impact of his college career, saying, "Ole Miss did a lot more for me than I did for Ole Miss."

Manning's 14-year NFL career included 10 years with the New Orleans Saints at a time when the team was known facetiously as the "Aints." Manning made the most of it, earning NFC Player of the Year in 1978 and All-Pro honors in 1978 and 1979. He finished his NFL career ranked 17th in completions. Hall of Fame coach Hank Stram, who coached Manning for two years with the Saints, called Manning, "a franchise quarterback without a franchise."

Younger football fans know Manning as the father of Indianapolis Colts quarterback Peyton Manning and New York Giants quarterback Eli Manning. However, his oldest son, Cooper, was an accomplished high school receiver who signed with Ole Miss before being diagnosed with spinal stenosis in 1992, ending his football career. The Mannings have always said Cooper was the son best suited to handle life without football, and he's done that with his own family and career.

Football was not the primary goal the Mannings held for their sons.

"I certainly never had any aspirations for them to play college and pro football," Manning said. "I never tried to push them toward that. That's just what they wanted to do."

Now Peyton and Eli both have won Super Bowls, something Manning never got the opportunity to do in his own career.

"People ask me if I knew all of this would happen—or any of it would," Manning said. "If in my wildest dreams I thought that Peyton would be so good, and that right on his heels would come his little brother [Eli] with similarly developing skills and credentials, as proud as I am, I didn't know. And wouldn't have dared [to predict it]."

Above: For many younger fans, Archie Manning is better known as the father of two Super Bowl–champion quarterbacks who also played for SEC teams as collegians. Peyton Manning (left) played at Tennessee, and Eli Manning followed in his father's footsteps at Ole Miss.

Opposite: Of all of Coach Johnny Vaught's great quarterbacks at Ole Miss, none was more accomplished or popular than Archie Manning. He remains one of the school's most honored and beloved figures.

Sullivan Steps Up

After Auburn beat Ole Miss 35-28 in Archie Manning's final college game, the 1971 Gator Bowl, Manning sought out Auburn junior quarterback Pat Sullivan to advise Sullivan on handling preseason Heisman Trophy and All-American hype.

Manning had seen enough to know Sullivan would need the counseling.

"That Pat Sullivan is tremendous," Manning said after watching Sullivan throw for 351 yards and two touchdowns and run for another score, "and I hope he gets the honors he deserves the next season."

Manning's instincts were right. After earning SEC Player of the Year and All-America honors in 1970, Sullivan won these awards again as a senior in 1971, and took his place in history as Auburn's first Heisman Trophy winner.

Sullivan set numerous SEC and school records in his Auburn career. He led the nation with 2,856 yards of total offense in 1970 and teamed with two-time All-American receiver Terry Beasley to lead the nation in passing offense, making Auburn the first SEC team ever to do so. He finished with a record of 25-5 as Auburn's starting quarterback and accounted for 71 touchdowns in three seasons.

Perhaps the highest praise Sullivan received came from Alabama coach Bear Bryant, who said, "He does more things to beat you than any quarterback I've ever seen."

Growing up in Birmingham, Sullivan chose Auburn over Alabama, knowing he had a chance to step in as the starting quarterback as a sophomore in 1969. By the time he passed for 248 yards and four touchdowns in a game at Georgia late in his senior season, Sullivan had the attention of Heisman Trophy voters—even though he had played in only one televised game before the final votes were counted.

This was before the Heisman Trophy had become one of the most visible awards in sports, and Sullivan admits that when he was a high school player he never even thought about winning the award. He didn't even find out about his Heisman selection in person.

"The year that I won it they made the announcement on Thanksgiving night at halftime of the Georgia-Georgia Tech game," Sullivan said. "I actually heard about it on national TV just like the millions of people that were watching."

The Heisman Trophy didn't guarantee future football success then, just as it doesn't now. The Tigers lost both remaining games after Sullivan won the Heisman. Sullivan spent only five seasons in the NFL before retiring to enter private business in Birmingham. In 1986 he returned to Auburn as the quarterback coach, and he became a head coach for the first time in 1992, at Texas Christian University. Even though his time at TCU didn't end well—the Horned Frogs posted a 1-10 record in 1997, Sullivan's final season there—he put the program back on solid ground and is now credited with laying the foundation for TCU's sustained success in the 2000s.

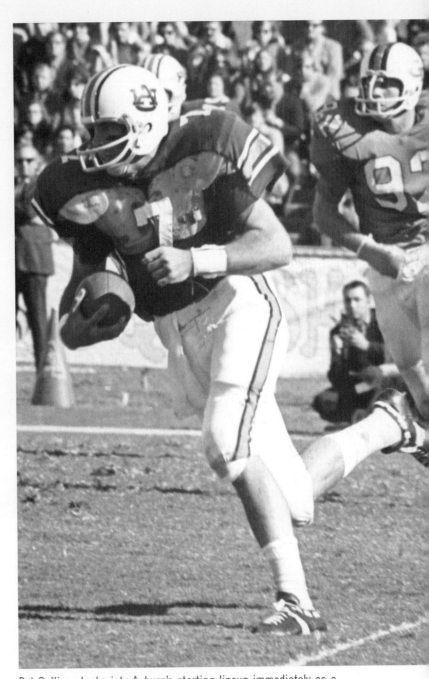

Pat Sullivan broke into Auburn's starting lineup immediately as a sophomore in 1969 and proceeded to break the school records for total offense and passing yardage. The young quarterback was just getting started. By the time he was done at Auburn, Sullivan held 24 school records, including 53 touchdown passes and a then–NCAA record by accounting for 71 touchdowns.

Opposite: Wide receiver Terry Beasley (left) and quarterback Pat Sullivan (right) teamed up in 1970 to make Auburn the first SEC team to lead the nation in passing offense. From 1969 to 1971, Sullivan and Beasley connected for 2,507 passing yards and 29 touchdowns.

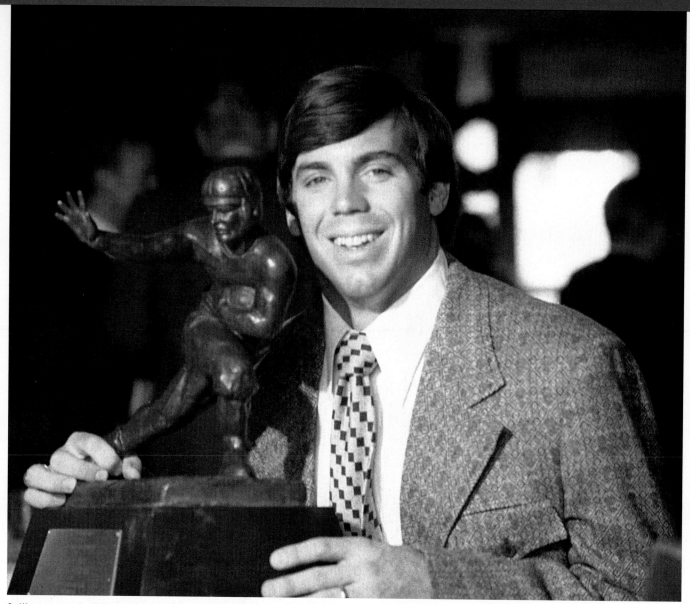

Sullivan topped off his college career by winning the Heisman Trophy as a senior in 1971. In the process, Sullivan became the fourth SEC player to win the award and the first from a school where John Heisman had coached. Sullivan is a member of the College Football Hall of Fame.

Sullivan returned to coaching in 1999 as the offensive coordinator and quarterback coach at the University of Alabama-Birmingham, where he met the toughest challenge of his life. In September 2003, Sullivan was diagnosed with throat cancer and began chemotherapy and radiation treatments in December. He lost more than 50 pounds, but missed only one game in the 2003 season.

He has made a strong comeback and received a clean bill of health. Sullivan is now a head coach once again, at Samford University in Birmingham. He speaks out against the use of smokeless tobacco, the likely source of his cancer.

A Southern Gentleman

When Ralph "Shug" Jordan sought the opportunity to change Auburn's sagging football fortunes in 1948, he thought his alma mater would surely turn to one of its own. Instead, Auburn chose former Notre Dame football player Earl Brown to be head coach.

"If they don't think an Auburn man can get the job done," Jordan said, "they ought to close the place down."

But Brown won only three games over the next three seasons. Auburn officials regretted their decision and came to their senses in 1951. First, they hired an Auburn man, Jeff Beard, to run the athletic department. Then they stepped out of the way and let Beard approach Jordan about becoming the school's next head coach.

"You have to come," Beard told Jordan. "We need you at home."

Jordan spent the next 25 years elevating the status of Auburn football, turning the Tigers from an SEC also-ran to a perennial winner. Under Jordan, Auburn won the 1957 national championship, played in 12 bowls, posted a winning record in 22 seasons, and finished ranked in the top 10 seven times.

Jordan and Beard worked together to build the athletic department into a successful venture equal to its SEC rivals. At the time, many SEC schools refused to play at Auburn because of its inferior facilities and remote location, so the Tigers played their home games in Birmingham, Montgomery, and Mobile, Alabama, as well as Columbus, Georgia. Jordan and Beard pushed for improvements to Cliff Hare Stadium and laid the foundation for Auburn's current status as an SEC power.

Jordan earned his nickname, Shug, for his penchant for chewing on sugar cane as a child in Selma, Alabama. He also earned a reputation as a true Southern gentleman. Coaches and sportswriters often spoke and wrote of his dignity and humility. Yet, Jordan possessed a firm resolve. He earned letters as a football center, as a basketball guard, and as a left-handed pitcher at Auburn. During World War II, Lieutenant Jordan became a decorated war hero and served during the invasions of North Africa, Sicily, Normandy, and Okinawa.

At various times Jordan coached football, basketball, or both—something unheard of in today's college athletics.

Auburn football had fallen on hard times when it called on one of its own to come home and put the program back on solid footing in the 1950s. Two decades earlier, Ralph "Shug" Jordan had played center on the Auburn football team, played forward on the basketball team, and pitched and played first base for the baseball team.

In ten seasons at Auburn, before and after the war, he compiled a record of 95-77 as head basketball coach. He won 45 more games as Georgia's head basketball coach before he returned to Auburn as head football coach.

His best early teams were built on strong defense and special teams and a conservative, mistake-free offensive style. In 1957, what looked to be his best team to date was dealt a blow when two key players, including the starting quarterback, were dismissed for team rules violations. Jordan moved left-handed halfback Lloyd Nix to quarterback, and the defense allowed only 28 points to help Auburn to a 10-0 finish and the Associated Press national championship. Auburn went 24 games without a loss, a streak that extended from November 10, 1956, to the 1959 season opener.

Jordan's most electric squads may have been the 1970 and 1971 teams led by quarterback Pat Sullivan and receiver Terry Beasley. As Heisman-winner Sullivan set NCAA and SEC records for passing in 1971, the Tigers won nine games and finished in the UPI top 10 in both seasons.

Jordan's best coaching job, however, came in 1972. The Tigers turned what was supposed to be a rebuilding year into a cause, finishing 10-1 and fifth in the final AP poll. Along the way, the team became "The Amazin's" and pulled off one of the most amazing victories in Auburn history.

In the 1972 Iron Bowl against Alabama, the Tigers had a difficult time moving the ball all day and trailed 16-3 in the fourth quarter. Auburn finally found a way to score when Bill Newton blocked two punts and David Langner picked up both and returned them for touchdowns. The 17-16 Auburn win has been immortalized as the "Punt, Bama, Punt" game.

"What I remember most is [Jordan] telling us that of all the teams he coached, including the national championship team, we were at the top of the list," Newton told the *Montgomery Advertiser* years later. "That was such a sense of pride for us. It was right after the Sullivan and Beasley era, and a lot of people said we didn't have any talent. What that team accomplished was pretty remarkable."

Jordan retired after the 1975 season with a career record of 176-83-6. He remains Auburn's all-time winningest coach and is a member of the National Football Foundation Hall of Fame. The stadium he helped to expand is now known as Jordan-Hare Stadium.

When Jordan's wife, Evelyn, planted pecan trees in the yard of their house after he became Auburn's head football coach, it symbolized their intentions to put down deep roots and be in Auburn for a long time. Jordan died on July 17, 1980, but those trees are still alive. The same can be said of Jordan's legacy.

"Winning the Heisman Trophy was only the second big thrill of my life," Sullivan said. "Number one was playing for Coach Jordan."

Coach Shug Jordan's best season at Auburn was in 1957, when the Tigers finished 10-0 and won the AP national championship, represented by the trophy held firmly in Jordan's embrace.

Coach Jordan was instrumental in putting Auburn on equal footing with many of its SEC competitors. His 25-year record at Auburn was 176-83-6, and during Jordan's tenure, the capacity of Cliff Hare Stadium was increased nearly three-fold, from 21,500 to 61,200. In 1973, it was renamed Jordan-Hare Stadium.

"Indescribable" Impact

Condredge Holloway was willing to listen to his mother when he chose college over professional baseball, but he wasn't about to compromise his goals for Bear Bryant and Shug Jordan.

Those decisions helped Holloway become a legend, not simply as the SEC's first African-American starting quarterback, but as a standout player who led the Volunteers to a bowl game in each of his three seasons as the starter (1972–1974).

He became the "Artful Dodger" to Tennessee fans for his electrifying way of turning trouble into triumph, by scrambling out of uncertainty—and turning it into success. His coach, Bill Battle, called him "Peanut," but Battle best described Holloway's impact as "well, indescribable."

As a three-sport star at Lee High School in Huntsville, Alabama, Holloway dreamed of playing baseball. The Montreal Expos drafted him in the first round of the 1971 draft, fourth overall. The only problem was that his mother, Dorothy, didn't want him to play pro baseball without earning an education first. Because Holloway was only 17 years old at the time, he was too young to sign a contract under Alabama law.

Dorothy got her way. Ultimately, so did her son. He wanted to play quarterback but when Bryant and Jordan offered scholarships, both made it clear that Holloway would play another position, most likely receiver or defensive back.

"I was told Alabama wasn't ready for a black quarterback," Holloway said. "There wasn't a whole lot of discussion after that. Coach Bryant was straight-up honest with me, and I respected him for that. He could have told me anything and gotten me to Alabama."

At Tennessee, however, Battle was ready for everything Holloway had to offer—as a quarterback. Battle promised Holloway he would get a legitimate chance to play quarterback.

Holloway proved he belonged at quarterback as a member of the freshman team, and he won the starting job for the varsity squad as a sophomore.

In the process of making SEC history, Holloway was just trying to win games. The same was true of his teammates.

"No one on my team ever brought [race] up," Holloway said. "I don't think anyone cared if I was black."

Tennessee coaches, players, and fans were too busy trying to follow the orange blur that Holloway became, running and passing his way to 3,102 passing yards, 18 touchdown passes, and 966 rushing yards. He led the Vols to two bowl victories and won MVP honors in the 1972 Bluebonnet Bowl and the 1975 Hula Bowl. Holloway also earned All-SEC honors in 1973. When Tennessee chose its "100 Years of Volunteers" team in 1990, Holloway was named quarterback.

"My coach, Bill Battle, paid me the greatest compliment when he said if I could play quarterback at UT, I could play quarterback anywhere," Holloway said.

Both the NFL's New England Patriots and the CFL's Ottawa Rough Riders drafted Holloway. With the Patriots selecting him in the 12th round and so few African-American quarterbacks in the NFL at that time, Holloway knew his best shot would come north of the border. His decision paid off and he became a star in Canada. He reached the high point of his pro career in 1982 when he led the Toronto Argonauts to their first Grey Cup championship in 31 years and won the CFL's Most Outstanding Player award.

Holloway is widely considered one of the CFL's all-time best players. He joined the Canadian Football Hall of Fame in 1998, the Tennessee Sports Hall of Fame in 1993, and the Alabama Sports Hall of Fame in 2008. A big piece of his heart remains at the University of Tennessee, where he is an assistant athletic director.

Opposite: Condredge Holloway grew up in Huntsville, Alabama, but neither the University of Alabama nor Auburn recruited him as quarterback. Tennessee Coach Bill Battle believed Holloway had everything the Vols needed for a successful quarterback.

When Condredge Holloway won the starting quarterback job at Tennessee as a sophomore, he became the first African American to start at quarterback in the SEC.

Holloway used a combination of running and passing skills to keep opponents on their toes. An All-SEC selection as a senior in 1973, he threw for 3,102 passing yards and 18 touchdown passes in his college career, while chipping in 966 yards rushing.

The Tide Stands Tall

In the fourth quarter of the 1979 Sugar Bowl, Penn State was facing fourth down with the ball about 10 inches from the Alabama goal line. Penn State quarterback Chuck Fusina and Alabama defensive tackle Marty Lyons both stood near the ball and pondered their next move.

With the national championship on the line, the Nittany Lions were trailing 14-7 and had to decide whether to go for the touchdown or kick a field goal and hope for another opportunity in the final minutes.

Fusina looked at Lyons and asked, "What do you think?" Lyons offered a straightforward response. "You should throw the ball."

Lyons wasn't being arrogant. He was just reflecting a matter-of-fact confidence that came from playing for Bear Bryant.

"It started with the way Coach Bryant and his assistants prepared us and coached us, the way they handled themselves and handled us," Lyons later recalled. He also referenced the special relationship among the Alabama players. "We [not only] weren't going to disappoint Coach Bryant or the university, but we weren't going to disappoint ourselves. We really played as a unit. We treated each other like family. We didn't have one star on the team—there were many, and we proved that by winning the national championship in our senior year on the goal-line stand against Penn State."

After winning three national championships and nearly winning a fourth in the 1960s, the Crimson Tide slid to 6-5 finishes in 1969 and again in 1970. All of a sudden, critics were insisting that it was time for Bryant to move on.

"If you win six games at Alabama, that's bad," said running back Johnny Musso, who played at Alabama from 1969 to 1971. "At least it was back then. We didn't have great teams and that was frustrating and hard. Coach Bryant was able to reach within himself and change what he was doing without changing who he was. He adjusted, he adapted, and I got to see that, but in the meantime it was frustrating. Teams that had been beaten by Alabama for years licked their chops when they saw that our talent wasn't as good as it had been."

Bryant adapted once again and proved why he belonged among the best coaches in college football history. One of the most significant changes was the decision to start all over on offense. Bryant took stock of Alabama's personnel and decided quarterback Terry Davis would be a much better fit for a triple-option attack such as the wishbone.

Bryant and his offensive assistants spent the summer of 1971 studying Texas' wishbone with Texas head coach Darrell Royal and assistant Emory Ballard. They installed the basic offense during the weeks leading up to the season opener against USC. One year after USC whipped Alabama 42-21, the Crimson Tide caught the Trojans by surprise with their new offense and won 17-10.

"Going to the wishbone made perfect sense," Musso said. "Even more important, Coach Bryant told us we could win seven or eight games in our old offense, or we could have a great team in the wishbone."

Alabama finished 11-1 in 1971 and won its first SEC championship since 1966. It would be the first of eight conference titles between 1971 and 1979.

Alabama went 11-1 in each of the next two seasons and won the UPI national championship in 1973. They dipped to 9-3 in 1976 and went right back to 11-1 in 1977 and 1978. The Tide finished in the final top 10 in 1974, 1975, and 1977, but the ultimate prize was on the line in 1978, when it came down to that decisive goal-line stand against Penn State.

After Alabama's defense stopped Penn State from getting into the end zone on three straight downs, the Nittany Lions had the ball less than a foot from the goal line with one down to go. Coach Joe Paterno called a timeout. He decided he wasn't going to settle for a field goal.

Opposite: End Ozzie Newsome started all four years at Alabama from 1974 to 1977, earned All-SEC honors in 1976 and 1977, and was an All-American in 1977. More important, the Crimson Tide had a record of 42-6 and won three SEC championships during Newsome's career. Bear Bryant said Newsome was the greatest end in school history, better than Bryant's teammate Don Hutson. Newsome is also in both the College and Pro Football Halls of Fame.

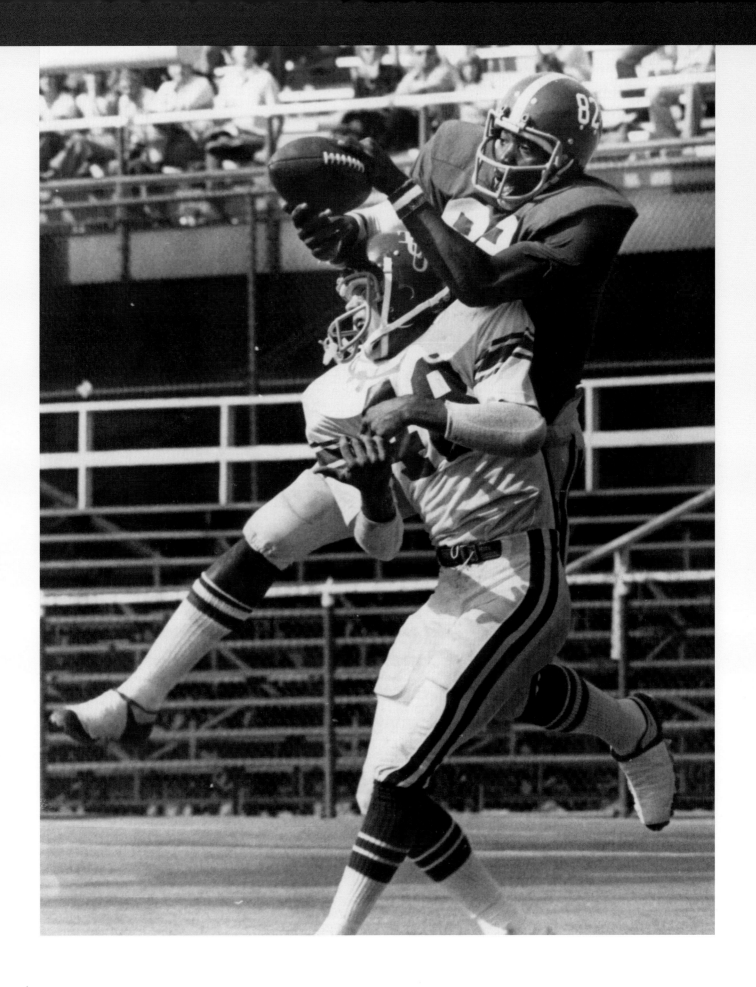

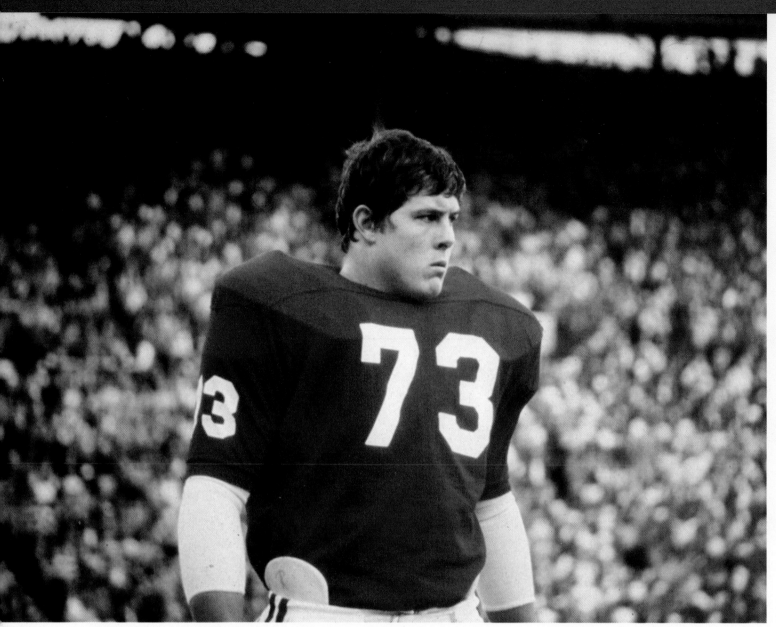

John Hannah stands tall as one of the SEC's greatest linemen and was a key part of Alabama's turnaround in the early 1970s. Bryant called him the finest offensive lineman he had ever been around. In 1981, *Sports Illustrated* named Hannah the best offensive lineman of all time. Hannah was selected to Alabama's all-century team, the SEC All-50-year team (1933–1982), the College Football Hall of Fame, and the Pro Football Hall of Fame.

Alabama's senior linebacker Barry Krauss recalled that moment. "He [Paterno] figured if we can't get one yard we don't deserve to be national champions, and I really respected that. He put it all on the line and we did, too. That's what champions are made of."

When Fusina handed the ball to running back Mike Guman, it seemed as if the entire Alabama defense surged to the point of attack. Lyons and fellow lineman David Hannah got underneath the Penn State offensive line and

forced them backwards. Then Krauss hit Guman head-first at the top of the pile, followed by Rich Wingo and Murray Legg. Alabama held in one of the most dramatic and memorable goal-line stands in college football.

"Murray Legg said it best: Coach Bryant had a great way of making us feel like we were a great team and a great bunch of football players, but we really weren't," Krauss said. "We were good football players who played well together because he made us feel like we were great football players. That play was the culmination of four years of hard work and believing in our coaches and ourselves."

Bryant would call the victory one of his proudest moments. "There was only one team that could have stopped Penn State on the goal line and that team was Alabama," he said. "It was a time of champions."

The Tide rode that momentum into the 1979 season.

They had a perfect 12-0 record and beat Arkansas 24-9 in the Sugar Bowl for what would be Bryant's sixth and final national championship. The victory capped a remarkable decade at the top of college football's mountain for Bryant and the Crimson Tide.

After the Sugar Bowl victory, Bryant said, "It's the greatest bunch of youngsters I've ever been around and I'm just happy to be a small part of it."

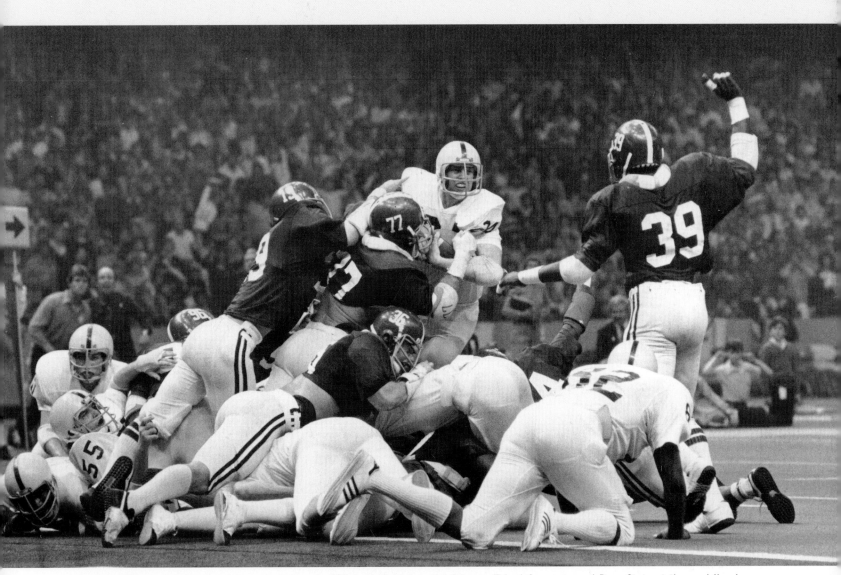

In one of the most famous and important plays in SEC football history, the Crimson Tide defense stopped Penn State at the goal line in the 1979 Sugar Bowl. Alabama won 14-7 and captured the national championship.

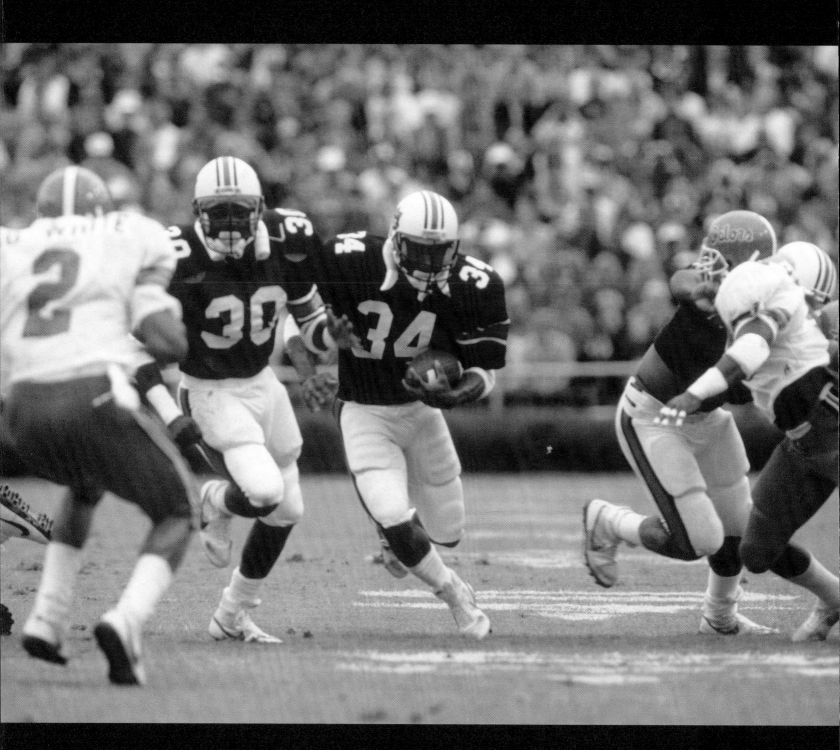

The 1980s
Opportunities Abound

The 1980s marked both the ends and beginnings of prominent eras in football for the Southeastern Conference.

The decade started with Alabama winning a national championship on January 1, 1980, and ended with Steve Spurrier being named the head coach at Florida on December 31, 1989. In between, Alabama lost a legendary coach and Auburn rose to prominence; Georgia won a national championship and lost a legendary coach; Florida rose and fell; two SEC players won the Heisman Trophy; and major college football programs took control over their own television rights.

The SEC played a prominent role in the College Football Association's lawsuit against the NCAA over television rights. The CFA, founded by a group of 63 college football programs in 1976, was formed in an effort to gain more autonomy for the schools from the NCAA. By the 1980s, televised college football games had become a significant source of income for the NCAA. However, the NCAA controlled all the television contracts and refused to allow individual institutions or their conferences to make their own deals with television networks.

In September 1981, the Board of Regents of the University of Oklahoma and the University of Georgia Athletic Association, representing the CFA, filed suit. In September 1982, the courts found in favor of the plaintiffs and ruled that the NCAA had violated antitrust laws. In June 1984, the United States Supreme Court upheld that ruling, finally breaking the NCAA's monopoly on television revenue.

College football programs and their fans benefited from the ruling because it—along with the arrival of cable television—led to widespread broadcast of games. Instead of seeing one or two games each Saturday, fans could see several. One month after the Supreme Court ruling, SEC Commissioner H. Boyd McWhorter signed an exclusive contract with Ted Turner and his WTBS network to televise the SEC Football Game of the Week. On September 8, 1984, LSU and Florida played in the first SEC Football Game of the Week. (The game ended in a 21-21 tie.)

Auburn's Bo Jackson was a uniquely gifted athlete who played running back for the football team, played centerfield for the baseball team, and ran sprints for the track team.

During H. Boyd McWhorter's tenure as SEC commissioner (1972–1986), the conference saw dramatic increases in both revenue and national exposure. In 1984, he closed a groundbreaking television deal with Ted Turner's WTBS network.

In September 1986, Dr. Harvey W. Schiller became the SEC's new commissioner. He oversaw the conference during a tremendous era of new growth in the areas of marketing, promotions, and corporate sponsorships. Schiller led the charge as the conference negotiated football and basketball television packages with networks ESPN, Turner Broadcasting, Jefferson-Pilot Teleproductions, and other programming on Sports Channel America. Under Schiller's leadership the conference also took a more assertive approach in the areas of compliance and enforcement of NCAA and SEC regulations.

The SEC's success was evident in the stands on autumn Saturdays of the 1988 season, when the conference led the nation in average football attendance for the first time, drawing 63,101 per game. Through the 2007 season, when more than 6.6 million fans attended SEC home games, the Southeastern Conference has led the nation in total attendance for 27 straight seasons. The passion surrounding SEC football was particularly evident on October 8, 1988, when a fourth-down TD pass from LSU quarterback Tommy Hodson to tailback Eddie Fuller with one minute and 41 seconds left in the game gave LSU a 7-6 win over No. 4 Auburn and set off a crowd reaction at Tiger Stadium that registered on a seismograph at the LSU Department of Geology.

On the field, the decade that started with Alabama winning its second straight national championship gave way to a time of greater uncertainty in the SEC.

In 1980, Florida's Charley Pell, Mississippi State's Emory Ballard, and Vanderbilt's George McIntyre were in their

Tennessee defensive end Reggie White was an ordained Baptist minister and was often referred to as the "Minister of Defense," but opposing quarterbacks thought he was more of a demon. White finished his college career as the Vols' record holder for most sacks in a game (4), a season (15), and a career (32). As a senior in 1983, White was all-conference, All-America, and the SEC Defensive Most Valuable Player.

When LSU quarterback Tommy Hodson connected with tailback Eddie Fuller on a fourth-down, game-winning touchdown pass with 1:41 remaining against Auburn on October 19, 1988, the crowd reaction at Tiger Stadium registered on a seismograph at the LSU Department of Geology.

second years as SEC head coaches, and Jerry Stoval was in his first year at LSU. Ole Miss' Steve Sloan and Tennessee's Johnny Majors were trying to rebuild their programs. Fran Curci had already peaked at Kentucky, and Doug Barfield was on his way out at Auburn. At Alabama, Bear Bryant was nearing the end of a legendary career.

At Georgia, Coach Vince Dooley and his staff were convinced that the Bulldogs were one good tailback away from putting it all together. Georgia realized it had that tailback in the 1980 season opener at Tennessee, when true freshman Herschel Walker took over with the Bulldogs down 15-0 in the second half and led them to a 16-15 victory.

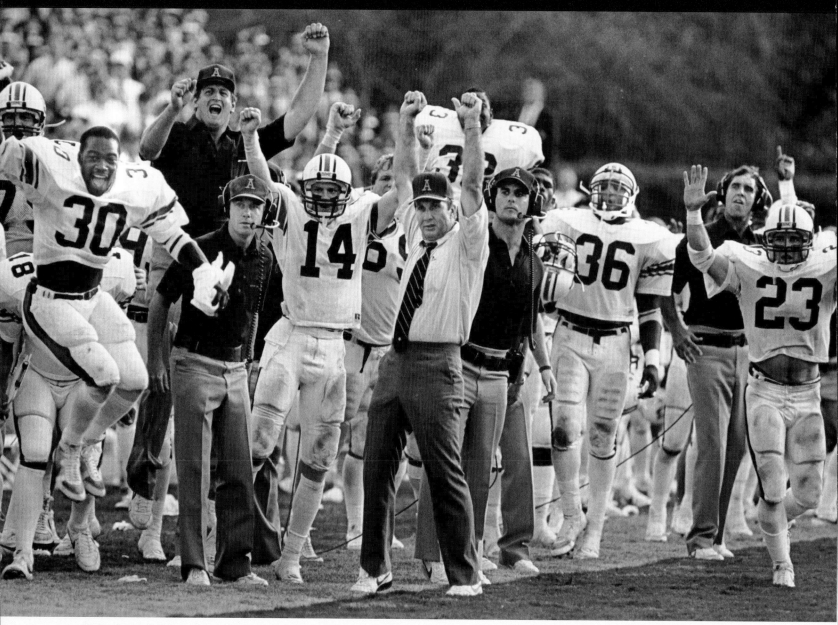

Under Coach Pat Dye, Auburn became a force in the SEC. The Tigers won a share of four conference titles, earned eight straight bowl bids, and beat Alabama six times from 1982 to 1989. Auburn also was finally able to get Alabama to play at Auburn's Jordan-Hare Stadium for the first time.

Georgia was named the consensus national champion that season and went on to win three SEC titles and 43 games from 1980 to 1984. Walker won the Heisman Trophy in 1982 and rushed for more yards in three years than any college player before or since. Walker then set another precedent by jumping to professional football after his junior season, a practice that was radical then but is more accepted today.

Dooley retired in 1988 after 25 years as Georgia's head coach. He ended his career with a record of 201 wins, 77 losses, and 10 ties. Dooley recommended former Bulldogs

defensive coordinator Erk Russell, then the head coach at Georgia Southern, to be his successor; Georgia hired running back coach Ray Goff, a former quarterback for the Bulldogs, instead.

Georgia produced the conference's one and only national champion in the 1980s, but the SEC nevertheless played a major role in the continued rise of college football's popularity. In addition to its surging attendance, the SEC became the first college football conference to place seven teams in one bowl season when Alabama, Auburn,

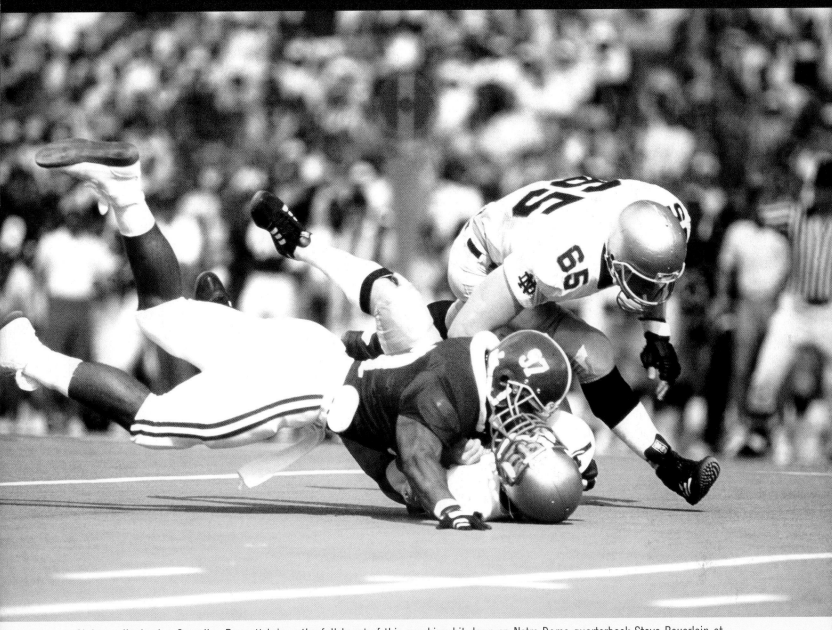

Alabama linebacker Cornelius Bennett brings the full brunt of this crushing hit down on Notre Dame quarterback Steve Beuerlein at Birmingham's Legion Field in October 1986. Bennett, a member of the College Football Hall of Fame, won the Lombardi Award as a senior in 1986.

Florida, Georgia, Kentucky, Ole Miss, and Tennessee all played in bowls at the end of the 1983 season.

By the end of the decade, all 10 SEC teams had played in a bowl, including Vanderbilt (the 1982 Hall of Fame Bowl). Vanderbilt had not played in a bowl game since 1974 and has not played in one since.

No SEC program experienced more change during the decade than Alabama. In 1980, Mississippi State defeated Alabama 6-3 in Jackson, Mississippi, ending the Crimson Tide's SEC record of 27 straight conference victories. In 1981, Bryant

became college football's all-time winningest coach when he earned his 315th victory with a 28-17 win over Auburn.

The victory was Alabama's 10th straight over Auburn, but things were already starting to change for the Tigers. Auburn had hired former Georgia lineman and Alabama assistant Pat Dye in 1981, and Dye led the Tigers to a 23-22 victory over Alabama on November 27, 1982. On December 15, with his health declining, Bryant announced his retirement. He coached his final game in the Liberty Bowl on December 29 and then passed away less than a month later.

Former Alabama wide receiver Ray Perkins left his job as the head coach of the New York Giants to accept the unenviable task of replacing Bryant. An often-rocky relationship between Perkins and long-time Alabama fans finally ended in 1986 when Perkins, following a 10-3 finish, left to become the head coach of the Tampa Bay Buccaneers. Many Alabama fans were infuriated when University of Alabama President Joab Thomas hired a Georgia Tech man, Bill Curry, to coach the Crimson Tide. Three tense years later, Curry left Alabama for Kentucky.

After Georgia dominated the SEC over the first four seasons of the decade, Auburn became the SEC's most dominant football program through the end of the '80s. Auburn won a share of four conference titles and earned eight straight bowl bids. The Tigers also beat Alabama six times

between 1982 and 1989 and, in 1989, finally got Alabama to play at Auburn's Jordan-Hare Stadium for the first time. Along the way, Tiger tailback Bo Jackson became the SEC's sixth Heisman Trophy winner, earning the award in 1985.

Other national award winners in the decade included Alabama linebacker Cornelius Bennett (1986 Lombardi Award), Auburn defensive tackle Tracy Rocker (1988 Outland Trophy and Lombardi Award) and Alabama linebacker Derrick Thomas (1988 Butkus Award). In an era that favored defense and the running game, the SEC also produced running backs such as Florida's Emmitt Smith, Alabama's Bobby Humphreys, and Georgia's Tim Worley, and defensive players such as Tennessee end Reggie White, Florida linebacker Wilber Marshall, and Mississippi State linebacker Johnnie Cooks.

Auburn defensive tackle Tracy Rocker was a dominating force on an Auburn defense that allowed only 7.6 points per game in 1988 and helped lead the Tigers to an SEC championship.

In 1988, Rocker became the first SEC player ever to win the Outland Trophy and the Lombardi Award in the same season. He was inducted into the College Football Hall of Fame in 2004.

Emmitt Smith wasn't particularly big or fast, but he used his outstanding vision and agility to set 58 school records, rush for 3,928 yards, and score 36 touchdowns in just three seasons at Florida. Smith, the SEC Player of the Year in 1989, was voted into the College Football Hall of Fame in 2006 and is a sure bet for the Pro Football Hall of Fame as well.

Meanwhile, at Florida, Charley Pell would leave an indelible mark on the program. The Gators went 0-10-1 in 1979, their first season under Pell. Pell had been a lineman under Bryant at Alabama, and his hard-nosed methods turned the Gators into winners over the next four years. His passionate pleas to Florida boosters allowed the university to make major improvements to the athletic facilities. Pell's aggressive approach also led to charges of NCAA rules violations, more than a hundred in all, that encompassed such indiscretions as spying on opponents' practices, giving money to players, and lying to NCAA officials. The NCAA put Florida's football program on a two-year probation, and the Gators had to forfeit their 1984 SEC championship.

Pell volunteered to take the blame for every violation both to protect his assistants and because he thought he had an agreement with the university to remain as coach through the end of the 1984 season. Instead, he was fired three games into the season and was replaced by Galen Hall. Hall, in turn, was fired midway through the 1989 season, in the wake of more NCAA rules violations.

For all the negative attention he brought to the program, Pell also laid the foundation of success that Steve Spurrier inherited when he returned to his alma mater as head coach on the final day of the decade. Spurrier would turn the Gators into consistent winners for the first time in school history and change the way the SEC plays football.

The Georgia Bulldogs gave their fans plenty to celebrate throughout the 1980 season, especially when they defeated Notre Dame 17-10 in the 1981 Sugar Bowl to secure the national championship.

How 'Bout Them Dawgs?

One day, early in the 1980 season, Georgia defensive coordinator Erk Russell was leaving the dormitory where the Bulldogs ate team meals, and he spotted a dime on the ground.

"I picked it up, put it in my left shoe," Russell recalled years later. "I was wearing saddle Oxfords, which I did all the time anyway, and we beat Clemson that day. Maybe it was the second or third game of the season. I taped the dime in my shoe so I wouldn't lose it, and made sure that I wore it throughout the season. We were 12-0 and won the national championship, and I'm sure the dime did it."

Maybe it was the dime, or maybe it was the product of an experienced coaching staff, a tough, hungry defense, a purloined pig, a capable quarterback, a big-play receiver, and a freshman tailback who proved to be the final piece of the puzzle.

Georgia coaches weren't sure what to expect from freshman tailback Herschel Walker, but he made a quick impression in preseason practice. With the Bulldogs trailing 15-0 in the second half of their season opener against Tennessee, Walker took over and led Georgia to a 16-15 win.

"He didn't really know where he was running that night," Georgia coach Vince Dooley said. "He was just running somewhere—and in a hurry."

Meanwhile the Georgia defense rarely let anyone get anywhere in a hurry. Russell's "Junkyard Dawgs" allowed 11.4 points per game and recorded three shutouts. An off-season incident provided an unexpected boost. Six seniors broke into the university stables, stole and killed a hog, and then attempted to eat the evidence.

"Those guys were punished pretty severely, but the whole squad, in knowing what happened, bonded together," Russell said. "I really believe it was the thing that started to unite our team."

Between the defense and the running game, Dooley had just the kind of team he wanted. But even a conservative coach needs a passing game now and then, and the Bulldogs got it when they needed it most.

In the ninth game of the season, the Bulldogs trailed Florida 21-20 with a little more than one minute left on the clock and the ball on their own 7-yard line. On third

Georgia safety Terry Hoage led the nation with 12 pass interceptions as a junior in 1982 and earned SEC Defensive Player of the Year in both his junior and senior seasons. He went on to have a long career in the NFL and became a member of the College Football Hall of Fame.

down and 11, quarterback Buck Belue dropped back deep into his end zone, rolled to escape the rush, and found receiver Lindsay Scott open on a route designed to pick up the first down. Scott jumped to make the catch, avoided a Florida safety, cut across the field, and then took off for the end zone. "I think it's [one] for the ages," Dooley said of the play. "We couldn't have won [the national title] without it."

One of the SEC's most memorable plays was celebrated by one of its most memorable calls, as Georgia's play-by-play announcer Larry Munson yelled "Lindsay Scott! Lindsay Scott! Lindsay Scott!" and added, "If you wanted a miracle, we just got one."

It looked like they would need another miracle to win the Sugar Bowl and capture the national championship. Georgia, which had won shares of the national title in 1927, 1942, and 1947, had posted only one undefeated season in school history, in 1946. Now it had the chance to do it again, but Notre Dame, the Sugar Bowl opponent, appeared to have every advantage over the Bulldogs.

"I remember how big they were and how we weren't supposed to have a chance," linebacker Keith Middleton told the *Athens Banner-Herald*. "They had all those guys over 300 pounds."

Georgia's slim chances seemed to get even slimmer when Walker sustained a dislocated shoulder on the Bulldogs' second offensive play. At first Georgia trainers and coaches feared the worst, but they were able to pop the shoulder back into place.

Walker returned to contribute two touchdown runs and Rex Robinson kicked a field goal, providing the scoring for Georgia. They got plenty of help from the defense and special teams, including blocked kicks by Terry Hoage and Greg Bell, fumble recoveries by Chris Welton and Bob Kelly, and interceptions by Mike Fisher and Scott Woerner. The Bulldogs defeated Notre Dame 17-10 and secured the school's first consensus national championship.

"We proved them wrong," Walker said of those who doubted the Bulldogs. "It wasn't Herschel Walker, [defensive captain] Frank Ros, or Buck Belue. It was the University of Georgia team, coaching staff, and everybody coming together and doing good things."

Defensive coordinator Erk Russell and the "Junkyard Dawg" defense played a big role in Georgia's perfect 12-0 season in 1980, allowing only 11.4 points per game during the Bulldogs' national championship run.

The experts insisted that the Notre Dame team was too big, too strong, and too powerful for Georgia, but the Bulldogs beat the Fighting Irish 17-10 in the 1981 Sugar Bowl and captured the national championship.

Nothing But a Winner

USC coach John McKay said, "He wasn't just a coach. He was *the* coach." Penn State's Joe Paterno said, "Even his peers in the coaching business felt in awe of him. . . . He was just a giant figure." Nebraska coach Bob Devaney said, "He was simply the best there ever was."

For all the words and phrases used to describe Paul Bryant, Bear himself put it best when he said, "I ain't nothing but a winner."

No coach before or since has done more to elevate the level of competition and the profile of Southeastern Conference football than Bryant. He achieved a lifetime record of 323-85-17 (.780) in 38 years as a head coach at Maryland, Kentucky, Texas A&M, and Alabama. He took 29 teams to bowl games and led 15 to conference championships. In 25 years under Bryant, Alabama went 232-46-9, finished with 10 or more wins 13 times, and most importantly, won six national championships (1961, 1964, 1965, 1973, 1978, 1979).

When he retired in 1982, Bryant was college football's winningest coach—a fitting achievement for a coach who always seemed to stand above whatever crowd he was in.

"Whatever he had, whatever it was, he had a lot of it," said Alabama athletic director Mal Moore, who played and coached for Bryant. "He had something about him that people simply didn't have or don't have."

Alabama had won national championships and widespread respect under Wallace Wade and Frank Thomas, but Bryant quickly led the Crimson Tide to unprecedented heights after becoming head coach in 1958. In less than a decade under Bryant, Alabama won three national championships between 1961 and 1965, and just missed out on a fourth in their undefeated 1966 season.

Those first teams, especially the 1961 champions, set the tone for two decades of success that put Alabama on top of the college football world. Even when the Crimson Tide slipped to 6-5 and 6-5-1 in 1969 and '70, Bryant dug in, made the necessary adjustments, switched to the wishbone offense and led the Tide to three more national titles in the 1970s.

Alabama players give Coach Bear Bryant a victory ride after the Crimson Tide beat Nebraska 34-7 in the 1966 Sugar Bowl. The victory gave the Tide its third national championship under Bryant.

During Bear Bryant's tenure at Alabama, Crimson Tide football and the houndstooth hat became synonymous with success. In his 25 years at Alabama, Bryant's teams won a total of six national championships.

In a familiar sight at Alabama practice sessions, Bryant leans against the goal post while watching his team run through pregame drills. Bryant's commanding presence could be intimidating to both his own players and his opponents.

"There was something about him . . . that was different from everybody, that made us always want to please him," said Ken Stabler, Alabama's quarterback from 1965 to 1967. "You'd do anything you could to make him slap you on the ass and say 'way to go' or recognize you in front of the rest of the team.

"People always ask, 'What is it like to play for Coach Bryant?' It's hard to explain that unless you've been around him and seen the effect he had on people. We would play teams that were always bigger, always faster, always more of them, and we always won. That was because of Coach Bryant. He out-coached the other guy. He out-motivated the other guy."

From 1980 to 1982, Bryant's Alabama teams won 27 games, lost eight, and tied one, and they shared the SEC championship with Georgia in 1981. But Bryant's health and age started to work against him, especially in recruiting against hungry young coaches.

"Coaching is a young man's game," Bryant said before the 1982 season. "You never see old men winning championships. All these [younger coaches] are recruiting better than we are."

On December 15, 1982, two weeks after Alabama closed out its regular season with its first loss to Auburn since 1972, Bryant announced his retirement. He agreed to remain as athletic director for the time being, even though the university chose not to honor his recommendation for a replacement and instead hired former Alabama wide receiver Ray Perkins as the new head coach.

Bryant's final game was an emotional 21-15 victory over Illinois in the Liberty Bowl on December 29. On January 26, 1983, Bryant died at age 69. He was buried wearing a ring presented at a reunion of former Texas A&M players who survived Junction.

"He literally coached himself to death," former Ohio State head coach Woody Hayes said at the funeral. "He was our greatest coach."

Bryant's legacy is still evident in numerous ways, from the Paul W. Bryant Museum, to Bryant-Denny Stadium, to the Paul "Bear" Bryant Award given annually to the nation's top college football coach. Those who were closest to Bryant insist he would be most proud of the enduring legacy of the Bryant Scholarship. In 1973 Bryant established an endowed scholarship fund at the University of Alabama to benefit the sons and daughters of his former players. Since its inception, more than 400 children of former players have attended the university on the Bryant Scholarship.

Coach Bryant is carried off the field by his players following his final game, a 21-15 win over Illinois in the Liberty Bowl on December 29, 1982. Bryant retired with 323 victories, a record for Division I coaches at the time.

Herschel for Heisman!

When University of Georgia assistant coach Mike Caver recruited and signed running back Herschel Walker out of Johnson County High School in Wrightsville, Georgia, the Bulldogs coaching staff thought Walker had the potential to be a star some day. They just weren't sure when that day would come.

"I really don't see Herschel giving us a whole lot of help next year," head coach Vince Dooley told *Sports Illustrated* in the summer of 1980. "Realistically, I think he's going to have a slow adjustment period from Class A football. I think everybody, and that includes coaches, fans, and Herschel himself, will have to wait and be patient."

That day arrived a lot sooner than anyone expected it to, but there were hints along the way. In Walker's first preseason at Georgia, one senior defender told his teammates that he planned to be the first to welcome the freshman with a big hit—he ended up flat on his back after a head-on collision. Another player, Steve Kelly, knew something was up when Dooley asked him to move from running back to safety so he could see more playing time that fall.

Still, no one really knew for sure until the second half of the 1980 season opener against Tennessee. With Georgia trailing 15-0, Walker entered the game and made an immediate impression on Tennessee safety and future Dallas Cowboys All-Pro Bill Bates by running over him at the 8-yard line on his way to a 16-yard touchdown. Walker added another touchdown on a 9-yard sweep, the Bulldogs defeated the Vols 16-15, and a legend was born.

"I knew he was strong, I knew he was fast—but Good Lord!" Georgia defensive end Freddie Gilbert told the *Athens Banner-Herald*. "After he ran over Bill Bates, nobody wanted to tackle him the next week."

Walker helped the Bulldogs finish the season 12-0 and win the 1980 national championship. During his 3 years at Georgia, the team went 33-3 with three straight SEC championships. Walker also won the 1982 Heisman Trophy and set conference career records with 5,259 rushing yards and 49 rushing touchdowns.

Walker's legendary strength was a product of considerable time spent sitting in front of the television as a child. He made a deal with his father that allowed him to watch TV if he exercised during the commercials. By the time he arrived at Georgia, those countless pushups, sit-ups, chin-ups, and sprints had turned him into a solid 6-foot-2, 220-pound mass of strength and speed.

Herschel Walker used a combination of raw power and speed to set 41 school records, 16 Southeastern Conference records, and 11 NCAA records in just three seasons at Georgia.

It didn't take long for Herschel Walker to make a big impact at Georgia. He rushed for 1,616 yards as a freshman during the 1980 championship season. The Bulldogs won 33 games and lost only 3 in Walker's three seasons.

After placing third in the Heisman Trophy voting as a freshman in 1980, Walker finished second in 1981. As a junior in 1982, Walker became the second Bulldog in history and the first in 40 years to win the award.

That combination, along with a reckless approach to running the football from point A to point B, made him as tough to stop as any back to ever play college football. He could run over, through, or past a defense like no one else before—or since.

"There have been better runners with starts and stops," Dooley said. "He didn't have the cutting ability of someone like a Rodney Hampton. If he did, he would be the greatest running back who ever lived."

Dooley commented that no runner had as impressive a combination of size, speed, and mental toughness. "He had world-class speed. Oh, was he big and strong, and I've never seen someone with the self-discipline he had."

Walker also left his mark as one of the first players to leave college early to play professional football. Although the NFL didn't accept underclassmen at that time, the rival USFL did and New Jersey Generals owner Donald Trump signed Walker to a then-stunning $3.9 million, three-year contract in 1983.

Walker spent three highly successful seasons with the Generals until the league folded. He then spent 12 up-and-down seasons in the NFL, during which he was constantly measured by the standard he set in college. Nothing, it seemed, was ever good enough.

History and perspective have been much kinder to Walker. Since the end of his pro career he was chosen as the top running back in college football history by ESPN and as the greatest player in Georgia history by the *Banner-Herald*.

"I'm honored, but it's strange," Walker said. "I don't see that I've done anything special. It seems to me that I was just doing what I was supposed to do."

Bo Knows Success

There have been college running backs with more impressive stats. Maybe some were bigger and stronger. Perhaps others were shiftier. Others may have had better vision.

But there was only one Vincent Edward "Bo" Jackson.

"Everybody in the world would like to coach somebody like Bo Jackson," said Pat Dye, who coached Jackson at Auburn from 1982 to 1985. "You really didn't have to coach him; you guided him."

Whether he was competing in football or baseball or engaging the public with his own particular charisma, Jackson brought a certain magic to nearly everything he touched during both his college and pro days as a rare two-sport star.

Sports Illustrated called Jackson the second-best two-sport athlete of all time behind Jackie Robinson. Dye didn't agree with that vote. "Jackie Robinson . . . couldn't do what Bo could do. Jackie Robinson wasn't close to being as fast as Bo was, or as big."

Jackson was unique from the start. Born the eighth of Florence Jackson Bond's 10 children in Bessemer, Alabama, he was a rambunctious boy who earned his nickname after being compared to a boar hog.

In his book *Bo Knows Bo*, Jackson wrote, "We never had enough food. But at least I could beat on other kids and steal their lunch money and buy myself something to eat. But I couldn't steal a father. I couldn't steal a father's hug when I needed one. I couldn't steal a father's whipping when I needed one."

His mother, however, was a different story.

"She was the only one who could whip my butt when I got into trouble," Jackson said. "She was the only person I feared, which was good."

Jackson didn't fear much when it came to sports. He emerged as a three-sport star at McAdory High School in McCalla, Alabama, where his all-around skills earned him two state decathlon championships. The New York Yankees saw enough pure baseball talent to select him in the second round of the 1982 draft, but Jackson turned down a multi-year contract offer from the Yankees and a scholarship offer from Alabama's Bear Bryant to play football at Auburn at a time when Dye was trying to build the program into a winner.

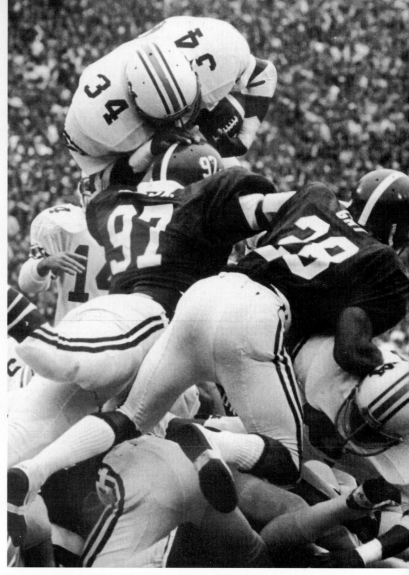

Bo Jackson's touchdown dive over the top of the Alabama defense gave the Tigers a 23-22 victory over the Crimson Tide in 1982. Jackson's decision to choose Auburn over Alabama was a significant moment in the long-standing rivalry between the two schools.

Jackson did his part to help Auburn usurp Alabama as the state's preeminent program in the 1980s. He hurdled over a goal-line pile as a freshman in 1982 to score the winning touchdown in the Tigers' first victory over the Crimson Tide since 1972.

In his four years at Auburn, Jackson ran for 4,303 yards, scored 43 touchdowns, and won the Heisman Trophy in 1985. Stats didn't define Jackson nearly as accurately as the awe he inspired with some of his electrifying runs.

"Bo was such a great athlete, it came easy to him," Dye said. "Besides that, he had a brilliant mind; he didn't forget."

Bo Jackson developed a habit of making big plays during his Auburn career. He accomplished runs of at least 50 yards on 11 occasions: 82, 80, 76 (twice), 71, 67, 53 (4 times), and 51 yards.

Those qualities also helped him excel in the spring as both a baseball player and sprinter for the track team. When the NFL's Tampa Bay Buccaneers made him the first pick of the 1986 NFL draft, Jackson rejected a five-year, multi-million dollar contract and the certainty of a pro football career to take his chances as a baseball player for the Kansas City Royals.

"My first love is baseball," he said, "and it has always been a dream of mine to be a major-league player."

Jackson proved he could play at the major league level—and play pro football at the same time by playing for both the Royals and the NFL's Oakland Raiders. He was a baseball All-Star in 1989 and a Pro Bowl running back in 1990, despite playing in only 10 football games. At the height of his popularity, his Nike "Bo Knows" ads had turned Jackson into a cultural icon.

It finally took a freak hip injury in an NFL playoff game in 1991 to slow him down. The injury led to a condition known as avascular necrosis and the deterioration of the cartilage and bone around his left hip joint. When Jackson opted for hip replacement surgery in 1992, few people ever expected to see him back on a field of any kind.

Instead, Jackson returned to the major leagues with the Chicago White Sox in 1993 and, typical of his flair for the dramatic, hit a pinch-hit home run in his first at-bat. Jackson played for the California Angels in 1994 and then retired for good.

Jackson has never been one to sit still or ponder his achievements for long. He fulfilled a promise he made to his mother before she died of cancer in 1992 and earned his Bachelor of Science degree in family and child development from Auburn in December 1995. Since then he has become active in the creation of several new business ventures, including a successful food company that distributes Bo Jackson Signature Meats.

The Top Dawg

With his team undefeated following the 1980 regular season and looking forward to a shot at Notre Dame and the national championship in the Sugar Bowl, the last thing Vince Dooley needed was a distraction. This wasn't just any distraction. It was Auburn, his alma mater, calling in late November with an offer.

"It had a lot of emotional pull," Dooley said. "They made me a very attractive offer, so I thought about it."

For three days Dooley pondered an offer that would make him both the head football coach and the athletic director, a title he did not hold at Georgia. He would also receive a contract worth $1.8 million, a substantial raise over what he was making at Georgia.

"I knew it was a tremendous opportunity," Dooley said. "Auburn was ripe at the time. That entered into my thinking. I knew it was going to be a good situation."

The more Dooley thought about it, though, the more his heart outweighed his head.

"I had too much invested here," Dooley told the *Athens Banner-Herald* years later. "I'd been here too long. I had too many players that I couldn't leave. My roots, as it turned out, were deeper and more recent [in Athens] than even at Auburn.... My children grew up here. They were all Georgia. I just couldn't leave. I had too much commitment here."

One month later, the Bulldogs completed their season with a 17-10 victory over Notre Dame and the school's first consensus national championship. In the process, Dooley backed up much of the faith Georgia athletic director Joel Eaves showed when he hired the young Auburn assistant as Georgia's head coach in December 1963.

"Looking back, it amazes me that somebody would hire a 31-year-old coach, and only a freshman coach at that, to be the head football coach at a rival school," Dooley said. "I was young enough to think it was a good decision, and I was probably the only one who did."

Dooley never lacked confidence as a kid growing up during the Great Depression, as the fourth of five kids in Mobile, Alabama, or as a star football and basketball player at McGill Catholic High School. He continued to play basketball for three years at Auburn, but his best success came on the football field as a quarterback for coach Ralph "Shug" Jordan.

Georgia's Vince Dooley achieved success as both a coach and an athletic director. In his 25 years as head coach at Georgia, Dooley's teams played in 20 bowl games and posted an overall record of 201-77-10. In his 25 years as athletic director, Georgia built a comprehensive athletics program that included 18 teams in men's and women's sports.

After two years in the Marine Corps, Dooley returned to Auburn to complete his master's degree and coach under Jordan. When Eaves called, no one was more surprised than Dooley, but he wasn't about to turn down the opportunity.

"All of this just came out of the blue," Dooley said. "It was sort of like ready or not, go."

Dooley inherited a program that had fallen on hard times and turned it into a consistent competitor in the SEC. With a penchant for tough defense and a hard-nosed running game, Dooley went on to win 201 games and six conference titles before he retired after the 1988 season. He became Georgia's full-time athletic director, a position he held until 2004.

The 1980 national championship gives Dooley a special place among his peers.

"It's one thing getting close and another thing winning," said former Georgia linebacker Frank Ros, a defensive captain in 1980. "He would have always been respected as one of the greatest coaches because he had always consistently been a winner. I think what the national championship game did was solidify his position as a legend. He really put our program [on] a whole other level."

Vince Dooley's best years as Georgia's head football coach came from 1980 to 1983, when the Bulldogs won a national championship and three SEC titles. They had a record of 43-4-1, and in those four seasons Georgia finished in the national rankings at number 1, 6, 4, and 4.

One of Coach Dooley's early stars was defensive tackle Bill Stanfill. Stanfill was the team captain and MVP in 1968 and winner of the Outland Trophy. A member of the College Football Hall of Fame, Stanfill was also chosen to the SEC's 25-year all-star team. Dooley called Stanfill the best defensive lineman he ever coached.

There were lean years along the way, but Dooley and his staff, particularly long-time defensive coordinator Erk Russell, developed a knack for adjusting, adapting, and getting the program back on the right track.

"I had a guy tell me a long time ago, 'The longer you are in this business, the more you will appreciate Coach Dooley,'" said Hugh Nall, a former Georgia lineman and the current offensive line coach at Auburn. "That's true. He had such a strong demand for excellence. . . . But probably the most impressive thing to me about him is the way he let his coaches coach and his kids play."

A number of honors reflect Dooley's impact on Georgia and college football. Dooley was inducted into the Georgia Sports Hall of Fame in 1978 and the College Football Hall of Fame in 1994, and he received the Amos Alonzo Stagg Award presented by the American Football Coaches Association in 2001. In 2004 Dooley joined Georgia's Circle of Honor, the school's highest tribute to former athletes and coaches. In 2007, Dooley received the Homer Rice Award, the highest honor given by the Division 1-A Athletic Directors Association.

The 1990s
Exploring and Expanding the Possibilities

Between expansion, the split into two divisions, the first NCAA Division I-A conference championship game, the arrival of Florida coach Steve Spurrier and his pass-oriented approach, the continued growth of television opportunities, and the evolution of the process to decide a national champion, the Southeastern Conference continued to expand its role as a leader on and off the field in the college football world in the 1990s.

One of the principal figures in those dramatic developments was Roy Kramer. The former Vanderbilt athletic director became the SEC's sixth commissioner on January 10, 1990. He didn't wait long to make a historic mark on the long-term future of the SEC.

On May 31, the SEC presidents unanimously approved a decision to allow Kramer to pursue expansion. With the Southwest Conference splintering and Division I-A independents looking for more solid ground as conference members, it was a time of enormous concern and speculation about the changing direction of college football. Against this background, the University of Arkansas left the SWC and accepted the SEC's invitation to become the 11th member of the conference on August 1. On September 25, South Carolina gave up its status as an independent to become the 12th member of the SEC. Now containing 12 teams for the first time since Georgia Tech and Tulane left the conference in the 1960s, the SEC split into Eastern and Western Divisions. Florida, Georgia, Kentucky, South Carolina, Tennessee, and Vanderbilt were placed in the Eastern Division, while Alabama, Arkansas, Auburn, LSU, Mississippi State, and Ole Miss went to the West.

"We wanted balance," Kramer said. "We also wanted the divisional championships to mean something. I think we got both."

The University of South Carolina had been a Division I-A independent in football since 1971, until the SEC extended an invitation to join the conference before the 1992 season. The program has struggled to compete with some of the SEC's established powerhouses, but the hiring of legendary coaches Lou Holtz and Steve Spurrier helped to make the Gamecocks consistently competitive.

The SEC's moves created a wave of change throughout college football. It eventually led members of the Big Eight and the defunct SWC to form the Big 12. The Big East added Miami in 1991, Florida State joined the Atlantic Coast Conference in 1992, and the Big Ten expanded with the addition of Penn State in 1993. Even the Western Athletic Conference expanded to 16 teams in 1996, only to have eight members split off and form the Mountain West Conference in 1999. In 1996, Conference USA was created to give six I-A independents a conference home.

The SEC also became the first conference to take advantage of a little-known NCAA rule allowing a conference with 12 teams to hold a postseason conference championship game. In 1991, the SEC presidents awarded the inaugural SEC Football Championship Game to Birmingham. After two years at historic Legion Field, the event moved in 1994 to the Georgia Dome in Atlanta, where the championship has been played since.

Between expansion and a championship game between division winners, critics insisted the SEC would never win another national championship. Instead, Alabama defeated Florida 28-21 in the SEC's first championship game in 1992, and then went on to defeat Miami in the Sugar Bowl to complete a 13-0 season and win the national championship.

By the end of the decade, Florida had played for two national championships and won one, in 1996, and Tennessee won the national title in 1998. The SEC also paved

With the Southeastern Conference looking to expand and the Southwest Conference weighed down by NCAA penalties for rules violations and declining performance and attendance, Arkansas made the jump from the SWC to the SEC in 1990.

Roy Kramer became the SEC's sixth commissioner in 1990 and oversaw the conference's expansion to 12 teams. He also spearheaded the establishment of the groundbreaking conference championship game and negotiated a lucrative national television package.

the way for other conferences to hold championship games, further cementing the SEC's place as a leader among the new power conferences.

Those power conferences—primarily the SEC, Big Ten, Pac-10, Big 12, and to a lesser degree, the ACC and Big East—also recognized the need for a system that would attempt to place the top two teams in a national championship game while working within the bowl structure. With Kramer playing a major role, the power conferences started the Bowl Coalition in 1992, which grew into the Bowl Alliance in 1995, and finally developed into the Bowl Championship Series (BCS) in 1997.

With each step, the BCS added more elements to the system in an attempt to bring the nation's two top-ranked teams together in the same bowl. The process uses a mix of polls and computer rankings to decide the candidates for the BCS National Championship Game as well as the Rose, Sugar, Fiesta, and Orange Bowls. The system still includes an element of tradition; the SEC champion plays in the Sugar Bowl when it's not playing for the national championship.

While the system remains a source of debate and controversy, and it continues to evolve, the BCS has been able to achieve its goal of creating a national championship game. From the creation of the BCA to the current BCS, the SEC has won six national championships and has continued to

Derrick Lassic outruns a Florida defender on his way to the end zone in the inaugural SEC Championship Game at Birmingham's Legion Field in 1992. More than 83,000 fans were on hand as the Crimson Tide defeated the Gators 28-21. Alabama made four more trips to the championship game in the 1990s, while Florida represented the Eastern Division in seven of the first nine SEC Championship Games.

build on its reputation as the nation's toughest football conference from top to bottom.

The conference was already deep enough before Florida emerged as a national power in the 1990s. The program had always been seen as a sleeping giant because of the state's vast talent pool. The Gators flirted with success briefly under coach Charley Pell in the 1980s, but two different run-ins with the NCAA kept Florida from taking full advantage of its resources.

That changed when Steve Spurrier returned to his alma mater on December 31, 1989. Spurrier, who won the Heisman Trophy as Florida's quarterback in 1967, put the Gators on the path toward five SEC championships from 1991 to 1996 and an additional SEC Eastern Division title in 1999. Spurrier also changed the way the SEC played football. Traditionally, SEC teams focused on defense, the running game, and special teams, with the passing game treated as somewhat of a last resort. Spurrier's dedicated and innovative approach to a wide-open, multiple-receiver passing game turned the SEC upside down.

"Everyone thought you couldn't be a passing team at all and win the championship," Spurrier said. "We proved that you can throw the ball."

SEC Championship Game Results, 1990s		
1992	Alabama 28	Florida 21
1993	Florida 28	Alabama 13
1994	Florida 24	Alabama 23
1995	Florida 34	Arkansas 3
1996	Florida 45	Alabama 30
1997	Tennessee 30	Auburn 29
1998	Tennessee 24	Mississippi State 14
1999	Alabama 34	Florida 7

Tennessee's Jamal Lewis dives over the Auburn defense for a touchdown in the 1997 SEC Championship Game. When the Vols emerged victorious 30-29, it marked the first time that a team other than Florida or Alabama had won the conference championship game.

Soon other teams were catching on—in a big way. Georgia threw the ball only when necessary under long-time coach Vince Dooley. One of his quarterbacks, Ray Goff, was the SEC player of the year in 1976 when he led the Bulldogs to the SEC championship, but Goff threw a total of just 74 passes in three seasons. As Georgia's head coach, Goff turned true freshman quarterback Eric Zeier loose in 1991, and Zeier rewrote the Bulldogs' single-season passing records. He threw 65 passes in a single game against Florida in 1993.

Right: Florida coach Steve Spurrier, in white sweater vest, keeps a close eye on the action in the 1994 SEC Championship Game. Under Spurrier's leadership, the Gators won five SEC Championship Games between 1993 and 2000.

As the passing game emerged as a valuable weapon, the SEC produced some of its all-time great passers. In addition to Zeier, Florida's Shane Matthews and Danny Wuerffel, Tennessee's Heath Shuler and Peyton Manning, Kentucky's Tim Couch, Alabama's Jay Barker, South Carolina's Steve Taneyhill, Arkansas' Clint Stoerner, and Auburn's Stan White and Dameyune Craig took their places among the nation's best passers. In 1996, Wuerffel became the SEC's seventh Heisman Trophy winner and the first Heisman winner to be coached by a Heisman recipient.

Of course, the passing game also led to occasional problems. When LSU played at Auburn in 1990, LSU held Auburn to 150 total offensive yards, a mere 18 second-half yards, and led 23-9 with just over 12 minutes left in the game. LSU kept passing anyway, and Auburn intercepted five fourth-quarter passes. Auburn returned three interceptions for touchdowns and won the game, 30-26.

"I've never seen anything like it in my life," Auburn coach Terry Bowden said afterwards.

The game was unusual enough, but it seemed a perfect fit during Auburn's 20-game winning streak in 1993–94. After a decade of prominence, Auburn won only 10 games combined in 1991 and 1992. The two sub-par seasons, a prolonged NCAA investigation, and health issues conspired to force coach Pat Dye into an early retirement.

Auburn surprised the college football world by hiring Terry Bowden, the coach at Division I-AA Samford and son of legendary Florida State coach Bobby Bowden. With a fresh start and a determined group of seniors, Auburn won all 11 of their games in 1993 and kept on winning until the final two games of the 1994 season. Just four seasons later Bowden resigned six games into the 1998 season when he became convinced he would be fired after the season. Auburn then hired Ole Miss coach Tommy Tuberville, who led the Tigers to an SEC West title in 2000.

Georgia quarterback Eric Zeier was a symbol of the SEC's changing game in the early 1990s. As the Bulldogs placed greater emphasis on the passing game, Zeier set dozens of school records and became the conference's all-time leader with 11,153 passing yards. (His record has since been surpassed by Tennessee's Peyton Manning, Georgia's David Greene, and Florida's Chris Leak.)

Auburn's turbulent decade was symbolic of the unpredictable nature of college football in the 1990s. Both Arkansas and Mississippi State represented the Western Division in the SEC Championship Game during the 1990s, and Kentucky played in consecutive bowl games for only the third time in school history. Meanwhile, perennial national powers such as Southern Cal and Oklahoma struggled to win and long-time losers Kansas State, Northwestern, and Virginia Tech rose to prominence.

Every member of the SEC benefited from the conference's growing success on and off the field. The SEC led the nation in total attendance throughout the decade and signed a groundbreaking television agreement with CBS Sports to televise SEC football as well as men's and women's basketball. In 1999, the SEC placed a record seven conference teams in the final AP top-25 football poll: Alabama (8), Tennessee (9), Florida (12), Mississippi State (13), Georgia (16), Arkansas (17), and Ole Miss (22).

Playing in Coach Hal Mumme's "Air Raid" offense, Tim Couch produced two of the SEC's biggest passing seasons in 1997 (3,884 passing yards and 37 touchdown passes) and 1998 (4,275 yards, 36 touchdown passes).

Putting Out the Welcome Mat

As college football entered the 1990s, rumors about conference alignment and expansion swarmed like bees. The only problem was, no one knew who would get the honey and who would get stung.

With the Southwest Conference on the verge of a nasty breakup and many prominent programs ready to give up their independent status for the security of conference affiliation, conjecture ran wild. Were Texas and Texas A&M headed for the Southeastern Conference? Or was it the Pac 10? Miami and Florida State were headed to the SEC as well to form a colossus. Colorado was leaving the Big Eight for the Pac-10. Missouri was leaving the Big Eight to join Penn State and turn the Big Ten into the Big 12.

"I expect a major upheaval," Arkansas athletic director Frank Broyles said on August 1990.

When the dust finally cleared on the storm of speculation, the SEC invited Arkansas to join on August 1 and South Carolina on September 25.

For Arkansas, the move meant leaving eight decades of tradition in the SWC for a brave new world in the SEC. With most of the SWC weighed down by NCAA penalties for rules violations, and with declining performance and attendance, Arkansas saw hope for a fresh start and a better future in the SEC.

South Carolina had been a Division I-A independent in football since 1971, but sought more than football success when it entered the SEC. University officials knew joining the SEC would benefit the entire athletic department by providing more financial and scheduling stability—and raising the department's athletic identity outside the Carolinas.

Mike McGee, South Carolina's athletic director from 1993 to 2005, recognized that the school would get much broader national exposure as a member of the SEC. "It's not 'College Football on CBS,'" McGee said. "It's 'The SEC on CBS.' You have a national stage that, in many respects, far outstrips the rest of the conferences."

The transition was challenging for both football programs in their early years in the SEC, but that was expected from both the conference and the schools. Then, in 1994, South Carolina earned its first bowl trip in six years, and in

While South Carolina's football tradition didn't match that of Arkansas, the school nevertheless brought a devoted following to the SEC. The Gamecocks appeared in four bowl games between 2000 and 2006, and they consistently draw crowds of more than 80,000 to Williams-Brice Stadium.

1995 Arkansas won the SEC Western Division title and played in the SEC Championship Game.

Arkansas went on to win the West again in 2002 and 2006, and the Razorbacks have played in bowls in eight of the past ten years.

When the SEC expanded to include the University of Arkansas in 1990, it added a program rich in football tradition and passionate fans. Since joining the SEC, the Razorbacks have appeared in nine bowl games and three SEC Championship Games.

South Carolina's fortunes took a turn for the better with two strong hires. First McGee hired former Notre Dame and Arkansas coach Lou Holtz. After Holtz put the program on solid ground and retired in 2004, McGee hired former Florida coach Steve Spurrier. Spurrier has put the Gamecocks in position to battle Florida, Georgia, and Tennessee for the East Division title.

Just as important, both universities brought loyal and enthusiastic fan bases as well as a commitment to building competitive athletic teams to the SEC. Both schools have undertaken significant construction projects, including new basketball arenas and baseball stadiums and additions to their football stadiums. By the 2006–07 season, a study by the U.S. Department of Education revealed that seven of the nation's top 13 revenue-producing football programs came from the SEC. Arkansas was ranked 12th and South Carolina was 13th.

In all, the SEC has won 121 national championships across all sports since 1990. In 2006–07 alone, the SEC won eight national titles and became the first conference to win national championships in football, men's basketball, and women's basketball in the same academic year.

"I think everybody felt [expansion] was a move that would strengthen our league and provide us a lot of opportunities that didn't exist in a 10-team structure," Mark Womack, the SEC's executive associate commissioner, said in 2003. "From our standpoint, we feel like it's turned out extremely well, maybe even better than we could have hoped for."

Decade of Champions

"The SEC will never win another championship." That phrase became a popular weapon for critics of the Southeastern Conference's decision to expand to 12 teams, split into two divisions, and play a conference championship game.

It was already difficult enough to survive the SEC's conference schedule undefeated, critics insisted, without adding another game between the two division winners.

Even some SEC coaches and players wondered if the SEC championship game would be a blessing or a curse.

"They should have waited until next year before they came up with this game," Alabama cornerback Antonio Langham said before the 11-0 Crimson Tide played 8-3 Florida in the first SEC championship game in 1992. "But they came up with it, and we're going to play it and move on."

Alabama made the most of it and beat Florida 28-21. The Tide then went on to defeat Miami 33-25 in the Sugar Bowl to take the national championship. Florida did the same in 1996, beating Alabama 45-30 in the championship game and then Florida State 52-20 in the Sugar Bowl for the national title. Then Tennessee pulled off the achievement in 1998, beating Mississippi State 24-14 in the conference championship game and winning the national crown by beating Florida State 23-16 in the Fiesta Bowl.

"You have to win the [SEC championship] game, of course," then-SEC commissioner Roy Kramer said, "but if you do win, your team is going to be battle-tested. Chances are they won't face anything in a bowl game they haven't seen before. If you ask the coaches who have been involved, they'll tell you that the SEC Championship Game is really

Alabama celebrates safety George Teague's 31-yard interception return for a touchdown in the 1993 Sugar Bowl. The Crimson Tide stymied Miami quarterback Gino Torretta and defeated the favored Hurricanes 34-13 to win the national championship.

Florida wide receiver Ike Hilliard hauls in a reception against Florida State during the 1997 Sugar Bowl. The Gators won their first national championship by defeating the Seminoles 52-20. Hilliard was one of the beneficiaries of an impressive outing by quarterback Danny Wuerffel.

more intense than most bowl games. It's more of a Super Bowl-type atmosphere. Once your kids have played in this thing, they are not going to have their heads turned by anything they see in a bowl."

In all three cases, the SEC championship game did a lot more to help than harm the eventual national champs.

For Alabama, playing Florida's pass-oriented offense and the Gators' overall speed helped the Crimson Tide prepare for Miami. Alabama's coaches came up with an offensive game plan to run right at Miami to negate its defensive speed, and a defensive game plan to pressure and confound the Hurricanes' Heisman Trophy–winning quarterback, Gino Torretta. The Tide even deployed 11-man fronts to freeze Torretta and slow his decision-making.

The game's most stunning moment came when Miami receiver Lamar Thomas appeared to have Alabama beaten badly for an 89-yard touchdown. The cocky and speedy Thomas had questioned Alabama's secondary in the days

leading up to the game. But Alabama safety George Teague, who had already returned an interception 31 yards for a touchdown, came out of nowhere to catch Thomas from behind and strip the ball away.

"That may have been the greatest individual effort in Alabama football history," defensive coordinator Bill Oliver said after the game.

Officially the game was an upset, but the Tide had refused to play the role of underdog on the way to its 12th national championship and seventh officially recognized national title.

"We did everything we set out to do," Alabama coach Gene Stallings said.

In 1995, Florida was 11-0 and ranked No. 2 when it beat Arkansas 34-3 in the SEC Championship Game and a earned a shot at the national championship in the Fiesta Bowl, where it lost to No. 1 Nebraska 62-24.

In 1996, Florida appeared to fall out of national championship contention with a 24-21 loss at Florida State on

Tennessee wide receiver Peerless Price outraces the Florida State defense for a 79-yard touchdown pass during the 1999 Fiesta Bowl. The Vols won 23-16 to capture the school's first national championship since 1951.

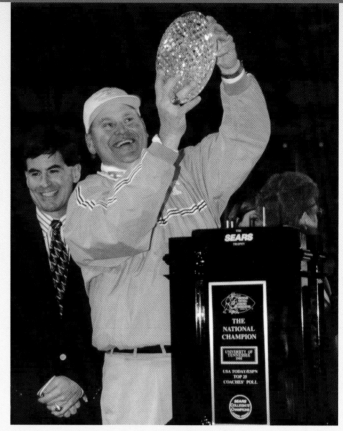

Tennessee coach Phillip Fulmer raises the 1998 national championship trophy after the Vols capped off their 12-0 season with a win in the first BCS Championship Game. It was a proud moment for Fulmer, a former offensive lineman and assistant coach for the Volunteers.

November 30. In that game, the Seminoles had given quite a beating to Florida's Heisman-winning quarterback, Danny Wuerffel.

The next week, Florida's victory over Alabama in the SEC Championship Game gave the Gators a chance to play for the national championship—and another shot at the Seminoles.

In the weeks before the Sugar Bowl game, Florida coach Steve Spurrier produced tapes of what he considered cheap shots and late hits by FSU defensive players. Spurrier did more than just plant psychological seeds in the heads of the Seminoles and the officials. He also came up with a game plan in which the Gators would make extensive use of the shotgun formation and use their tight end and a back to provide extra protection for Wuerffel.

With a little more time to find his receivers and get the ball away, Wuerffel completed 18 of 34 passes for 306 yards and three touchdowns in a 52-20 romp.

"That's probably the smartest thing Steve has done," FSU coach Bobby Bowden said. "You can see why I didn't want to play them again. I didn't know it would be this bad, but I didn't want to play them again."

In 1998, Tennessee entered the conference championship game hoping to emerge from a crowd of contenders for the national championship. As the Vols did their part by beating Mississippi State, UCLA lost at Miami, and Kansas State lost to Texas A&M in the Big 12 championship game. When the smoke cleared, the Vols and Seminoles emerged to play for the national championship.

Like Alabama in 1992 and Florida in 1998, the Vols were supposed to be underdogs. Instead, in a game marred by turnovers and mistakes, Tennessee came through with the right plays at the right time. One year after quarterback Peyton Manning left Tennessee to become the NFL's No. 1 draft choice, quarterback Tee Martin led a team that won a lot of ugly games in a beautiful season.

"It's not just one or two guys," Tennessee coach Phillip Fulmer said. "It's a whole football team believing that it could get it done, working hard and finally getting it done."

A Dye-hard Commitment

In mid-December 1980, Auburn was looking for a coach when 40-year-old Pat Dye walked into an interview with the search committee and said, "I'm your man."

With his experience as a player at Georgia, as an assistant coach under Bear Bryant at Alabama, and as a head coach at both East Carolina and Wyoming, Dye believed he knew exactly what Auburn needed.

"I played at Georgia and I coached at Alabama . . . they are your biggest rivals," Dye told the search committee. "I know what it takes to win and I know what it takes to beat them."

When one of the members of the search committee asked Dye how long it would take to beat Alabama, Dye didn't flinch.

"Sixty minutes."

Dye's point was simple. It would take a total commitment to beat Alabama, and he was the man to lead the way. It actually took Auburn 120 minutes to get the job done, but when the Tigers beat the Crimson Tide in 1982, it signaled a changing of the guard in the state of Alabama and the SEC. Auburn's first win over Alabama since 1972 proved to be Bryant's last game against Auburn and a big step toward Auburn becoming an SEC power.

Auburn went on to win outright SEC titles in 1983 and 1987 and a share of two others in 1988 and 1989. The Tigers also played in nine straight bowl games from 1982 to 1990. With a team that mirrored Dye's own toughness, the Tigers won most of their games with defense, the running game, and special teams.

Dye's toughness came from his childhood in rural Blythe, Georgia, as the youngest of five children. His father raised cotton and his mother taught school, so Dye learned the benefits of both hard work and education. Those lessons took him to Georgia, where he played for Wally Butts and earned All-America honors as a lineman in 1959 and 1960.

After graduation Dye spent time in the Army and played in the Canadian Football League before sending a letter to Bryant asking for a job. When Bryant called Butts to ask if Dye had what it took to coach at Alabama, Butts said, "I don't know, but he sure could have played for you." Soon after, Bryant hired the 26-year-old Dye as a defensive assistant.

Even after six seasons as the head man at East Carolina and Wyoming, Dye still had a lot to prove at Auburn. In his first game against Alabama, Dye knew Bryant would try to use his size and presence to intimidate Dye when the coaches met at midfield. Instead, Dye spoke first and said, "Coach I just want you to know we're coming after your ass." Bryant laughed and said, "What are you trying to do, boy, scare me?" Dye responded, "I ain't trying to scare you, Coach. I just want you to know we ain't scared of you any more."

Auburn emerged as an SEC and national powerhouse under Coach Pat Dye, who led the Tigers to a record of 99-39-4 in 12 seasons. Before Dye came on the scene, the Tigers had won only one SEC championship in 48 years. During his tenure, Auburn captured four conference titles, including three straight from 1987 to 1989.

Pat Dye brought a hard-nosed mentality to Auburn when he became the head coach in 1981. He also helped Auburn level the playing field against archrival Alabama following two decades of domination by the Crimson Tide. The teams split their 12 head-to-head matchups between 1981 and 1992, with six wins apiece. In 1989, the Tigers hosted the Crimson Tide at Jordan-Hare for the first time and emerged with a 30-20 victory in the historic and emotional game.

In a nine-year span from 1982 to 1990, Auburn's .771 winning percentage (84-22-3) was the nation's third best. Dye also served as athletic director during this time and oversaw the expansion and renovation of Jordan-Hare Stadium, which now seats more than 85,000 fans.

Dye's most significant achievement came in his combined roles as coach and athletic director. Auburn had always played Alabama at Birmingham's Legion Field, but Auburn people never saw it as an neutral field, especially because Alabama still played three homes game in Birmingham each year at that point.

With Auburn's contract to play the game at Legion Field coming to an end in 1988, Dye informed Alabama that Auburn would play all of its 1989 home games in Jordan-Hare. Alabama coach Ray Perkins had once vowed "it won't happen," but on December 2, 1989, Alabama played at Auburn.

During Pat Dye's tenure as athletic director, Auburn expanded Jordan-Hare Stadium to 85,214 seats, and in 2005 the playing field at the stadium was renamed "Pat Dye Field."

The Crimson Tide came in undefeated and ranked second in the nation, but the Tigers fed off an emotional crowd that had waited for this day for decades. The Tigers won 30-20 in a game Dye called, "the last brick in our house."

There would be tough days ahead for Dye, including a prolonged NCAA investigation into rules violations, two five-win seasons, and health problems that led to widespread rumors of his departure. On the night before the 1992 Alabama game, Dye resigned.

In 1993, the nucleus of a team toughened by hard times in 1991 and 1992 finished 11-0 under first-year coach Terry Bowden, but many seniors were quick to credit Dye for laying the foundation for the perfect season. Still, because of NCAA sanctions, the Tigers could not play in the SEC Championship Game or a bowl game.

In 2005, Auburn honored Dye by naming the field at Jordan-Hare Stadium "Pat Dye Field." Later that year, Pat Dye was inducted into the College Football Hall of Fame.

Pat Dye was named the National Coach of the Year in 1983 and is one of only seven coaches in history to have coached winners of the Heisman (Bo Jackson in 1985), Outland (Tracy Rocker in 1988), and Lombardi (Rocker, 1988) trophies.

Great Quarterback, Better Person

Of all the things that have been said of Danny Wuerffel, the best description of who Wuerffel really is came from his coach.

"Danny Wuerffel is a better person than he is a quarterback," former Florida coach Steve Spurrier said, "and he is a great, great quarterback."

To Florida fans, Wuerffel is the epitome of the all-American boy: a strong student, a record-setting quarterback, a winner who led Florida to a national championship, and a man of faith who used his success to share his faith.

Even opponents and fans of Florida's rivals had to admire Wuerffel. He was difficult to hate, no matter how hard they tried.

Danny Wuerffel and the Gators had a lot to celebrate during his four years as Florida's starting quarterback. From 1993 to 1996, the Gators won one national championship and four SEC titles and posted a record of 45-6-1. Here he celebrates a touchdown during Florida's 62-37 thrashing of Tennessee in September 1995, handing the Vols their only loss of the season.

"If you were describing a winner," Florida State coach Bobby Bowden said, "he's a winner."

The son of an Air Force Chaplain, Wuerffel lived in South Carolina, Spain, Nebraska, and Colorado before attending Fort Walton Beach (Florida) High School, where he led the Vikings to an undefeated season and the Florida AAAA state football championship as a senior in 1991. He also graduated as valedictorian.

Wuerffel nearly signed with Alabama, but with Spurrier turning the SEC upside down with his passing offense and Florida on the cusp of national success, Wuerffel became a Gator.

It didn't take long for the decision to work for both Wuerffel and Florida. As a first-year player in 1993, Wuerffel had been splitting time with junior Terry Dean. When Spurrier gave Wuerffel the start against Tennessee and the Gators won 41-34, the Wuerffel era was officially underway.

The Gators won the SEC championship in each of the next four seasons, and Wuerffel grew into one of the nation's top quarterbacks in Spurrier's system. On the field, he set 17 NCAA and Florida passing records and still holds the SEC record with 114 career touchdown passes. Off the field, he earned a 3.75 grade-point average and rarely turned down an opportunity to speak in public or talk to a fan. Wuerffel did, however, turn down *Playboy* magazine's award as the 1996 National Scholar Athlete of the year.

"He's just too nice a guy, just way too nice," Spurrier said in 1996. "I tell Danny he's just got to learn to say no, but he won't do it. I can be a jerk. He can never be a jerk."

Wuerffel finished his 1996 season by winning the Heisman Trophy and the Draddy Award that goes to the nation's top student-athlete. But his most important accomplishment came in his final game when he completed 18 of 34 passes for 306 yards and three touchdowns, and ran for a fourth score in a 52-20 Sugar Bowl victory that gave the Gators the national championship.

After the game Spurrier called Wuerffel, "the best quarterback that ever played college football. If one of those NFL teams wants to win a Super Bowl, they better get Danny Wuerffel on their team."

Quarterback Danny Wuerffel was a good fit for Coach Steve Spurrier's "fun 'n' gun" offense at Florida. He set numerous NCAA and school passing records. His 114 career touchdown passes still stand as the SEC's all-time mark.

Wuerffel was at his best as a senior in 1996. He completed 207 of 360 passes for 3,625 yards and an SEC-record 39 TDs. He also became the second Gator quarterback to win the Heisman Trophy, following in the footsteps of his coach, Steve Spurrier, who won it 30 years earlier.

Wuerffel never experienced the same level of success in a seven-year NFL career with the New Orleans Saints, Green Bay Packers, Chicago Bears, and Washington Redskins. When he retired from pro football in 2002, he turned his energies toward working for Desire Street Ministries, a nonprofit, faith-based organization with a mission to revitalize impoverished neighborhoods in New Orleans through spiritual and community development.

When Hurricane Katrina destroyed Wuerffel's home and Desire Street Ministries in 2005, Wuerffel once again used his fame to do something positive. The Ministry turned its efforts toward victims of Katrina and eventually reopened Desire Street Academy in Baton Rouge, where it continues to educate and house male African-American high school students displaced by the hurricane.

"Don't worry about me and my family. . . . We've lost everything, but we need nothing. If you want to help me, then help me help others," Wuerffel wrote weeks after the hurricane hit. "If using my name to get Desire Street in the door so people will listen is my God-given purpose, then so be it."

Peyton Paves His Path

Peyton Manning had a big decision to make as a high school senior. If he followed his heart, he would most likely sign with Ole Miss, where his father Archie had been a star quarterback and his mother Olivia had been homecoming queen.

If it came down to his head, it would be somewhere else. Showing the kind of diligence that has served him well as a college and pro quarterback, Manning studied his options carefully and decided Tennessee had everything he wanted in terms of resources, tradition, and a commitment to the passing game.

When he sat down with his parents to make the big decision he told them he would go to Ole Miss if they wanted him to. When his parents left the decision up to him, Tennessee fans rejoiced, Ole Miss fans responded with angry letters and calls, and Archie saw something special in the son's steadfast resolve.

"With my Ole Miss hat on, I'm disappointed, like a lot of people," Archie said at the time. "But with my daddy hat on, I'm proud of the way he handled things. At 17, I couldn't have stood up to the stuff he has."

From his decision to attend Tennessee to his evolution into one of the NFL's best quarterbacks and a Super Bowl champion, Manning has usually relied on his head to help him see the right path. It helped him when he arrived at Tennessee the summer before his freshman season. Manning immersed himself in learning the offense. When senior quarterback Jerry Colquitt suffered a season-ending knee injury early in the 1994 season opener at UCLA, Manning found himself sharing time with two other quarterbacks. When he entered the huddle for the first time he told his teammates, "I know I'm just a freshman but I can take us down the field." A veteran lineman responded, "Shut up and call the play."

Following an injury to junior quarterback Todd Helton (now better known as first baseman for the Colorado Rockies), Manning split the starting job with fellow freshman Branndon Stewart. Manning eventually became SEC Freshman of the Year, while Stewart transferred.

Left: Because of injuries to upperclassmen—and thanks to his own talents—Peyton Manning was able to step into the starting quarterback job as a true freshman in 1994. Here he turns to hand the ball off during his debut game, against UCLA, on September 2, 1994.

Opposite: Even though his father, Archie, played quarterback at Ole Miss, the Manning family supported Peyton Manning's decision to play for the Tennessee Volunteers.

With Manning as the full-time starter from 1995 to 1997, Tennessee posted a record of 32-5 and appeared in three bowl games. Manning himself set SEC career records for completions (863), passing yards (11,201) and total offense (11,020), although those marks have since been bested.

Manning spent the 1995 and 1996 seasons passing for 6,241 and 42 touchdowns, but the Vols lost to Florida and fell short of the SEC championship in both seasons. After the Vols finished 10-2 overall and ninth in the final AP poll in 1996, many assumed Manning would leave for the NFL after his junior season.

In his mind, it seemed like the right thing to do. NFL people told him he was ready, so why spend another year in college and risk getting hurt when the money and fame of the NFL awaited? This time, however, Manning listened to his heart.

He decided to return to Tennessee for his senior season—not just for the opportunities to beat Florida, win the Heisman Trophy, and lead his team to the national championship. He had already graduated in three years and decided it was time to enjoy a once-in-a-lifetime opportunity.

"My college experience was a really good one, so I decided to stay all four years," Manning said. "I just didn't want to look back and say I wish I would have stayed my senior year. For months I was asked the same question repeatedly every day: 'Why did you really stay?' I just wanted to enjoy being a college senior. For some reason people had a very hard time believing that."

Manning came up short in the pursuit of Florida, the Heisman, and the national title. But he did lead the Vols to their first SEC championship since 1990 and an 11-2 finish while passing for 3,819 yards and 36 touchdowns. He broke the SEC career records for completions (863), passing yards (11,201), and total offense (11,020). He also earned the Maxwell, Davey O'Brien, Johnny Unitas Golden Arm, and Draddy Awards.

While Manning is now best known for his NFL career with the Indianapolis Colts—he started as the first selection in the 1998 draft and became one of the NFL's most accomplished quarterbacks and the MVP of Super Bowl XLI in 2007—his legacy goes far beyond his professional achievements.

During his college career, the Knoxville Zoo named a baby giraffe in his honor. After his career, the university retired his No. 16 jersey and renamed the street on which players walk to Neyland Stadium on game days as Peyton Manning Pass.

The Manning Scholarship, originated from funds generated by Manning's numerous collegiate awards, annually awards a first-year student participating in the University of Tennessee's Honors Program. In 2006, Manning pledged $1 million toward improvements to Tennessee's football complex and stadium locker rooms. Even more importantly, a children's hospital in Indianapolis was renamed the Peyton Manning Children's Hospital at St. Vincent in September 2007, and his Peyback Foundation continues to serve numerous family and child-related causes.

Peyton Manning defied expectations when he decided to return to Tennessee for his senior season in 1997. In the SEC Championship Game on December 6, he threw four touchdown passes and rallied the Vols to a 30-29 victory over Auburn to bring Tennessee its first conference title since 1990.

The 2000s

Sitting on Top of the World

By any measure—be it national championships, national polls, bowl appearances, wins against non-conference opponents, attendance, or revenue—the Southeastern Conference has solidified its status as the nation's best college football conference during the first decade of the new millennium.

National championships by LSU in 2003 and 2007, another by Florida in 2006, plus a perfect season by Auburn in 2004 make for a strong case.

But national championships haven't provided the only big stories of the decade for the SEC. One of the most important stories took place in 2002 when Roy Kramer retired after 12 years as the SEC's sixth commissioner. While the SEC has experienced significant strides under each commissioner, the SEC's growth exploded under Kramer's leadership.

The SEC expanded with the addition of Arkansas and South Carolina, became the first Division I conference to play a postseason conference championship game, took the leading role in the formation of the Bowl Championship Series

and won three football national championships. In all, the SEC won 85 national championships and distributed more than $654 million to its members during Kramer's term.

"This conference was great before I ever got here and will be great after Roy Kramer is gone," Kramer said upon his retirement.

Three months after Kramer's retirement, the SEC hired Michael L. Slive as its new commissioner. The SEC continues to build its competitive and financial success under Slive, but he has also taken a leadership role in the SEC's renewed commitment to academics, scholarship and integrity of competition. Slive served as the coordinator of the BCS for the 2006 and 2007 seasons. He is also a member of the NCAA Division I Men's Basketball Committee through 2009 and will serve as the committee's chairman for the 2008–2009 season.

Former Alabama player Sylvester Croom and former Georgia player Damon Evans also played monumental roles in the conference's growth. In December 2003, Croom

Receiver Devery Henderson is mobbed by teammates after his 74-yard touchdown reception with no time remaining on the clock secured a remarkable 33-30 win over Kentucky on November 9, 2002. Wildcat fans had stormed the field as time ran out, thinking they had the victory, but LSU quarterback Marcus Randall heaved a "Hail Mary" pass from the Tigers' 18-yard line, and Henderson reeled in the ball and ran it in for the score.

became the SEC's first African-American head football coach when he was hired at Mississippi State. After three seasons spent rebuilding the program from the ground up, Croom earned 2007 SEC Coach of the Year honors when the Bulldogs defeated Auburn, Alabama, and Kentucky, won the Liberty Bowl, and posted the school's first winning season (8-5) since 2001.

After a subpar 2003 season nearly led to a coaching change, Auburn came together in 2004 and compiled a 13-0 record. In most seasons that would have meant a national championship, but the Tigers finished the year with a number 2 ranking in the polls, behind undefeated USC.

In July 2004, Evans became the SEC's first African-American athletic director when he took over at his alma mater, succeeding legendary football coach and athletic director Vince Dooley. At the time of his hiring, Evans was just 34 years old, but in 2006 and 2007, Georgia led the SEC and ranked fourth nationally with $59.5 million in revenue.

Others excelled on the field by winning some of the nation's college football awards. In 2007, Florida quarterback Tim Tebow became the first sophomore to win the Heisman Trophy. Arkansas running back Darren McFadden finished second in the Heisman Trophy voting in 2006 and 2007 and won the Doak Walker Award as the nation's top running back both years.

Tennessee defensive tackle John Henderson won the Outland Trophy in 2000, Georgia defensive end David Pollack won the Lombardi Award and the Bednarik Trophy in 2004, Auburn cornerback Carlos Rogers won the Thorpe Award in 2004, and Ole Miss linebacker Patrick Willis won the Butkus Award in 2006. No SEC player earned more individual success than LSU defensive tackle Glenn Dorsey in 2007. Dorsey completed a sweep of every possible award for a defensive lineman, winning the Nagurski, Lombardi, Outland, and Bednarik awards, as well as consensus All-America honors.

Dorsey's favorite individual award was the Lott Award because it recognized his combination of on-field performance and personal character. Dorsey, who followed Pollack and Alabama linebacker DeMeco Ryans as the third SEC player to win the Lott, passed up a shot to be a certain first-round NFL Draft pick to return for his senior season and a chance to win the national championship.

For all those individual awards, nothing measures a conference as accurately as its team success. Just winning in the SEC has never been more difficult than it has been in

SEC Championship Game Results, 2000–2007		
2000	Florida 28	Auburn 6
2001	LSU 31	Tennessee 20
2002	Georgia 30	Arkansas 3
2003	LSU 34	Georgia 13
2004	Auburn 38	Tennessee 28
2005	Georgia 34	LSU 14
2006	Florida 38	Arkansas 28
2007	LSU 21	Tennessee 14

With his explosive running style, Arkansas running back Darren McFadden ended his three-year college career ranked second on the SEC's all-time rushing list with 4,950 yards. He twice finished second in the Heisman Trophy voting and won the Doak Walker Award as a junior before entering the NFL Draft. He was selected by the Oakland Raiders with the fourth overall pick in the 2008 draft.

the past decade. Six different schools have played in the SEC Championship Game, and four different schools have won the title game. Eleven of the conference's 12 teams have played in bowl games and the 12th (Vanderbilt) has come up just one win short of bowl eligibility twice while pulling off historic upsets over Tennessee and Georgia. Kentucky has earned three straight bowl games for the first time since 1949–1951, when Bear Bryant coached the Wildcats.

LSU defensive tackle Glenn Dorsey decided to return for his senior season in 2007, and it all paid off when the Tigers won the national championship. Dorsey also swept every possible award for a defensive lineman, winning the Nagurski, Lombardi, Outland, Bednarik, and Lott Awards. Dorsey was the fifth overall selection in the 2008 NFL Draft, and the second SEC player taken with a top-five pick.

When LSU won the 2007 national title by beating Ohio State 38-24 in the Louisiana Superdome on January 7, 2008, it marked the SEC's fourth national championship in the first 10 years of the BCS. The SEC also became the first conference to win back-to-back BCS titles. No other conference claims more than two national titles in that span.

The SEC won two BCS bowl games each in 2006 and 2007 and set a national record with seven bowl wins in the 2007 postseason, breaking its own record of six set during the 2006 postseason. The SEC entered the 2008 season with 184 bowl wins, best among all Division I-A conferences.

The list of SEC accomplishments in this decade is both long and impressive. Since 2000, the SEC has had more teams ranked in the final *USA Today* Coaches Poll than any other conference, with 39 overall (the Big 12 is second with 31). The SEC has also earned the nation's top non-conference winning percentage (including bowl games) since 2000, at .737 (294-105).

The 2007 season also saw the SEC lead the nation in attendance for the 27th straight season, with a total of 6,687,342 fans attending 89 games, an average of 75,139 per game. Six SEC schools finished among the nation's top 10 in attendance, with Tennessee fourth, Auburn fifth, Georgia sixth, LSU seventh, Alabama eighth, and Florida ninth.

Following the 2006–2007 academic year, the SEC distributed approximately $122 million to its members, the highest total in conference history. In a 2008 *Birmingham News* story, Kramer reflected on a time when, as the athletic director at Vanderbilt, receiving $200,000 from the SEC in the late 1970s was a big deal. "Today, schools would think it's pocket change," Kramer said.

More important than they money itself, every dollar is a reflection of the SEC's immense popularity among its passionate and devoted fan base. The revenue is a result of every ticket sold, every televised game, and every postseason game, as well as every cap, T-shirt, and car tag bearing the name of an SEC team.

"You have to be a little amazed at it all," Kramer said.

The Southeastern Conference is home to the nation's most passionate and devoted fans, such as these enthusiastic Auburn fans at Jordan-Hare Stadium. In 2007, the SEC led the nation in attendance for the 27th consecutive season. A total of 6,687,342 fans attended 89 SEC games in 2007, for an average of 75,139 per game.

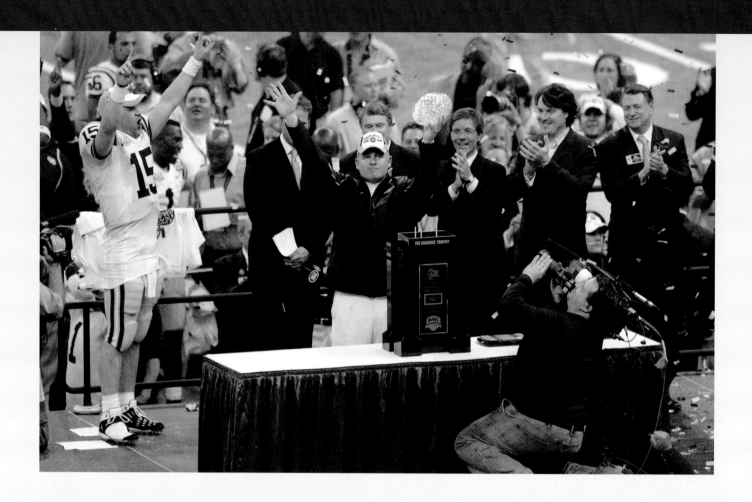

Above: Coach Les Miles and his LSU Tigers celebrate their national championship on January 7, 2008, following a 38-24 victory over Ohio State in the BCS National Championship Game. The national title was the second in five years for LSU.

Left: Michael L. Slive was hired to be the seventh person to head the SEC when Roy Kramer retired after 12 years as the conference commissioner. Slive has taken a leadership role in the conference's renewed commitment to academics, scholarship, and competitive integrity.

Opposite: Defensive tackle Chad Lavalais, wide receiver Michael Clayton, and Coach Nick Saban (left to right) celebrate LSU's 21-14 victory over Oklahoma in the 2004 Sugar Bowl. The win secured the first national championship for the Tigers since 1958.

The Hits Keep Coming

When LSU fell behind 10-0 against top-ranked Ohio State in the 2008 BCS Championship Game at the Louisiana Superdome, it may have appeared that Ohio State had everything under control.

Everyone who watched LSU play through adversity all season, including three previous 10-point deficits, knew the Tigers had the Buckeyes right where they wanted them.

"We had to keep playing," LSU quarterback Matt Flynn said. "We knew they were going to come out with a big surge. We knew we just had to stay in there and keep playing our game."

When LSU went on to win 38-24 for its second national championship in five years, it provided just another example of the perseverance and faith that have been so vital to the SEC's success in this decade. From LSU's national championship teams in 2003 and 2007, to Florida's 2006 BCS title game winners, to Auburn's undefeated 2004 squad, all four teams possessed a special quality that went beyond talent and coaching.

In 2003, LSU and coach Nick Saban opened the season ranked 15th in the preseason polls and spent the season taking one step at a time toward the top. Along the way, the Tigers needed a 34-yard touchdown pass from Matt Mauck to Skyler Green to beat Georgia 17-10 and had to overcome a 19-7 home loss to Florida to reach the SEC Championship Game. LSU entered the game stuck in

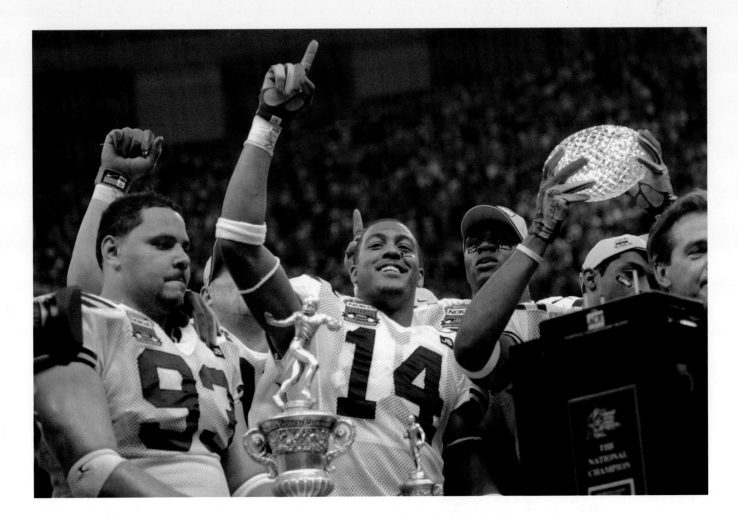

LSU quarterback Matt Flynn signals for a touchdown after Jacob Hester's 1-yard scoring run during the Tigers' 38-24 victory over Ohio State in the 2008 BCS National Championship Game. Flynn and Hester were two of eleven senior starters who played a key role for the national-champion Tigers.

third place in the BCS behind USC and Oklahoma, but the Tigers beat Georgia 34-13 in the conference title game while Oklahoma lost to Kansas State in the Big 12 championship game. The Oklahoma loss gave LSU a shot at the national championship against Oklahoma in the BCS National Championship game at the Superdome in New Orleans.

When LSU beat Oklahoma 21-14 in the championship game, it won the BCS share of the national championship, while USC finished No. 1 in the final AP poll.

"All I know is the powers that be selected us to be in this game," Mauck said. "We just received the trophy."

Auburn faced its own BCS controversy the next season and experienced a rare situation in which playing in the SEC wasn't enough for a shot at the national title.

Auburn's pursuit of a championship in 2004 actually started late in the 2003 season, when coach Tommy Tuberville nearly lost his job. Instead, Auburn finished with a win over rival Alabama and the media exposed a trip by Auburn officials to meet with Louisville coach Bobby Petrino before the Alabama game. Fans sided with Tuberville, the players rallied around him, and star running backs Carnell Williams and Ronnie Brown returned for their senior seasons.

The Tigers opened the season ranked 17th and faced some stiff challenges during the season. They needed two dramatic pass completions on fourth and 12 and on third and 16 from Jason Campbell to Courtney Taylor late in a 10-9 win over LSU. Week by week, Auburn inched closer to the top of the national polls on their way to a 13-0 finish. Unfortunately for the Tigers, USC and Oklahoma also remained undefeated and played for the national championship, with USC winning and the Tigers on the outside looking in.

"We're national champions in our hearts, even if no one else thinks so," Campbell said. "No one can take that away from us."

In 2006, Florida faced the nation's toughest schedule, with five games against ranked SEC teams. The Gators lost 27-17 to Auburn but came through with dramatic wins against Tennessee (21-20), Georgia (21-14), and South Carolina (17-16) on their way to the SEC Championship Game.

Despite their success in close games against quality opponents, the Gators trailed No. 1 Ohio State, No. 2 Michigan and No. 3 USC late in the season, even after Ohio State defeated Michigan on November 18. Over the next three weeks, UCLA knocked off USC and Florida made its case with the 21-14 win over Florida State and a 38-28 win over Arkansas in the SEC Championship Game. When the smoke cleared and the final BCS rankings came out, Florida had earned a shot at Ohio State in the BCS National Championship Game in Glendale, Arizona.

Florida addressed any criticism and doubts with its play on the field, dominating Ohio State for a 41-14 victory that left all the questions answered.

Auburn quarterback Jason Campbell prepares to pass against LSU in September 2004. Campbell led the Tigers on a game-winning drive, concluding with the go-ahead touchdown on a third-and-12 completion with 1:14 left in the game. Auburn's 10-9 win was the third victory in what would be a perfect, if ultimately disappointing, 13-0 season.

Florida wide receiver Dallas Baker, No. 81, distracts Coach Urban Meyer as his teammates prepare to dump a cooler of ice on the coach at the conclusion of the 2007 BCS National Championship Game. The Gators beat Ohio State 41-14 to win their second national championship.

Coach Les Miles holds up the national championship trophy following the victory over Ohio State in the 2008 BCS National Championship Game. Miles was the fourth different SEC coach to hoist the crystal trophy since the institution of the BCS in 1998.

"We became a better team every game as the season went on," Florida cornerback Ryan Smith said. "In the last game of the season, the national championship, we played our best game."

"Honestly, we've played a lot better teams than them," Florida defensive end Jarvis Moss added. "I could name four or five teams in the SEC that could probably compete with them and play the same type of game we did against them."

LSU's rugged SEC schedule played a big part in its journey to the national championship in 2007. The Tigers, in their third season under coach Les Miles, overcame a number of obstacles throughout one of the wildest seasons in the college football history.

The Tigers were ranked No. 1 on October 6 when Miles gambled on five fourth-down plays against No. 9 Florida. The Tigers converted all five attempts for a 28-24 comeback win. One week later at No. 17 Kentucky, LSU failed to convert on fourth-and-two in the third overtime of a 43-37 loss that dropped the Tigers to fifth in the polls. On October 20 against No. 18 Auburn, the Tigers passed up a field goal attempt for the win and instead scored on a 22-yard touchdown pass from Matt Flynn to Demetrius Byrd with one second left to take a 30-24 victory.

On November 3 against an Alabama team now coached by Saban, the Tigers took the game deep into the fourth quarter before scoring the winning touchdown with one minute and 26 seconds left in a 41-34 victory. Just when it appeared LSU was in good shape for a shot at the national title, it lost 50-48 in three overtimes to Arkansas the day after Thanksgiving and appeared to be out of the race.

Instead, the Tigers overcame constant speculation about Miles leaving for Michigan, his alma mater, and an injury that sidelined starting quarterback Matt Flynn, and they beat Tennessee 21-14 in the SEC Championship Game. On the same day, Oklahoma beat No. 1 Missouri in the Big 12 title game and 4-7 Pittsburgh stunned No. 2 West Virginia. LSU jumped No. 6 Virginia Tech, No. 5 Kansas, and No. 4 Georgia in the BCS standings on its way to a spot in the National Championship Game against Ohio State.

Just as Florida had done the year before, the Tigers put all the controversy to rest by beating Ohio State and becoming the first team with two losses to win the BCS national title.

"We're a team of fight, a team of destiny," LSU defensive end Kirston Pittman said. "People said we didn't belong. We belong. Look who's holding up the crystal trophy."

Coach Superior

Ever since Steve Spurrier returned to the SEC on December 31, 1989, as the head coach at Florida, the rest of the conference has had a love-hate relationship with him.

Florida fans love him. He made good on the potential of a program that had long fallen short of its promise, turning the Gators into a national power by winning a national championship in 1996 and winning six SEC championships from 1991 to 2000.

South Carolina fans love him because in 2004 he accepted the challenge to make the Gamecocks a true contender in the SEC East. While the Gamecocks have yet to win an East title, the program is closer than it's ever been before.

Fans of the passing game admire him because he entered a conference in which teams always had emphasized defense, the running game, and special teams, and Spurrier showed a different, more exciting way to win championships by spreading the field with multiple receivers and passing the ball frequently and effectively with his fun 'n' gun offense.

Those who don't like him tend to be fans of teams that have lost so many games to his teams over the past two decades. They don't like what they perceive to be his arrogance and his tendency to say whatever's on his mind. Spurrier once referred to Florida State as "Free Shoes University" after FSU players were suspended for receiving free shoes in violation of NCAA rules. He also reminded frustrated Tennessee fans, "You can't spell Citrus Bowl without UT."

"I don't really think I say all that much," Spurrier said in response to criticism. "It just gets interpreted stronger because no other coaches say anything."

Even FSU coach Bobby Bowden admitted, "He says things a lot of us think but don't have enough guts to say."

Of course, most of those same fans who call him "Coach Superior," "the Evil Genius," or "Darth Visor" would feel a whole lot different if Spurrier were coaching their team to a championship.

"Teams are not supposed to like their opponents if the opponents are beating them," Spurrier once told *Sports Illustrated*. "And I am a little different. I read something once

When Steve Spurrier took over at Florida, he instituted a pass-oriented offense that changed the way football is played in the SEC. The Gators won six SEC titles under Spurrier. Here he is being carried off the field following Florida's victory over Auburn in the 2000 SEC Championship Game.

that I think is so true: If you want to be successful, you have to do it the way everybody else does it and do it a lot better—or you have to do it differently.

"I can't outwork anybody and I can't coach the off-tackle play better than anybody else. So I figured I'd try to coach some different ball plays and instead of poor-mouthing my team I'd try to build it up to the point where the players think 'Coach believes we're pretty good; by golly, let's go prove it.'"

Spurrier rarely lacked confidence as a high school athlete in Tennessee, as a Heisman Trophy–winning quarterback at Florida in 1966, as a struggling NFL quarterback—even when he started for an 0-14 Tampa Bay Bucs team in 1976—or when he was let go by two different head coaches in the late 1970s. Every time someone believed he wasn't good enough, Spurrier vowed to prove him wrong by beating him. He did that as the head coach at Duke from 1987 to 1989, leading the Blue Devils to rare success. And he did it time

Above: Steve Spurrier's arrival at South Carolina spurred an already devoted fan base and brought the promise of more success in the rugged SEC Eastern Division.

Below: After leaving Florida for an unsuccessful two-year stint with the Washington Redskins of the NFL, Spurrier was happy to be back in the college game. He led South Carolina to winning records in the conference and overall in 2005, his first season with the team, and to a 44-36 win in the 2006 Liberty Bowl against the University of Houston.

and time again in the 1990s, establishing himself as the SEC's most successful coach since Bear Bryant and becoming the first Heisman winner to coach a Heisman winner when quarterback Danny Wuerffel won the award in 1996.

Even legends have their tough times. The Gators went 10-2 in 2001 but became the target of criticism when they didn't win the SEC. At that point Spurrier realized nothing short of a national championship would ever do, so he resigned and became the coach of the Washington Redskins. Two 7-9 seasons led to his resignation and more criticism, but Spurrier wasn't done with football.

The challenge at South Carolina hasn't been easy, but it has reignited his fire to win and do something critics insist can't be done: surpass SEC East powers Florida, Georgia, and Tennessee to win a division title.

"We're still trying to make it better. We haven't done it yet," Spurrier said.

Maroon Is All That Matters

Born the son of a minister and a school teacher in Tuscaloosa, Alabama, in 1954, Sylvester Croom learned to be one of those people who didn't focus on the obstacles but instead learned how to overcome them and move forward.

Croom didn't let anything stand in his way when he became one of the first African-American athletes to play for Alabama and coach Bear Bryant. He didn't let anything stop him from earning a varsity letter as a freshman, even as he moved around from linebacker to tight end and tackle. He didn't let anything prevent him from becoming the starting center as a junior, a team captain as a senior, or earning All-America honors while playing for three straight SEC championship teams and a national championship team in 1973. Nothing was going to keep him from earning a bachelor's degree in history with a minor in biology by the time he was 20 years old.

"In my career, I've been around a lot of great leaders," said Ozzie Newsome, who was Croom's teammate at Alabama and who went to become a Hall of Fame tight end and general manager of the Baltimore Ravens. "And he led that huddle, trust me. He was impressive at a lot of things, but mostly as a leader."

Anyone who knows Croom wasn't surprised when he became the first African-American head coach in the Southeastern Conference. They may have been surprised it took an SEC school so long to see all Croom had to offer, but they also knew Croom was the right one to break that barrier when Mississippi State hired him on December 1, 2003.

"I talked to people I knew in the business, and Sylvester's name came up again and again, so I went to Green Bay to interview him," Mississippi State athletic director Larry Templeton said. "Afterward, I called the president and told him the search was over."

Sylvester Croom's background as the son of a minister and a teacher and as a player and assistant coach for Bear Bryant at Alabama helped prepare him to become the SEC's first African-American head football coach.

After Mississippi State finished 8-5 in 2007, including wins over Auburn, Kentucky, and Alabama, and then defeated Central Florida in the Liberty Bowl Croom was honored as the SEC Coach of the Year.

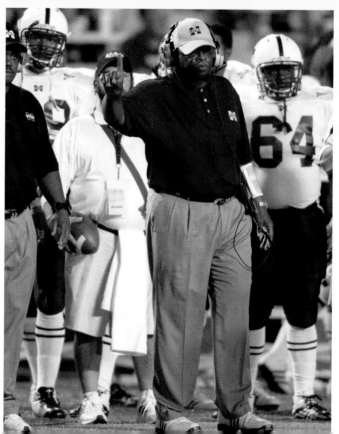

The Mississippi State Bulldogs celebrate a 10-3 victory over Central Florida in the 2007 Liberty Bowl. It was Mississippi State's first bowl trip since 2000 and just the seventh bowl win in school history.

It was an opportunity Croom had been preparing for as soon as he became a graduate assistant under Bryant in 1976. Through stints as a full-time assistant under Bryant and his successor, Ray Perkins, as well as the 16 years he spent as an NFL assistant, Croom had readied himself for the chance to prove himself as a head coach. One year after Alabama passed him over to hire Mike Shula, Croom already had a detailed plan in place when Templeton came calling.

"He whips out a piece of paper from his pocket and showed it to me," Templeton said. "He had his whole staff put together—the staff he brought with him to Starkville."

Croom accepted the job with only one condition. He wasn't coming to Mississippi State to make history or make anyone look good. He was coming to build a winning football program and do it the right way. When he took the job, Croom said, "I am the first African-American coach in the SEC but there ain't but one color that matters here, and that color is maroon."

"I've said all along, it's not about me," Croom later added. "I understand the historical significance of my hiring. The game is about the players. I didn't get into this to break any kind of barrier or make some kind of history."

Doing it the right way wasn't easy. Croom took over a program hurt by NCAA probation and scholarship reductions. He lost many of the players he inherited because they weren't willing to pay the price on and off the field. His first three teams won only three games each. One morning after a painful loss, he woke to find a "for sale" sign in his front yard. While many fans wondered if Croom could do the job, his players were convinced he was the right man for the job.

"Anybody who criticizes him, I don't have much for 'em," said offensive lineman Brian Anderson, a senior on the 2006 team. "I'm behind him 100 percent. If every man was as good a guy as he is, as good a person and as good a man, we wouldn't have as much stuff going on in the world today. If anybody needs a role model, he's it. I'm sorry he has to take all the heat and stuff for the losses."

In 2007, all of Croom's hard work, patience, and commitment started to show on the field when the hard-nosed and resilient Bulldogs won at Auburn and Kentucky and beat Alabama for the second straight year on the way to an 8-5 finish and a Liberty Bowl victory.

"I made it very clear when I took this job that I was not in it for the quick fix," said Croom, who won SEC Coach of the Year honors. "I said I wanted to build a championship program that would stand the test of time. I knew this day was gonna come if [people] gave me the time."

Eli Makes His Own Way

When you're the youngest son of Ole Miss legend Archie Manning and the younger brother of current NFL star Peyton Manning, it's not easy being your own man. Somehow, Eli Manning has been able to set himself apart without straying from his roots.

"Peyton's the guardian type. Eli, to everybody who has known the Mannings, he's been everybody's little brother," said Duke coach David Cutcliffe, Peyton's quarterback coach at Tennessee and Eli's head coach at Ole Miss. "I hear criticism from people who say he doesn't show emotion or he's not intense. He's intense, he just has a gift of never getting too high or never getting too low, which has equipped him extremely well for not only having a big brother but a father precede him that were so famous."

From his youth growing up in New Orleans, Eli Manning was well aware that his father was the quarterback of the hometown Saints and immensely popular at Ole Miss.

Manning often lived in the shadows of his gregarious oldest brother, Cooper, and his driven older brother, Peyton, who would pin Eli down and beat on him until he could name all the teams in the SEC. With Archie, Cooper, and Peyton always on the move, Eli learned many valuable life lessons from his mother, Olivia.

His older brother Peyton decided to play his college football at Tennessee, but Eli Manning opted to follow in the footsteps of his famous father, Archie, and went to play for the Rebels of Ole Miss. Eli quickly established his own legacy by setting several school passing records.

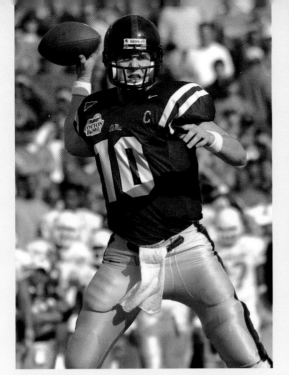
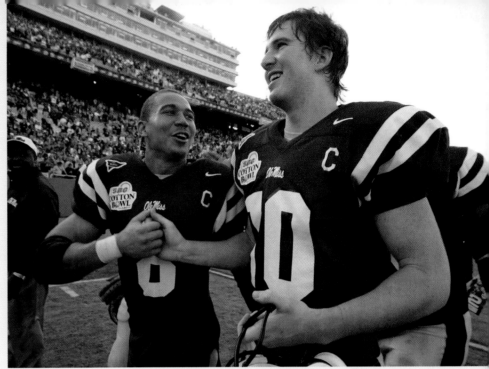

Above left: As a senior in 2003, quarterback Eli Manning helped lead Ole Miss to a 10-3 record, a share of the SEC Western Division title, and a Cotton Bowl victory. He also won the Maxwell and Johnny Unitas Golden Arm Awards.

Above right: Manning celebrates with receiver Chris Collins following the Rebels' 31-28 victory over Oklahoma State in the 2004 Cotton Bowl. Less than five months later, Manning was selected number one overall in the 2004 NFL Draft.

"She can take a crisis and get it right back to normal because she's very levelheaded," Archie said. "She doesn't holler and scream. She just handles it. It's a great trait. I'm grateful Eli picked up on it."

That cool, calm demeanor allowed Eli Manning to follow in his father's footsteps at Ole Miss without feeling the sort of weighty pressure that could crush many quarterbacks. Even though Manning was seen as the immediate answer at Ole Miss, Cutcliffe took his time with his new quarterback, redshirting him as a freshman and not playing him much in his first season—until the Music City Bowl, when Manning came off the bench to complete 12 of 20 passes for 167 yards and three touchdowns.

Manning spent the rest of his Ole Miss career setting or tying 45 single-game, season, and career records with 10,119 career passing yards and 81 touchdown passes. He led the 2003 Rebels to their best season since 1971 with a 10-3 record and a 31-28 Cotton Bowl victory over Oklahoma State. Along the way, Manning also received his share of honors, including the Maxwell and Johnny Unitas Golden Arm Awards and the National Football Foundation and College Hall of Fame Scholar Athlete Award.

After becoming the second Manning to be selected first overall in the NFL Draft, Manning endured his share of struggles with the New York Giants but handled them with his usual unflappable demeanor.

"Eli is laid back. He's not going to be rattled," Cutcliffe said. "He's had continuous criticism since he's been in New York, and he never let it affect him. He's well equipped for the hype in that town."

Those same qualities helped Manning lead the Giants through a rough start in 2007, all the way through the playoffs, and to the Super Bowl, where he earned MVP honors after the Giants upset the previously undefeated New England Patriots, 17-14. One year after Peyton led the Indianapolis Colts to a Super Bowl victory, Archie's youngest son and Peyton's little brother made his own statement.

The relationship shared by the brothers was evident in the postgame locker room when Peyton embraced and congratulated his brother and they spent the next two minutes talking—what else—football before Peyton finally said, "I love you, man, I love you, very much" as they hugged again.

"He said I'm past the point where he can give me advice anymore," Eli said of Peyton. "He wants it the other way now. I don't know if I agree with him, but it's great to hear it from him."

Raising the Standard

In his four years at Vanderbilt, Jay Cutler took a tough job and made it better. His success led to one of the best jobs in pro football.

As the Commodores' starting quarterback from 2002 to 2005, Cutler completed his college career as Vanderbilt's all-time passing leader. More importantly, Cutler did his part to make the Commodores a competitive threat in the SEC.

"Jay was a big part of setting a standard here," said linebacker Jonathon Goff, a sophomore in Cutler's senior season at Vandy. "People notice Vanderbilt football now because of him."

When Cutler came to Vanderbilt from Santa Claus, Indiana, the Commodores had finished 2-9 overall and 0-8 in the SEC the previous season. Cutler started as a true freshman for new coach Bobby Johnson and took his share of beatings as Vandy finished with just two wins in each of his first seasons.

Cutler earned the respect of his teammates for taking those hits and bouncing back without complaint. He also became a leader, often letting as many as nine players live with him in the summer just so more Commodores could work together in the offseason. He even passed up a chance to enter the NFL Draft after his junior season, saying, "There is some stuff that I still want to get done here. Obviously I'd like to win more games."

When SEC coaches selected Cutler to the preseason all-SEC first-team before his senior season, it was easy for critics to wonder if the coaches were just throwing Cutler and the Commodores a bone. SEC players and coaches knew better.

"Their quarterback is a really good football player—hands down he's the best football player I've ever faced," Florida defensive end Jarvis Moss said.

"He's a real special player," Tennessee coach Phillip Fulmer said. "I've said for a couple of years Jay Cutler is the best quarterback in the league."

Fulmer's team found out just how good Cutler could be when he led the Commodores to a 28-24 victory over Tennessee in Cutler's last game at Vanderbilt. It was Vandy's first win over the Vols since 1982 and its first at Neyland Stadium since 1975.

Even when Vanderbilt was outmatched by better SEC teams, Jay Cutler's skills and fierce competitive nature often gave the Commodores a chance. As a senior in 2005, he led Vandy to its first win over Tennessee since 1982—the year Cutler was born.

"You see grown men crying and you realize how long it's been since we've won," Cutler said. "It tells us how much [this victory] means to this program."

Even though the Commodores missed out on a bowl with a 5-6 record, Cutler had done his part to move the program forward.

"He helped us recruit when he was here—and he still helps us recruit," Johnson said. "He proved that if you want to get to the NFL, you can do it from Vanderbilt."

NFL teams looked past Vandy's won-loss record and focused on Cutler's combination of arm strength, toughness, and intelligence. Cutler became Vandy's third-ever first-round NFL draft choice when the Denver Broncos picked him 11th overall in 2006. He became the Broncos' starting quarterback late in his rookie season and finished as the NFL's 12th-ranked passer.

Jay Cutler came to Vanderbilt for the chance to play right away and put the Commodores on the right path. He accomplished both in the course of his four-year career. Cutler started all 45 games at quarterback for the Commodores from 2002 to 2005 and, in his final year, took Vandy to the brink of its first winning season since 1982.

Quarterback of the Future

When Florida coach Urban Meyer started recruiting quarterback Tim Tebow, he sent Tebow a text message that read "National Championships and Heismans are waiting for u here."

No one who knows Tebow was shocked when Tebow accomplished those goals during his college career. The surprise was that he had achieved both in his first two seasons at Florida.

As a freshman in 2006, Tebow played a critical role as a part-time situational quarterback on Florida's national championship team. As a sophomore in 2007, he took over as the full-time starter and became the first sophomore to win the Heisman Trophy.

Legendary Florida State coach Bobby Bowden acclaimed Tebow as "the quarterback of the future" and added, "I can't believe how good he is as a sophomore. The guy has broken all kinds of records."

The quarterback of the future has established an impressive standard in the present as a 6-foot, 3-inch, 235-pound quarterback willing and able to run over and through defenders while still making play after play as a passer.

"The kid is unbelievable," sophomore wide receiver David Nelson told the *Gainesville Sun* during the 2007 season. "He's the toughest person I've ever met in my life, physically and mentally. I'm 100 percent confident in him. If it's fourth-and-six and we run a quarterback sneak, I know he'll carry seven guys on his back to get the six yards. Whatever it takes, I'm confident he'll get it done."

In addition to being the first sophomore to win the Heisman, Tebow is also the first to be born in the Philippines. The son of missionaries Bob and Pam Tebow, he survived his first battle before he was born, when his mother had to fight off an infection and recommendations from doctors that her baby should be aborted to protect her health.

When the Tebow family returned to Florida, their youngest son grew up working the family's farm with his four siblings. Tebow is also the first Heisman winner to be home-schooled. Florida state law allowed him to compete in high school sports, and he became a star at Nease High School in Ponte Vedra Beach, Florida.

Quarterback Tim Tebow confers with Coach Urban Meyer during the 2008 Capital One Bowl in Orlando. Florida lost to Michigan in the game, but Tebow continued to assert his place among the elite quarterbacks in college football.

Tebow received scholarship offers from a long list of schools but chose Florida, where his parents both attended. His combination of talent, toughness, and maturity allowed him to play as a true freshman and Tebow often alternated with senior starter Chris Leak, especially on short-yardage and goal-line situations.

After the Gators won their national title and Leak completed his career, Tebow faced questions about his ability to lead the Gators as a full-time quarterback. On a young team dominated by sophomores and freshman, Tebow answered by leading the nation's third-ranked offense to 42.5 points and 457.2 yards per game. He completed 66.9 percent of his passes for 3,286 yards and 32 touchdowns with only six interceptions. He also led Florida in rushing with 895 yards on the ground, set an NCAA single-season record for running touchdowns by a quarterback with 23 scores and became the first player in major college history to produce 20 rushing touchdowns and 20 passing touchdowns in the same season.

In addition to winning the Heisman, Tebow won the Davey O'Brien and Maxwell awards as well as first-team AP All-America and SEC Offensive Player of the Year honors. He also became an ESPN.com Academic All-American first-team selection and a member of the SEC Football Community Service Team.

After achieving so much so soon, one of Tebow's biggest challenges will be handling all the pressure and expectations that come with success and notoriety. Some of the best advice he could ever receive came from former Florida quarterback Danny Wuerffel, the son of a preacher and the 1996 Heisman Trophy winner.

"Plain and simple, you don't change," Tebow said, paraphrasing Wuerffel's message. "You are the same person. You go about everything the exact same. You work as hard as you can. You do everything you did before you won it. Maybe other people's perception is different about you, but your perception about you and how you do things isn't different at all."

Above: As a freshman in 2006, Tebow was effective as a part-time quarterback on Florida's national championship team. He took over as the full-time starter a year later and earned numerous honors as a sophomore, including the Maxwell Award and the Heisman Trophy.

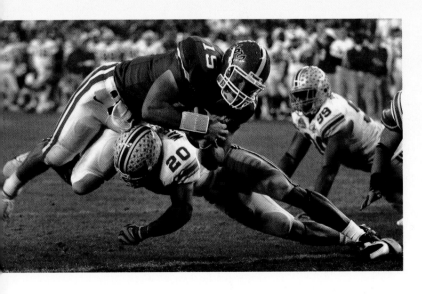

Left: Tebow is just as effective running with the ball as he is passing it, as Ohio State defenders learned on this touchdown run in the fourth quarter of the 2007 BCS National Championship Game. The score provided the final points in Florida's 41-14 victory. Tebow also chipped in with a one-yard touchdown pass to Andre Caldwell in the second quarter.

APPENDIX

The SEC Record Book

Southeastern Conference National Championship Teams

(officially recognized by the SEC)

1951	Tennessee (AP, UPI)
1957	Auburn (AP)
1958	LSU (AP, UPI)
1960	Ole Miss (FWAA)
1961	Alabama (AP, UPI)
1964	Alabama (AP, UPI)
1965	Alabama (AP, FWAA)
1973	Alabama (UPI)
1978	Alabama (AP, FWAA)
1979	Alabama (AP, UPI, FWAA)
1980	Georgia (AP, UPI, FWAA)
1992	Alabama (AP, USA Today/CNN, FWAA)
1996	Florida (AP, USA Today/CNN, FWAA)
1998	Tennessee (AP, BCS, FWAA, FWAA)
2003	LSU (BCS)
2006	Florida (AP, BCS)
2007	LSU (AP, BCS)

FWAA = Football Writers Association of America

SEC Players and Coaches in the College Football Hall Of Fame

PLAYERS

ALABAMA

A. T. S. "Pooley" Hubert	halfback	1922–1925
Johnny Mack Brown	halfback	1923–1925
Fred Sington	tackle	1928–1930
Johnny Cain	fullback	1930–1932
Don Hutson	end	1932–1934
Millard "Dixie" Howell	tailback	1932–1934
Riley Smith	quarterback	1933–1935
Don Whitmire	tackle	1941–1944
Harry Gilmer	halfback	1944–1947
Vaughn Mancha	center	1944–1947
Billy Neighbors	tackle	1959–1961
Lee Roy Jordan	center	1960–1962
Johnny Musso	halfback	1969–1971
John Hannah	guard	1970–1972
Ozzie Newsome	end	1974–1977
Cornelius Bennett	linebacker	1983–1986

ARKANSAS

Wear K. Schoonover	end	1927–1929
Clyde Scott	halfback	1944–1948
Wayne Harris	guard/linebacker	1958–1960
Lance Alworth	halfback	1959–1961
Loyd Phillips	offensive lineman	1964–1966
Chuck Dicus	end	1968–1970
Billy Ray Smith	defensive end	1979–1982

AUBURN

Jimmy Hitchcock	halfback	1930–1932
Walter Gilbert	center	1934–1936
Tucker Frederickson	back	1962–1964
Pat Sullivan	quarterback	1969–1971
Terry Beasley	wide receiver	1969–1971
Bo Jackson	running back	1982–1985
Tracy Rocker	defensive tackle	1985–1988

FLORIDA

Dale Van Sickel	end	1927–1929
Steve Spurrier	quarterback	1964–1966
Jack Youngblood	defensive lineman	1968–1970
Emmitt Smith	running back	1987–1989

GEORGIA

Robert McWhorter	halfback	1910–1913
Vernon "Catfish" Smith	end	1929–1931
Bill Hartman	fullback	1935–1937
Frank Sinkwich	halfback	1940–1942
Charles Trippi	halfback	1942, 1945–1946
John Rauch	quarterback	1945–1948
Fran Tarkenton	quarterback	1958–1960
Bill Stanfill	defensive tackle	1966–1968
Herschel Walker	running back	1980–1982
Terry Hoage	defensive back	1980–1983
Kevin Butler	place kicker	1981–1984

KENTUCKY

Jerry Claiborne	defensive back/running back/end	1946, 1948–1949
Bob Gain	tackle	1947–1950
Vito "Babe" Parilli	quarterback	1949–1951
Lou Michaels	offensive lineman	1955–1957

LSU

G. E. "Doc" Fenton	quarterback	1904–1909
Abe Mickal	quarterback	1933–1935
Gaynell Tinsley	end	1934–1936
Ken Kavanaugh	end	1937–1939
Tommy Casanova	defensive back	1969–1971

OLE MISS

Frank "Bruiser" Kinard	tackle	1935–1937
Parker Hall	halfback	1936–1938
Doug Kenna	halfback	1941–1942
Charlie Conerly	tailback	1942, 1946–1947
Barney Poole	end	1942–1948
Charlie Flowers	fullback	1957–1959
Jake Gibbs	quarterback	1958–1960
Archie Manning	quarterback	1968–1970

MISSISSIPPI STATE

Jackie Parker	back	1952–1953
D. D. Lewis	linebacker	1965–1967

SOUTH CAROLINA

George Rogers	running back	1977–1980

TENNESSEE

Nate Dougherty	guard	1906–1909
Eugene McEver	halfback	1928–1929, 1931
Robert Lee Dodd	quarterback	1928–1930
Herman Hickman	guard	1929–1931
Beattie Feathers	halfback	1931–1933
Bowden Wyatt	end	1936–1938
George Cafego	halfback	1937–1939
Robert Suffridge	guard	1938–1940
Edward Molinski	guard	1938–1940
Hank Lauricella	halfback	1949–1951
Doug Atkins	end	1950–1952
John Michels	guard	1950–1952
Johnny Majors	back	1954–1956
Steve DeLong	guard	1962–1964
Frank Emanuel	linebacker	1963–1965
Bob Johnson	center	1965–1967
Steve Kiner	linebacker	1967–1969
Chip Kell	offensive guard	1968–1970
Reggie White	defensive tackle	1980–1983

VANDERBILT

John J. Tigert	fullback	1901–1903
Josh Cody	tackle	1914–1916, 1919
Lynn Bomar	end	1921–1924
William Spears	quarterback	1925–1927
Carl Hinkle	center	1935–1937

COACHES

NAME	ALMA MATER	SEC SCHOOL(S) COACHED
Bill Alexander	Georgia Tech	Georgia Tech (1920–1944)
Charles Bachman	Florida	Florida (1928–1932)
Dana X. Bible	Carson-Newman	LSU (1916)
Bernie Bierman	Minnesota	Mississippi State (1925–1926), Tulane (1927–1931)
Frank Broyles	Georgia Tech	Arkansas (1958–1976)
Paul "Bear" Bryant	Alabama	Kentucky (1946–53), Alabama (1958–1982)
Wally Butts	Mercer	Georgia (1939–1960)
Bobby Dodd	Tennessee	Georgia Tech (1945–1966)
Jerry Claiborne	Kentucky	Kentucky (1982–1989)
Doug Dickey	Florida	Tennessee (1964–1969), Florida (1970–1978)
Mike Donahue	Yale	Auburn (1904–1906; 1908–1922), LSU (1923–1927)
Vince Dooley	Auburn	Georgia (1964–1988)
Pat Dye	Georgia	Auburn (1981–1992)
Bill Edwards	Wittenberg	Vanderbilt (1949–1952)
Ray Graves	Tennessee	Florida (1960–1969)
John Heisman	Penn	Auburn (1895–1899), Georgia Tech (1904–1919)
L. M. "Biff" Jones	Army	LSU (1932–1934)
Ralph "Shug" Jordan	Auburn	Auburn (1951–1975)
Charlie McClendon	Kentucky	LSU (1962–1979)
Dan McGugin	Michigan	Vanderbilt (1904–1917; 1918–1934)
Allyn McKeen	Tennessee	Mississippi State (1939–1948)
Bernie Moore	Carson-Newman	LSU (1935–1947)
Ray Morrison	Vanderbilt	Vanderbilt (1936–1939)
Robert R. Neyland	Army	Tennessee (1926–1934; 1936–1940; 1946–1952)
Darrell Royal	Oklahoma	Mississippi State (1954–1955)
Henry "Red" Sanders	Vanderbilt	Vanderbilt (1940–1942; 1946–1948)
Clark Shaughnessy	Minnesota	Tulane (1915–1926)
Francis Schmidt	Nebraska	Arkansas (1922–1928)
Frank Thomas	Notre Dame	Alabama (1931–1946)
John Vaught	Texas Christian	Ole Miss (1947–1970; 1973)
Wallace Wade	Brown	Alabama (1923–1930)
G. S. "Pop" Warner	Cornell	Georgia (1895–1896)
Bowden Wyatt	Tennessee	Arkansas (1953–1954), Tennessee (1955–1962)

SEC Award Winners

HEISMAN TROPHY

1942	Frank Sinkwich, halfback	Georgia
1959	Billy Cannon, halfback	LSU
1966	Steve Spurrier, quarterback	Florida
1971	Pat Sullivan, wide receiver	Auburn
1982	Herschel Walker, running back	Georgia
1985	Bo Jackson, running back	Auburn
1996	Danny Wuerffel, quarterback	Florida
2007	Tim Tebow, quarterback	Florida

MAXWELL AWARD

1946	Charley Trippi, halfback	Georgia
1982	Herschel Walker, running back	Georgia
1996	Danny Wuerffel, quarterback	Florida
1997	Peyton Manning, quarterback	Tennessee
2003	Eli Manning, quarterback	Ole Miss
2007	Tim Tebow, quarterback	Florida

WALTER CAMP AWARD

1971	Pat Sullivan, quarterback	Auburn
1982	Herschel Walker, running back	Georgia
1985	Bo Jackson, running back	Auburn
1996	Danny Wuerrfel, quarterback	Florida
2007	Darren McFadden, running back	Arkansas

OUTLAND TROPHY

1950	Bob Gain, tackle	Kentucky
1958	Zeke Smith, guard	Auburn
1964	Steve DeLong, tackle	Tennessee
1968	Bill Stanfill, tackle	Georgia
1988	Tracy Rocker, defensive tackle	Auburn
1999	Chris Samuels, offensive tackle	Alabama
2000	John Henderson, defensive tackle	Tennessee
2007	Glenn Dorsey, defensive tackle	LSU

MANNING AWARD

2006	JaMarcus Russell	LSU

JIM THORPE AWARD

1993	Antonio Langham	Alabama
1996	Lawrence Wright	Florida
2004	Carlos Rogers	Auburn

FRED BILETNIKOFF AWARD

2001	Josh Reed	LSU

VINCE LOMBARDI/ROTARY AWARD

1986	Cornelius Bennett, linebacker	Alabama
1988	Tracy Rocker, defensive tackle	Auburn
2004	David Pollack, defensive end	Georgia
2007	Glenn Dorsey, defensive tackle	LSU

BUTKUS AWARD

1988	Derrick Thomas	Alabama
2006	Patrick Willis	Ole Miss

LOU GROZA AWARD

1993	Judd Davis	Florida
2003	Jonathan Nichols	Ole Miss

DAVEY O'BRIEN AWARD

1995	Danny Wuerffel	Florida
1996	Danny Wuerffel	Florida
1997	Peyton Manning	Tennessee
2007	Tim Tebow	Florida

BRONKO NAGURSKI AWARD

1998	Champ Bailey	Georgia
2007	Glenn Dorsey	LSU

JOHNNY UNITAS GOLDEN ARM AWARD

1994	Jay Barker	Alabama
1996	Danny Wuerffel	Florida
1997	Peyton Manning	Tennessee
2003	Eli Manning	Ole Miss

CHUCK BEDNARIK TROPHY

2004	David Pollack, defensive end	Georgia

MOSI TATUPU AWARD

2002	Glenn Pakulak	Kentucky

DOAK WALKER AWARD

1992	Garrison Hearst	Georgia
2006	Darren McFadden	Arkansas
2007	Darren McFadden	Arkansas

RIMINGTON AWARD

2004	Ben Wilkerson	LSU
2007	Jonathan Luigs	Arkansas

TED HENDRICKS AWARD

2004	David Pollack	Georgia

LOTT TROPHY

2004	David Pollack	Georgia
2005	DeMeco Ryans	Alabama
2007	Glenn Dorsey	LSU

WUERFFEL TROPHY

2004	David Pollack	Georgia

SEC MOST VALUABLE PLAYERS

Beginning in 2003, separate awards were given for offensive player of the year and defensive player of the year. In 2004, an award for special teams player of the year was added.

Year	Player	Team
1933	Beattie Feathers, halfback	Tennessee
1934	Dixie Howell, tailback	Alabama
1935	Willie Geny, end	Vanderbilt
1936	Walter Gilbert, center	Auburn
1937	Carl Hinkle, center	Vanderbilt
1938	George Cafego, halfback	Tennessee
1939	Ken Kavanaugh, end	LSU
1939	Bob Foxx, wingback	Tennessee
1940	Erwin Elrod, end	Miss. State
1941	Jack Jenkins, fullback	Vanderbilt
1942	Frank Sinkwich, tailback	Georgia
1943	no selection made	
1944	Tom McWilliams, halfback	Miss. State
1945	Harry Gilmer, tailback	Alabama
1946	Charley Trippi, halfback	Georgia
1947	Charlie Conerly, tailback	Ole Miss
1948	John Rauch, quarterback	Georgia
1949	Travis Tidwell, quarterback	Auburn
1950	Babe Parilli, quarterback	Kentucky
1951	Bill Wade, quarterback	Vanderbilt
1952	Jackie Parker, quarterback	Miss. State
1953	Jackie Parker, quarterback	Miss. State
1954	Art Davis, halfback	Miss. State
1955	John Majors, tailback	Tennessee
1956	John Majors, tailback	Tennessee
1957	Lou Michaels, tackle	Kentucky
1958	Billy Cannon, halfback	LSU
1959	Billy Cannon, halfback	LSU
1960	Jake Gibbs, quarterback	Ole Miss
1961	Pat Trammell, quarterback	Alabama
1962	Jerry Stovall, halfback	LSU
1963	Jimmy Sidle, quarterback	Auburn
1964	Tucker Frederickson, fullback	Auburn
1965	Steve Sloan, quarterback	Alabama
1966	Steve Spurrier, quarterback	Florida
1967	Bob Goodridge, end	Vanderbilt
1968	Jake Scott, safety	Georgia
1969	Archie Manning, quarterback	Ole Miss
1970	Pat Sullivan, quarterback	Auburn
1971	Johnny Musso, tailback	Alabama
1972	Terry Davis, quarterback	Alabama
1973	Sonny Collins, tailback	Kentucky
1974	Rockey Felker, quarterback	Miss. State
1975	Jimmy DuBose, fullback	Florida
1976	Ray Goff, quarterback	Georgia
1977	Charles Alexander, tailback	LSU
1978	Willie McClendon, tailback	Georgia
1979	Joe Cribbs, running back	Auburn
1980	Herschel Walker, running back	Georgia
1981	Herschel Walker, running back	Georgia
1982	Herschel Walker, running back	Georgia
1983	Reggie White, defensive tackle	Tennessee
1984	Kerwin Bell, quarterback	Florida
1985	Bo Jackson, running back	Auburn
1986	Cornelius Bennett, linebacker	Alabama
1987	Wendell Davis, wide receiver	LSU
1988	Tracy Rocker, defensive tackle	Auburn
1989	Emmitt Smith, running back	Florida
1990	Shane Matthews, quarterback	Florida
1991	Shane Matthews, quarterback	Florida
1992	Garrison Hearst, running back	Georgia
1993	Heath Shuler, quarterback	Tennessee
1994	Jay Barker, quarterback	Alabama
1995	Danny Wuerffel, quarterback	Florida
1996	Danny Wuerffel, quarterback	Florida
1997	Peyton Manning, quarterback	Tennessee
1998	Tim Couch, quarterback	Kentucky
1999	Shaun Alexander, running back	Alabama
2000	Rudi Johnson, running back	Auburn
2001	Rex Grossman, quarterback	Florida
2002	David Pollack, defensive end	Georgia
2003	Eli Manning, quarterback	Ole Miss
	Chad Lavalais, defensive tackle	LSU
2004	Jason Campbell, quarterback	Auburn
	David Pollack, defensive end	Georgia
	Carnell Williams, running back (special teams)	Auburn
2005	Jay Cutler, quarterback	Vanderbilt
	DeMeco Ryans, Linebacker	Alabama
	Skyler Green, return specialist	LSU
2006	Darren McFadden, running back	Arkansas
	Patrick Willis, linebacker	Ole Miss
	John Vaughn, place kicker	Auburn
2007	Darren McFadden, running back	Arkansas
	Glenn Dorsey, defensive tackle	LSU
	Felix Jones, running back (special teams)	Arkansas

NATIONAL COACH OF THE YEAR

Year	Coach	School	Award
1942	Bill Alexander	Georgia Tech	AFCA
1956	Bowden Wyatt	Tennessee	AFCA
1958	Paul Dietzel	LSU	AFCA, FWAA
1961	Paul "Bear" Bryant	Alabama	AFCA
1970	Charlie McClendon	LSU	AFCA
1971	Paul "Bear" Bryant	Alabama	AFCA
1973	Paul "Bear" Bryant	Alabama	AFCA
1980	Vince Dooley	Georgia	AFCA, FWAA, WC
1982	Jerry Stovall	LSU	WC
1992	Gene Stallings	Alabama	AFCA, FWAA, WC
1993	Terry Bowden	Auburn	AFCA, FWAA, WC
1998	Phillip Fulmer	Tennessee	FWAA
2003	Nick Saban	LSU	FWAA, AP
2004	Tommy Tuberville	Auburn	WC, AP

AFCA = American Football Coaches Association
FWAA = Football Writers Association of America
WC = Walter Camp

AP SEC COACH OF THE YEAR

Year	Coach	School
1946	Wally Butts	Georgia
1947	John Vaught	Ole Miss
1948	John Vaught	Ole Miss
1949	Gaynell Tinsley	LSU
1950	Paul "Bear" Bryant	Kentucky
1951	Bob Neyland	Tennessee
1952	Bobby Dodd	Georgia Tech
1953	Ralph "Shug" Jordan	Auburn
1954	John Vaught	Ole Miss
1955	John Vaught	Ole Miss
1956	Bowden Wyatt	Tennessee
1957	Ralph "Shug" Jordan	Auburn
1958	Paul Dietzel	LSU
1959	Paul "Bear" Bryant	Alabama
1960	John Vaught	Ole Miss
1961	Paul "Bear" Bryant	Alabama
1962	John Vaught	Ole Miss
1963	Paul Davis	Mississippi State
1964	Paul "Bear" Bryant	Alabama
1965	Paul "Bear" Bryant	Alabama
1966	Vince Dooley	Georgia
1967	Doug Dickey	Tennessee
1968	Vince Dooley	Georgia
1969	Charlie McClendon	LSU
1970	Charlie Shira	Mississippi State
1971	Paul "Bear" Bryant	Alabama
1972	Ralph "Shug" Jordan	Auburn
1973	Paul "Bear" Bryant	Alabama
1974	Steve Sloan	Vanderbilt
1975	Ken Cooper	Ole Miss
1976	Vince Dooley	Georgia
1977	Fran Curci	Kentucky
1978	Paul "Bear" Bryant	Alabama
1979	Paul "Bear" Bryant	Alabama
1980	Vince Dooley	Georgia
1981	Paul "Bear" Bryant	Alabama
1982	Jerry Stovall	LSU
1983	Billy Brewer	Ole Miss
	Jerry Claiborne	Kentucky
1984	Galen Hall	Florida
1985	Johnny Majors	Tennessee
1986	Bill Arnsparger	LSU
1987	Pat Dye	Auburn
1988	Pat Dye	Auburn
1989	Bill Curry	Alabama
1990	Steve Spurrier	Florida
1991	Gerry DiNardo	Vanderbilt
1992	Gene Stallings	Alabama
1993	Terry Bowden	Auburn
1994	Gene Stallings	Alabama
1995	Steve Spurrier	Florida
1996	Steve Spurrier	Florida
1997	Tommy Tuberville	Ole Miss
1998	Phillip Fulmer	Tennessee
1999	Mike DuBose	Alabama
2000	Lou Holtz	South Carolina
2001	Houston Nutt	Arkansas
2002	Mark Richt	Georgia
2003	David Cutcliffe	Ole Miss
	Nick Saban	LSU
2004	Tommy Tuberville	Auburn
2005	Steve Spurrier	South Carolina
2006	Houston Nutt	Arkansas
2007	Sylvester Croom	Mississippi State

SEC COACH OF THE YEAR

(voted by the SEC coaches)

Year	Coach	School
1935	Jack Meagher	Auburn
1936	Bob Neyland	Tennessee
1937	Ray Morrison	Vanderbilt
1938	Bob Neyland	Tennessee
1939	Bill Alexander	Georgia Tech
1940	Allyn McKeen	Mississippi State
1941	Red Sanders	Vanderbilt
1942	Wally Butts	Georgia
1943	No Selection Made	
1944	John Barnhill	Tennessee
1945	Frank Thomas	Alabama
1946	Wally Butts	Georgia
1947	John Vaught	Ole Miss
1948	Henry Frnka	Tulane
1949	Gaynell Tinsley	LSU
1950	Bob Neyland	Tennessee
1951	Bobby Dodd	Georgia Tech
1952	Harold Drew	Alabama
1953	Ralph "Shug" Jordan	Auburn
1954	Blanton Collier	Kentucky
1955	Art Guepe	Vanderbilt
1956	Bowden Wyatt	Tennessee
1957	Wade Walker	Mississippi State
1958	Paul Dietzel	LSU
1959	Wally Butts	Georgia
1960	Ray Graves	Florida
1961	Paul "Bear" Bryant	Alabama
1962	John Vaught	Ole Miss
1963	Ralph "Shug" Jordan	Auburn
1964	Paul "Bear" Bryant	Alabama
1965	Doug Dickey	Tennessee
1966	Vince Dooley	Georgia
1967	Doug Dickey	Tennessee
1968	Vince Dooley	Georgia
1969	Charlie McClendon	LSU
1970	Charlie McClendon	LSU
1971	Paul "Bear" Bryant	Alabama
1972	Ralph "Shug" Jordan	Auburn
1973	Paul "Bear" Bryant	Alabama
1974	Paul "Bear" Bryant	Alabama
1975	Ken Cooper	Ole Miss
1976	Vince Dooley	Georgia
1977	Paul "Bear" Bryant	Alabama
1978	Vince Dooley	Georgia
1979	Paul "Bear" Bryant	Alabama
1980	Vince Dooley	Georgia
1981	Paul "Bear" Bryant	Alabama
1982	George MacIntyre	Vanderbilt
1983	Pat Dye	Auburn
1984	Bill Arnsparger	LSU
1985	Johnny Majors	Tennessee
1986	Bill Arnsparger	LSU
1987	Pat Dye	Auburn
1988	Pat Dye	Auburn
1989	Bill Curry	Alabama
1990	Billy Brewer	Ole Miss
1991	Steve Spurrier	Florida
1992	Gene Stallings	Alabama
1993	Terry Bowden	Auburn
1994	Steve Spurrier	Florida
1995	Steve Spurrier	Florida
1996	Steve Spurrier	Florida
1997	Jim Donnan	Georgia
1998	Phillip Fulmer	Tennessee
1999	Mike DuBose	Alabama
2000	Lou Holtz	South Carolina
2001	Houston Nutt	Arkansas
2002	Mark Richt	Georgia
2003	David Cutcliffe	Ole Miss
2004	Tommy Tuberville	Auburn
2005	Mark Richt	Georgia
2006	Houston Nutt	Arkansas
2007	Sylvester Croom	Mississippi State

UPI SEC COACH OF THE YEAR

(discontinued following the 1990 season)

1960	John Vaught	Ole Miss
1961	Paul "Bear" Bryant	Alabama
1962	John Vaught	Ole Miss
1963	Ralph "Shug" Jordan	Auburn
1964	Paul "Bear" Bryant	Alabama
1965	Paul "Bear" Bryant	Alabama
1966	Vince Dooley	Georgia
1967	Doug Dickey	Tennessee
1968	Vince Dooley	Georgia
1969	Charlie McClendon	LSU
1970	Charlie McClendon	LSU
1971	Paul "Bear" Bryant	Alabama
1972	Ralph "Shug" Jordan	Auburn
1973	Paul "Bear" Bryant	Alabama
1974	Paul "Bear" Bryant	Alabama
1975	Ken Cooper	Ole Miss
1976	Vince Dooley	Georgia
1977	Paul "Bear" Bryant	Alabama
1978	Paul "Bear" Bryant	Alabama
1979	Paul "Bear" Bryant	Alabama
1980	Charley Pell	Florida
1981	Paul "Bear" Bryant	Alabama
1982	George MacIntyre	Vanderbilt
1983	Pat Dye	Auburn
1984	Galen Hall	Florida
1985	Johnny Majors	Tennessee
1986	Billy Brewer	Ole Miss
1987	Bill Curry	Alabama
1988	Pat Dye	Auburn
1989	Bill Curry	Alabama
1990	Steve Spurrier	Florida

SEC CHAMPIONSHIP COACHES

(including ties)

Paul "Bear" Bryant (14) — Kentucky 1950; Alabama 1961, 1964, 1965, 1966, 1971, 1972, 1973, 1974, 1975, 1977, 1978, 1979, 1981

Johnny Vaught (6) — Ole Miss 1947, 1954, 1955, 1960, 1962, 1963

Vince Dooley (6) — Georgia 1966, 1968, 1976, 1980, 1981, 1982

Steve Spurrier (6) — Florida 1991, 1993, 1994, 1995, 1996, 2000

Bob Neyland (5) — Tennessee 1938, 1939, 1940, 1946, 1951

Frank Thomas (4) — Alabama 1933, 1934, 1937, 1945

Wally Butts (4) — Georgia 1942, 1946, 1948, 1959

Pat Dye (4) — Auburn 1983, 1987, 1988, 1989

Bill Alexander (3) — Georgia Tech 1939, 1943, 1944

Johnny Majors (3) — Tennessee 1985, 1989, 1990

Bernie Moore (2) — LSU 1935, 1936

Paul Dietzel (2) — LSU 1958, 1961

Doug Dickey (2) — Tennessee 1967, 1969

Bobby Dodd (2) — Georgia Tech 1951, 1952

Phillip Fulmer (2) — Tennessee 1997, 1998

Nick Saban (2) — LSU 2001, 2003

Mark Richt (2) — Georgia 2002, 2005

Ted Cox (1) — Tulane 1934

Red Dawson (1) — Tulane 1939

Allyn McKeen (1) — Mississippi State 1941

Henry Frnka (1) — Tulane 1949

Red Drew (1) — Alabama 1953

Bowden Wyatt (1) — Tennessee 1956

Ralph "Shug" Jordan (1) — Auburn 1957

Charlie McClendon (1) — LSU 1970

Fran Curci (1) — Kentucky 1976

Bill Arnsparger (1) — LSU 1986

Mike Archer (1) — LSU 1988

Bill Curry (1) — Alabama 1989

Gene Stallings (1) — Alabama 1992

Mike DuBose (1) — Alabama 1999

Tommy Tuberville (1) — Auburn 2004

Urban Meyer (1) — Florida, 2006

Les Miles (1) — LSU, 2007

SEC Individual Career Statistical Leaders

(through 2007 season)

TOTAL OFFENSIVE YARDS GAINED

11,350 Chris Leak, Florida (137 rushing, 11,213 passing), 2003–2006

11,270 David Greene, Georgia (–258 rushing, 11,528 passing), 2001–2004

11,020 Peyton Manning, Tennessee (–181 rushing, 11,201 passing), 1994–1997

10,841 Eric Zeier, Georgia (–312 rushing, 11,153 passing), 1991–1994

10,637 Jared Lorenzen, Kentucky (279 rushing, 10,354 passing), 2000–2003

10,500 Danny Wuerffel, Florida (–375 rushing, 10,875 passing), 1993–1996

9,989 Eli Manning, Ole Miss (–130 rushing, 10,119 passing), 2000–2003

9,953 Jay Cutler, Vanderbilt (1,256 rushing, 8,697 passing), 2002–2005

9,577 Casey Clausen, Tennessee (–130 rushing, 9,707 passing), 2000–2003

9,241 Shane Matthews, Florida (–46 rushing, 9,287 passing), 1989–1992

TOUCHDOWN RESPONSIBILITY

122 Danny Wuerffel, Florida (8 rushing, 114 passing), 1993–1996

118 Eli Manning, Ole Miss (8 rushing, 110 passing), 2000–2003

101 Peyton Manning, Tennessee (12 rushing, 89 passing), 1994–1997

101 Chris Leak, Florida (13 rushing, 88 passing), 2003–2006

90 Jared Lorenzen, Kentucky (12 rushing, 78 passing), 2000–2003

83 Rex Grossman, Florida (6 rushing, 77 passing), 2000–2002

82 Shane Matthews, Florida (7 rushing, 74 passing, 1 receiving), 1989–1992

82 Andre' Woodson, Kentucky (3 rushing, 79 passing), 2004–2007

81 Casey Clausen, Tennessee (6 rushing, 75 passing), 2000–2003

78 Tim Couch, Kentucky (4 rushing, 74 passing), 1996–1998

RUSHING YARDS

5,259 Herschel Walker, Georgia (33 games), 1980–1982

4,589 Darren McFadden, Arkansas (38 games), 2005–2007

4,557 Kevin Faulk, LSU (41 games), 1995–1998

4,303 Bo Jackson, Auburn (38 games), 1982–1985

4,163 Errict Rhett, Florida (48 games), 1990–1993

4,050 Dalton Hilliard, LSU (44 games), 1982–1985

4,035 Charles Alexander, LSU (44 games), 1975–1978

3,928 Emmitt Smith, Florida (31 games), 1987–1989

3,835 Sonny Collins, Kentucky (41 games), 1972–1975

3,831 Carnell Williams, Auburn (42 games), 2001–2004

ALL-PURPOSE YARDS

6,833 Kevin Faulk, LSU (4,557 rush, 600 rec., 832 PR, 844 KOR), 1995–1998

5,856 Derek Abney, Kentucky (160 rush, 2,339 rec., 1,042 PR, 2,315 KOR), 2000–2003

5,831 Darren McFadden, Arkansas (4,589 rush, 365 rec., 877 KOR), 2005–2007

5,749 Herschel Walker, Georgia (5,249 rush, 243 rec., 247 KOR), 1980–1982

5,743 Domanick Davis, LSU (2056 rush, 393 rec., 1126 PR, 2168 KOR), 1999–2002

5,596 James Brooks, Auburn (3,523 rush, 347 rec., 1,726 KOR), 1977–1980

5,393 Errict Rhett, Florida (4,163 rush, 1,230 rec.), 1990–1993

5,343 Rafael Little, Kentucky (2996 rush, 1324 rec., 854 PR, 169 KOR), 2004–2007

5,326 Dalton Hilliard, LSU (4,050 rush, 1,133 rec., 143 KOR),.1982–1985

5,084 Carnell Williams, Auburn (3,831 rush, 342 rec., 302 PR, 609 KOR), 2001–2004

PASS COMPLETIONS

895 Chris Leak, Florida (1,458 attempts, 11,213 yards), 2003–2006

863 Peyton Manning, Tennessee (1,402 attempts, 11,201 yards), 1994–1997

862 Jared Lorenzen, Kentucky (1,514 attempts, 10,354 yards), 2000–2003

849 David Greene, Georgia (1,440 attempts, 11,528 yards), 2001–2004

838 Eric Zeier, Georgia (1,402 attempts, 11,153 yards), 1991–1994

829 Eli Manning, Ole Miss (1,363 attempts, 10,119 yards), 2000–2003

795 Tim Couch, Kentucky (1,184 attempts, 8,435 yards), 1996–1998

791 Andre' Woodson, Kentucky (1,278 attempts, 9,360 yards), 2004–2007

775 Casey Clausen, Tennessee (1,270 attempts, 9,707 yards), 2000–2003

727 Steve Taneyhill, South Carolina (1,209 attempts, 8,555 yards), 1992–1995

PASSING YARDS

11,528 David Greene, Georgia (849 of 1,440), 2001–2004

11,213 Chris Leak, Florida (895 of 1,458), 2003–2006

11,201 Peyton Manning, Tennessee (863 of 1,381), 1994–1997

11,153 Eric Zeier, Georgia (838 of 1,402), 1991–1994

10,875 Danny Wuerffel, Florida (708 of 1,170), 1993–1996

10,354 Jared Lorenzen, Kentucky (862 of 1,514), 2000–2003

10,119 Eli Manning, Ole Miss (829 of 1,363), 2000–2003

9,707 Casey Clausen, Tennessee (774 of 1,269), 2000–2003

9,360 Andre' Woodson, Kentucky (791 of 1,278), 2004–2007

9,287 Shane Matthews, Florida (722 of 1,202),1989–1992

TOUCHDOWN PASSES

114 Danny Wuerffel, Florida 1993–1996

89 Peyton Manning, Tennessee 1994–1997

88 Chris Leak, Florida 2003–2006

81	Eli Manning, Ole Miss 2000–2003	
79	Andre' Woodson, Kentucky 2004–2007	
78	Jared Lorenzen, Kentucky 2000–2003	
77	Rex Grossman, Florida 2000–2002	
75	Casey Clausen, Tennessee 2000–2003	
74	Shane Matthews, Florida 1989–1992	
74	Tim Couch, Kentucky 1996–1998	

RECEPTIONS

236	Earl Bennett, Vanderbilt (2,852 yards), 2005–2007
208	Craig Yeast, Kentucky (2,899 yards), 1995–1998
204	Terrence Edwards, Georgia (3,093 yards), 1999–2002
200	Keith Edwards, Vanderbilt (1,757 yards), 1980, 1982–1984
198	Chris Collins, Ole Miss (2,621 yards), 2000–2003
197	Derek Abney, Kentucky (2,339 yards), 2000–2003
194	Anthony White, Kentucky (1,519 yards), 1996–1999
194	D. J. Hall, Alabama (2,923 yards), 2004–2007
189	Keenan Burton, Kentucky (2,376 yards), 2003–2007
188	Boo Mitchell, Vanderbilt (2,964 yards), 1985–1988

RECEPTION YARDAGE

3,093	Terrence Edwards, Georgia (204 catches), 1999–2002
3,001	Josh Reed, LSU (167 catches), 1999–2001
2,964	Boo Mitchell, Vanderbilt (188 catches), 1985–1988
2,923	D. J. Hall, Alabama (194 catches), 2004–2007
2,899	Craig Yeast, Kentucky (208 catches), 1995–1998
2,884	Fred Gibson, Georgia (161 catches), 2001–2004
2,880	Dan Stricker, Vanderbilt (182 catches), 1999–2002
2,879	Anthony Lucas, Arkansas (137 catches), 1995–1999
2,852	Earl Bennett, Vanderbilt (236 catches), 2005–2007
2,814	Joey Kent, Tennessee (183 catches), 1993–1996

TOUCHDOWN RECEPTIONS

31	Chris Doering, Florida (40 games), 1992–1995
30	Terrence Edwards, Georgia (45 games), 1999–2002
29	Ike Hilliard, Florida (32 games), 1994–1996
29	Terry Beasley, Auburn (30 games), 1969–1971
29	Jack Jackson, Florida (38 games), 1992–1994
28	Craig Yeast, Kentucky (43 games), 1995–1998
27	Jabar Gaffney, Florida (23 games), 2000–2001
27	Marcus Monk, Arkansas (40 games), 2004–2007
26	Reidel Anthony, Florida (33 games), 1994–1996
25	Joey Kent, Tennessee (44 games), 1993–1996
25	Dwayne Bowe, LSU (42 games), 2003–2006
25	Keenan Burton, Kentucky (55 games), 2003–2007

SEC Single-Season Team Records

SCORING OFFENSE

POINTS

559   Florida (12 games), 1996

POINTS PER GAME

46.6   Florida (559 in 12 games), 1996

MOST TOUCHDOWNS

76   Florida (12 games), 1996

MOST FIELD GOALS MADE

31   Georgia, 2003

MOST PATS MADE

72   Florida, 1995

PASSING OFFENSE

ATTEMPTS

574   Kentucky (414 completions), 1998

COMPLETIONS

414   Kentucky (574 attempts), 1998

COMPLETION PERCENTAGE

72.1   Kentucky (414 of 574), 1998

TOUCHDOWNS

48   Florida (12 games), 1995

KICKOFF RETURNS

RETURNS

63   Kentucky, 2007

RETURN YARDS

1,462   Tennessee 2007

RUSHING OFFENSE

YARDS

4,027   Alabama (664 rushes in 11 games), 1973

YARDS PER RUSH

6.8   LSU (360 rushes for 2,632 yards), 1945

TOTAL OFFENSE

PLAYS

1,054   LSU (6,152 yards), 2007

YARDS

6,413   Florida (12 games), 1995

YARDS PER PLAY

7.4   Florida (6,413 yards in 867 plays), 1995

FIRST DOWNS

335   Kentucky (13 games), 2007

Index

Acknowledgments

Several individuals went out of their way to help make this book possible, none more so than Charles Bloom, the associate commissioner of media relations for the Southeastern Conference. Charles went above and beyond the call of duty numerous times and opened up the vaults of the SEC office for research and guidance. Thanks also to DeWayne Peevy, associate director of media relations.

In addition, a number of university media-relations directors were especially helpful in this project, notably: Claude Felton, University of Georgia; Bud Ford, University of Tennessee; Langston Rogers, Ole Miss; Larry Leathers, Vanderbilt University; Mike Nemeth, Mississippi State University; and Michael Bonnette, Louisiana State University.

I am also grateful for the continued assistance of Brad Green of the Paul W. Bryant Museum, who has helped me through two books. Thanks also to Pratt Patterson of the University of the South (Sewanee).

I relied on numerous sources for research, some more bountiful than others, particularly Tony Barnhart's *Southern Fried Football*, Christopher J. Walsh's *Where Football Is King*, David Housel's *Auburn University Football Vault*, Keith Dunnavant's *The Missing Ring*, and Marvin West's *Legends of Tennessee Football*.

Finally, thanks to Karen, Colin, Taylor, Bo, and Grace, and everyone who had to be patient and understanding throughout the process.

Photo Credits

We wish to acknowledge the following for providing the illustrations included in the book. Every effort has been made to locate the copyright holders for materials used, and we apologize for any oversights.

AP Images: p. 43, 49, 52, 56 (Frank Filan), 61 (Ed Widdis), 63, 65, 67, 69, 70 left, 71 (Ed Widdis), 77, 78, 79, 84 (Dave Taylor), 88, 89, 96, 99, 101, 107 (Jacob Harris), 109, 116 (University of Kentucky Archive), 123, 129, 132, 133 (Porfirio Solorzano), 150 (Anthony Camerano), 161, 177 (Tannen Maury).

Auburn University Athletic Media Relations: p. 20, 90, 110, 151–153, 166, 168 both, 181, 195, 196, 197 bottom.

Auburn University/Collegiate Images: p. 148, 149, 180, 213.

College Football Hall of Fame: p. 25 both, 38 right.

Georgia Tech Sports Information: p. 59.

Georgia Tech/Collegiate Images: p. 26, 27 both, 29.

Getty Images: p. 2 (Joe Murphy/WireImage), 6 (Doug Benc), 8 (Streeter Lecka), 9 top (Rex Brown), 10 (Joe Murphy), 11 top (Kevin C. Cox), 12 (Mike Zarrilli), 95 (Streeter Lecka), 104 (George Silk/Time Life Pictures), 106 (George Silk/Time Life Pictures), 120 (Hulton Archive), 130 (Focus On Sport), 134 (Bill Eppridge/Time Life Pictures), 135 (Bill Eppridge/Time Life Pictures), 138 (Frederic Lewis/Hulton Archive), 146 (Jamie Squire), 162 (Focus On Sport), 169 (Allen Steele), 178 (Tony Tomsic/WireImage), 188 top (Andy Lyons), 188 bottom (Doug Pensinger), 189 top right (Bernstein Associates), 193 (Brian Bahr), 197 top (Scott Cunningham), 198 (Scott Halleran), 199 left (Scott Halleran), 199 right (Andy Lyons), 200 (Stephen Dunn), 203 (Andy Lyons), 212 (Andy Lyons), 216 (Jamie Squire), 217 top (Grant Halverson), 219 (Joe Murphy), 220 (Jamie Squire), 221 right (Ronald Martinez), 224 (Tom Hauck), 225 bottom left (Stephen Dunn).

Kenan Research Center at the Atlanta History Center: p. 18 top.

Louisiana State University Sports Information: p. 37, 40, 41 both, 48, 86 right, 105, 108, 139 left, 165, 204, 215.

Louisiana State University/Collegiate Images: p. 140, 208.

Mississippi State University Athletic Media and Public Relations: p. 62, 102, 103, 114 left, 218 both.

Orange Bowl Committee/Collegiate Images: p. 124, 125.

Paul W. Bryant Museum: p. 21, 30–33, 42, 45, 68, 70 right, 75, 121, 122 both, 131, 136, 139 right, 159, 160, 175, 176, 187, 192.

Southeastern Conference: p. 9 bottom, 11 bottom left and bottom right, 13, 58, 164 top left, 184, 186 both, 189 bottom left, 190, 191, 202, 206, 207, 209–211, 214, 217 bottom, 225 top right.

University of Alabama/Collegiate Images: p. 72, 73, 74, 113, 167, 174.

University of Florida/Collegiate Images: p. 115 right.

University of Georgia Sports Communications: p. 14, 17, 19 both, 38 left, 64, 76, 81, 126–128, 170–173, 179 both, 182, 183 both.

University of Georgia/Collegiate Images: p. 66, 80.

University of Kentucky/Collegiate Images: p. 97 both, 98, 117, 118.

University of Mississippi Athletic Media Relations: p. 46, 47 bottom right, 60, 82, 83, 112, 115 left, 141–145, 147, 221 left (photo by Nathan Latil).

University of Mississippi/Collegiate Images: p. 47 top left.

University of Tennessee Sports Information: p. 18 bottom, 28, 34, 36, 51, 53–55, 87, 91–93, 114 right, 119, 155–157, 164 bottom right, 194 both, 201.

University of Tennessee/Collegiate Images: p. 86 left.

University of the South Sports Information: p. 23.

Vanderbilt University Athletic Media Relations: p. 24 both, 222, 223.

Vanderbilt University Special Collections and Archives: p. 100.